SIX PORTRAITS

MADAME DE STAËL AS "CORINNE"
(From a portrait by Mme Vigée-Lebrun.)

SIX PORTRAITS

By ISABEL C. CLARKE

MADAME DE STAËL. JANE AUSTEN.
GEORGE ELIOT. MRS. OLIPHANT.
JOHN OLIVER HOBBES (MRS. CRAIGIE).
: : KATHERINE MANSFIELD : :

Essay Index Reprint Series

With Eight Illustrations

BOOKS FOR LIBRARIES PRESS, INC.
FREEPORT, NEW YORK

First Published 1935
Reprinted 1967

LIBRARY OF CONGRESS CATALOG CARD NUMBER: 67-26725

PRINTED IN THE UNITED STATES OF AMERICA

Preface

IN these portraits of literary women I have endeavoured to trace the story of their lives, the aims and motives that guided them in their career as well as the circumstances in which they achieved their task, rather than to add to the already abundant criticism of their books. The period under discussion extends over more than a hundred and fifty years, and it will be observed that except for one brief interval the dates overlap, thus forming a sequence of literary activity and achievement across nearly a century and a half.

In preparing this book my thanks are due in various quarters for much courteous assistance. To Mr. R. A. Austen-Leigh for permission to quote copyright material from the *Life and Letters of Jane Austen* edited by W. and R. A. Austen-Leigh ; to Mrs. Ouvry for similar courtesy in regard to excerpts from *The Family Life and Letters of George Eliot* by Arthur Paterson ; to Miss Janet Oliphant for valuable help in preparing the portrait of her aunt as well as for allowing me to use material from *The Autobiography and Letters of Mrs. Oliphant* ; to Captain John Craigie for similar courtesy in regard to the *Life of John Oliver Hobbes* ; to Mr. Middleton Murry for allowing me to quote from the *Journal* and *Letters* of Katherine Mansfield, and also to Miss Clara Palmer for her reminiscences of the early life of that gifted writer. I am also indebted to M. Schopfer for the photograph of the Château de Coppet, scene of so many episodes in the life of Mme de Staël.

ISABEL C. CLARKE.

Rome, 1935.

Contents

List of Illustrations

Madame de Staël

MADAME DE STAËL

§

JACQUES NECKER, father of Mme de Staël, was the grandson of a German lawyer of Küstrin in Brandenburg. Charles Frederic Necker, father of Jacques, was educated with a view to adopting the same profession in his native town. But he accompanied some young men of rank on a tour of Europe, and spending some time with them at Geneva took a liking to that city. Eventually he settled there and was granted permission to teach law at the University, in which post he was installed in 1725 at the age of thirty-nine. In the following year Geneva bestowed upon him the singular favour of her citizenship.

He had been in England and was granted a pension by George I to enable him to receive English pupils at Geneva. In the eighteenth century there were many points of sympathy between England and the Swiss republics.

It is said that Charles Necker remained always completely German. He married in 1726 Jeanne Marie Gautier, the daughter of a former mayor of Geneva, who was about seven years younger than himself. She bore him four children, of whom two only survived, Louis, who changed his name to de Germany, and Jacques who was born in 1732. Although they mingled with the most exclusive circles of Genevan upper-middle class society, Jeanne Necker Gautier continued to keep a pension for young English students.

The elder son studied science in Paris, but returned eventually to Geneva where he became professor of mathematics, and assisted his father at the Academy. The younger son, Jacques, was a precocious child who completed his classical studies at the age of fourteen, about two years earlier than was usual for boys, and forthwith entered a bank. But his love of science and literature prevented him from applying his mind to figures and his father wisely perceived that a wider sphere was necessary. At the suggestion of his friend, Jacob Vernet, he sent his son to the latter's brother, a banker in Paris. Jacques was fifteen, but so prematurely developed that he not only visited at his employer's house but was introduced to his friends.

Society, however, did not interest him ; he was silent, slightly morose. He saw almost exclusively his own countrymen of whom there was a large colony in Paris. The Swiss from the Catholic cantons mingled far more in French society than those from Geneva.

The boy worked hard. He became absorbed in those figures which at Geneva he had disdained. Fifteen years later when he was only thirty years old he founded the house of Thélusson-Necker, of which he opened a branch in London at the conclusion of the Seven Years' War. His father died about that time ; his mother was already dead, and a scandal had forced Louis de Germany to quit the shores of his native lake. He too migrated to Paris where he founded a bank.

Jacques was about thirty-two years of age when destiny flung across his path the beautiful Suzanne Curchod, daughter of the Calvinist pastor of Crassier, a village some four miles from Geneva, to which post he had been appointed in the year 1729. Curchod married about that time Madeleine Albert de Nasse whom he had met at Lausanne. She was a Frenchwoman, being the daughter of a lawyer at Montélimar who, fleeing from the persecutions under Louis XV sought sanctuary in Switzerland, that happy hunting-ground of Protestant refugees. Unkind persons said that the lawyer's real name was Jean Albert and that he had no right to that of de Nasse. Suzanne Curchod thought differently for late in life she would sign herself C. de Nasse Necker.

Mme Curchod lived for thirty years at Crassier, an exemplary wife and mother. She saw her only child, Suzanne, grow up charming, beautiful and attractive. Moreover, she was highly educated according to the standards of that day. She read Latin, a little Greek ; she spoke English and studied geometry and physics. She was something too of a musician. She was fair, with blond hair, blue eyes and a delicate complexion. Men found her attractive. . . .

Her parents took her to Lausanne which offered a wider matrimonial field than Crassier. For many years a legend prevailed in that city concerning " la belle Curchod." Among her admirers two were especially noticeable, Georges Deyverdun or d'Yverdon, the last of the noble family of Grandson-Belmont, and a young Englishman, Edward Gibbon, who had been sent thither to live in a pastor's family where it was hoped he would be cured of the Catholicism he had so impetuously embraced. So effective was the remedy that he never ceased to indulge in the bitterest diatribes against Christianity in general and Catholicism in particular.

In his journal of 1757 he made the following significant entry: I have seen Mlle Curchod. *Omnia vincit amor.* . . . She was about twenty at that time, fair, fresh, extremely pretty. Very soon they became engaged. Gibbon returned to England in April of that year terrified at the prospect of revealing the fact to his father. Everything happened according to plan. He announced his engagement, the expected storm followed, his stepmother intercepted the " belle Curchod's " letters. And even as Gibbon had apostatized to please his father, so now he wrote to break off the engagement. Suzanne even then was the prey to that morbid melancholy she bequeathed to her daughter, and cries of despair emanated from Crassier. She wrote a letter of piteous appeal, now preserved in the British Museum, to which Gibbon responded evasively. He did not return to Lausanne for five years when he might reasonably have expected the whole affair to have blown over. He found Suzanne still unmarried and now alone with her mother and in reduced circumstances. Her father had been dead some years, and they had little to subsist upon except the meagre pension Mme Curchod received as the widow of a pastor.

Suzanne did her utmost to reconquer her lover but without success. A Genevan friend of hers—Moulton—was pressed into the service, and he appealed for help to Jean-Jacques Rousseau whom Gibbon was visiting at the time. Gibbon was obdurate, moreover, in order to put her in the wrong he endeavoured to assure himself and those about him that in his absence she had consoled herself with Georges Deyverdun who had remained faithful to her through those years of hopeless waiting. " False and dangerous girl," was Gibbon's comment, when she wrote to tell him that neither Deyverdun nor anyone else had for a moment effaced his image in her heart.

Defeated, she retired to Geneva with her mother and occupied herself with teaching. She gave lessons for seven hours daily, despite her delicate health. It would have been impossible then to predict the brilliant and opulent future which awaited the disappointed, impoverished girl, no longer in her first youth.

In 1763 her mother died and Moulton came to her assistance, engaging her to look after his children while she continued to give lessons in her spare time. She was supposed to be engaged to a lawyer, M. Correvon, but her heart was not in it ; she continually deferred the marriage.

In the early weeks of 1764 she went to Lausanne to stay with her friend, Mme de Brenles. Gibbon was then at Mézery staying with its Seigneur, M. de Crousaz. They met on quite amicable terms. Did it make any difference to him that she should attend a large

brilliant reception at which the Prince of Würtemburg was present ?
There is no doubt that the thought of her obsessed him though he
considered her explanation equivocal. They had an interview later
which lasted two hours and he returned her letters. Soon afterwards
she went back to Geneva where an unexpected destiny awaited her.

§

Mme de Verménoux, a young rich widow with one son, was
staying in Geneva for the purpose of consulting the famous doctor
Tronchin who had a European reputation at that time. She was
on the point of returning to Paris, and almost at the eleventh hour
she invited Suzanne Curchod to accompany her as her companion.
Moulton approved of the plan ; the preparations were hurriedly
made, and thus Suzanne left Geneva.

Among Mme Verménoux's many admirers was Jacques Necker,
rich, prosperous, lonely. He constantly visited her house and they
were supposed to be engaged. Whether that was the case or not
cannot clearly be ascertained, but seeing Suzanne Curchod there he
fell in love with her and they were married within six months of her
arrival in Paris. Necker then lived in a large house in rue Michel le
Comte. Not long afterwards Gibbon arrived in Paris and visited
Suzanne every day. She never felt the slightest bitterness towards
him for his ungenerous treatment of her and they always remained
friends.

Mme de Verménoux caused to come from Zürich a young man
as tutor to her son. His name was Meister and he became an intimate
friend of the Necker family and it was to him that many of Mme
de Staël's most intimate and self-revealing letters were addressed.

Suzanne was lonely in her new, splendid *ambiente*. Necker was an
extremely busy man, deeply preoccupied with affairs of all kinds. Not
only banking, but also finance and speculation engaged that fertile
mind. Especially did he see the advisability of speculating in wheat
since one of the most lamentable results of a long war is inevitably
famine. . . .

" A country barren of friendship and only useful in forming the
taste," was Suzanne's cynical description of France. But she had a
strong natural tendency to melancholy and depression, and she had
not yet embarked upon that social career which was to make Necker's
house so famous. Moreover, she was expecting a child and her mind
was full of foreboding and fear.

On April 22, 1766, she gave birth to a girl after prolonged agony.
The baby was christened in the chapel of the Dutch Embassy by M.
Duvoisin, a pastor from the Pays de Vaud. She was called Anne-

Louise-Germaine—the latter name being given out of compliment to her godmother, Mme Verménoux.

Mme Necker was then as always definitely opposed to the Catholic religion and from the moment the child could speak she was surrounded by Swiss and Protestant influences.

They went to Lausanne to stay with Suzanne's old friend, Mme de Brenles. She wrote afterwards to apologize for Necker's gloomy sullenness which she said had greatly displeased her. The fact was he was intent upon fresh plans. Shortly afterwards he was appointed Resident Minister of the Republic of Geneva at Paris, his first definitely political post. For him it was an important step. It gave him the entrée at Court. He combined the rôles of financier and diplomat, always a slightly hazardous and ambiguous adventure.

Germaine was ten years old, dark, plain with rather coarse features and masses of black hair. Her large brilliant intelligent black eyes went far to redeem the plainness of her face. She was tall for her age and precociously intelligent. Already she appeared at the famous Fridays inaugurated at the sumptuous Hôtel Leblanc, whither Necker had removed after his accession to power, and where his wife, " the beautiful Hypatia " with whom Suard was said to be in love, dispensed such a gracious hospitality. Necker, silent and sullen as was his wont, contributed little to the gaiety of these gatherings.

Suzanne's principal preoccupation was the education of her daughter. She taught her for the most part herself, her former strenuous apprenticeship qualifying her admirably for the task. But she sought to repress her ; to freeze that abounding vitality, to mould her to the pattern of her own Calvinism. Thus it was to her father rather than to her mother the child instinctively turned. Necker in his spare hours was diverted by the precocious chatter of his daughter. He admired her, and admiration was then as always the breath of life to her. Sometimes he would even take her part against Suzanne. . . .

On one occasion Suard came into the salon just as Mme Necker was leaving it and discovered Germaine standing there, alone and in tears. He went up to her and said : " One kiss from papa will make up to you for all that, won't it ? " She answered with something of bitterness : " Yes, monsieur, my father thinks of my present happiness, my mother only thinks of my future."

Germaine had been dangerously ill and was not fully recovered when Necker suddenly announced his intention of going to London. They stayed in some rather squalid lodgings in Suffolk Street. Horace Walpole and Gibbon entertained them. Gibbon had just published the first volume of his *Decline and Fall* and waṣ enjoying the fruits of its practically instantaneous success.

They remained two months in England and then returned to find Paris in the throes of a political crisis. The Treasury, deeply compromised by the fall of Turgot, needed a master-mind to conduct its affairs. This was found in Necker. He was called to the post in October, 1776. There was something stupefying in such an appointment. A foreigner, a Swiss banker, to be Minister to the King of France ! Probably he was as much astonished as anyone. When the news penetrated to the shores of Lake Léman, where it excited as much amazement as it had done on the boulevards of Paris, a medal was struck in his honour. Geneva appointed Necker's brother, de Germany, to succeed him as their diplomatic representative. Its honour and prestige must surely be secure in the hands of such a family. . . .

§

Germaine was eleven years old ; it was considered desirable that she should have a suitable companion of her own age. This was found in a little Genevan Protestant, Jeanne Huber, who remained her intimate friend for many years. Germaine's eloquence made a profound impression upon her. They did not play games together, Germaine was far too serious for that. She enquired as to the nature of Jeanne's studies. Did she speak any foreign language ? Did she often go to the play ? She was perfectly *au fait* with current politics as indeed were the little Brontë children at the same age. Probably she heard little else discussed in the Hôtel Leblanc. There at her mother's Friday receptions Jeanne could recall her sitting on a low stool beside Mme Necker, holding herself very upright and almost always surrounded by several elderly people who addressed her with kindly interest.

Tall for her age Germaine looked older than she was. But the hectic life of the salon ruined her health, her vitality deteriorated, and she gave signs of debility and languor. Tronchin, then established in Paris as physician to the duc d'Orleans, recommended such modern treatment as complete rest, liberty, a life spent in the open air. 'She was removed from the exacting, intensive system of education imposed by Suzanne to the complete freedom of their country house at St. Ouen whither Jeanne Huber accompanied her.

They recited poems and composed verses and dramas. Germaine loved her friend despite the difference in their natures. She wept over the very things which aroused the laughter of little Jeanne. That melancholy sensibility, then regarded as a desirable quality in women, was beginning to manifest itself.

Necker came to see her. Sullen, silent, impenetrable with the rest of the world, he relaxed with his little daughter. But even to her he rarely lifted the mask. He suffered from the fears and scruples engendered by his terrible Calvinist upbringing, from the effects of which he was never wholly to free himself. His wife also suffered from it, but with her it produced that profound melancholy less comprehensible in Mme Necker of the opulent Hôtel Leblanc than in the impoverished governess giving lessons for seven hours a day to keep the wolf from the door at Geneva.

At fifteen years old Germaine decided that she would marry her mother's old admirer, Gibbon. And even then Mme Necker was beginning to weave plans for her daughter's future. She was jealous of this precocious, brilliant, adolescent girl, who attracted so many of the important visitors to her side. Something must be done about it. . . .

She thought at first of the younger Pitt, whom she described as a great and noble character, as a possible husband for her. While these negotiations were in progress the family went, in 1784, to Lausanne where Germaine enjoyed herself amid the scenes of her mother's youthful triumphs. It was then that Necker bought from a member of the Thélusson family the Château of Coppet, for which he paid the sum of five hundred thousand *livres* of French money. Originally given by the Count of Savoy to the Counts of Gruyère, Coppet had passed in the seventeenth century to the duc de Lesdiguières. It was, however, badly in need of repair and in the meantime Necker rented Beaulieu, a large country house near by, where he settled himself for the summer. While there he imprudently published his *De l'Administration des Finances de la France*. . . .

Twenty years had passed since " la belle Curchod " had left Lausanne for Paris, and she was less happy in her old haunts now that she had returned to them. But Necker was recovering something of calm after the feverish years of speculation and money-making, and Germaine caught up in a whirl of gaiety was happier than she had ever been before. Was she not one of the richest heiresses in Europe ? . . .

" She is less good-looking than I expected," M. de Charrière, who had known Suzanne in her youth, wrote to his wife. " She is even ugly, but there is something pleasant about her eyes ; they are not soft but suggest a natural intelligence."

Lausanne was at that time one of the most fashionable resorts in Europe. People from all countries sought health and amusement in Switzerland and the Alps. Tissot, who had succeeded the famous

B

Tronchin as its prominent physician, attracted hosts of invalids. Many English spent the winter at Nice, the summer in the Pays de Vaud.

Gibbon was there, sharing a house with his old rival Deyverdun and writing the last volume of his famous history. Sarcastically he observed when he heard of the purchase of Coppet, that it was merely another proof that those who had once tasted grandeur were unable to return to their primitive condition. Still, he was friendly, deeming that it would be an agreeable place wherein to spend a few weeks of the summer. He described Germaine as badly brought up, wild, vain, but good-natured.

Necker was happiest at Coppet, Germaine decided ; his ambitious projects seemed to dwindle in the face of those immense mountains rising to the sky. A free country with happy faces about one . . . so different from France where already the clouds were gathering. And the society " more virtuous than that of Paris," as her mother said, was agreeable to her.

Now that they were actually established at Coppet it seemed as if Necker would never again wish to leave it. Had France been but a place of magnificent exile to him ? Suzanne fell a prey to one of her fits of profound nervous depression, and Germaine who had enjoyed Lausanne was bored in this splendid house standing in its own park, watered by streams and surrounded by trees.

In 1785 they returned to Paris, and now Mme Necker was more than ever resolved to secure a husband for her daughter. But where to find a Protestant of noble birth ? The girl had already rejected the idea of marrying an Englishman. She wished to live in Paris, the home of her childhood and girlhood.

Her twenty years residence in France had done nothing to reconcile Mme Necker to Catholicism. She clung to her gloomy Calvinism, and she was determined that Germaine should also cling to it. Looking around for possible suitors she fixed upon the Swedish Ambassador, Eric Magnus, Baron de Staël-Holstein, a man of the fair Nordic type, greatly admired by the French beauties of the day and very deeply in debt. What did it matter that he was sixteen years older than Germaine and that she did not pretend to love him ? Indeed, she was so unnerved at the prospect that she was ill for a whole month beforehand with fever, for like her mother profound mental agitation affected her physically.

Her fortune attracted the Ambassador who had little of his own, and who was, moreover, addicted to gambling. They were married at the chapel of the Swedish Embassy in January, 1786.

" It will be hard for me to begin a new life," the girl wrote

desolately to her mother, "and fear of the unknown adds to my
uneasiness about the whole business." With her clear penetrating
vision she must have discerned that de Staël needed money above
all things, and that was why he had agreed to marry a girl without
looks or birth. . . .

However, thenceforth life was changed for her, and the Embassy
in the rue du Bac became a centre to which the personality of the
Ambassadress attracted all that was intellectual in the Paris of that
day.   A couple of weeks after her marriage she was presented to
Marie Antoinette, but performed the traditional three curtsies so
clumsily that she finally stumbled and put her foot through her
gown.   And the Queen did not like her.   She had nothing of the calm
and dignity so essential to Court life.   She was plain, ungraceful,
rather rough, with a fondness for wearing brilliant colours that did
not suit her.   Indeed, she seemed to have little to recommend her
except Necker's vast fortune and her own eternal conversation.

There were indeed several reasons why she failed to make a good
impression at Court even before Necker's fall from power.   She was
a foreigner, she was of middle-class origin, and by education she was
a Calvinist.   To the French Court, Catholic and aristocratic, she
must have seemed something of an interloper.

Still, shortly after her marriage a Court banquet of twenty-four
guests was given in her honour, presided over by the Princesse de
Chimay, a lady-in-waiting.   Mme de Polignac who had had a ten-
dresse for the good-looking ambassador, frequently invited her to
supper.   She lived, as she said, in a whirl of gaiety, entertaining both
at her own house and at the Embassy.

She began to write in September of that year and in a few months
had tossed off a couple of novels and some poetic dramas.   When she
could not for any reason talk she wrote, and with her both activities
were equally fluent and copious.   She went out less during the
following spring for she was expecting her first child and was almost
as full of gloomy foreboding as Suzanne had been before her own
birth.   Her little daughter was born in July, 1787 ; it did not live
long and she showed it little care or attention.

Two of her girlhood's friends were married and living in Paris.
One was her former playfellow, Jeanne Huber, now Mme Rilliet-
Huber.   The other was her cousin's wife, Albertine Necker de Saus-
sure, who had married the son of Louis de Germany and was living
with her husband and father-in-law.   She was a daughter of de
Saussure, the famous naturalist, and was much of her own age.
But she noticed with something of mortification that the Ambas-
sadress only invited her to meet the Genevan colony. . . .

§

The clouds on the horizon thickened. One autumn night when Mme de Staël was entertaining her parents and some friends the festivities were interrupted by a grim and significant incident almost reminiscent of the Writing on the Wall. A messenger who wished most urgently to speak with M. Necker was announced. This was no other than Le Noir, a lieutenant of police, bearer of a *lettre de cachet* from the King, commanding Necker's immediate departure from Paris, and forbidding him to approach within a hundred miles of the capital. For many years he had been the Controller-General of finance, and it had fallen to him to obtain funds to pay for the lamentable Seven Years' War. But he had disobeyed his monarch by publishing, despite royal prohibition, his *Mémoire Justificatif*, and thus had undoubtedly incurred punishment. He left immediately for his country house at St. Ouen, and on the following day Mme de Staël went to Versailles in her quality of Ambassadress to be received in audience by the Queen so that she might intercede for her father. Marie Antoinette was not then prepared—as at a later date— to approach the King on the subject, and Mme de Staël retired discomfited from the royal presence, secretly bent on revenge. . . .

Despite her plain face only redeemed by the dark burning eyes, her thick clumsy figure, she was capable of attracting some of the most brilliant men of liberal tendencies to her salon. From thence she could disseminate " ideas " as Napoleon was later to say of her. And her ideas at that time were to propagate hatred of the Royal Family. Revolutionary mutterings were already to be heard in France, since hunger, that grim prelude to all social upheavals, was fastening its claws upon the people. Mme de Staël worked to promote those sinister murmurings. Liberty, a constitution such as England possessed, formed the principal items of her programme.

Necker's banishment was of brief duration for Brienne his successor failed, and it had been decided that the King should summon the States-General which had not met for a hundred and seventy-five years. Necker was deemed the one financier who could co-operate adequately with that assemblage. Mme de Staël made a hurried journey to St. Ouen to inform her father he was about to be recalled. King Louis XVI little dreamed what that gesture of his was destined to entail.

It has been said, if somewhat cynically, that the chief task of a Government is to obtain funds to pay for the expenses of the country it serves. This problem which has pressed with considerable weight upon the statesmen of our own day, was then more or less in its infancy, and it is hardly surprising to find that the task was beyond Necker. He was a banker, even a stock-jobber, but he was in no sense a statesman and he did not in the least foresee the temper of the body with which he was called upon to deal. It does not follow because a man can make a very large fortune for himself at the dubious game of finance, that he can conduct similar operations upon a vaster scale for a country, and that country not his own. He was really something of an adventurer as well as being a very shrewd profiteer of that unpleasant description which knows how to enrich itself from the blood and travail of protracted war. His political outlook was narrow, and he was further that strange anomaly, a man of foreign origin and of no outstanding qualities who had risen to a prominent position in a country not his own.

The history of the next few years is the history of the French Revolution. But it is impossible to give any account of Mme de Staël without referring to certain significant events of that epoch, so closely was Necker allied to them and so intimately was his daughter implicated in all that concerned him.

There was, for instance, the historic meeting of the States-General with its three Orders, the Clergy, the Nobles and the Commons, preceded by that marvellous religious procession which made its slow progress from the church of Notre Dame at Versailles to that of St. Louis on May 4, 1789. The two thousand persons of whom it was composed carried lighted tapers, for such was the solemnity of the occasion that the Archbishop of Paris bore the Monstrance with the Blessed Sacrament, above which the canopy was upheld by the King, his brother, and two Princes of the Blood Royal. The clergy of Versailles headed the long procession, then came the Commons, the Nobles and the Clergy—the three Orders that composed the States-General. The Queen and her ladies brought up the rear, behind the Archbishop of Paris. Beneath the struggling May sunshine—for the morning had been wet—the serpent-like ribbon of people illuminated by those pale, flickering pyramids of flame contributed by the candles made an unforgettable sight.

From a window Mme de Staël watched that slow and solemn progress. There was triumph in her heart. For this her father had been recalled to Paris as the only man capable of coping with the burning economic questions of the hour. She singled out the conspicuous figure of Mirabeau from among the six hundred Commons, which included also such names as Robespierre and Sieyès. He had been returned as Deputy by the people of Marseilles whose hearts he had won by his powerful eloquence. This man who in his youth had been persecuted beyond human desert by his father, who had

even caused him to be imprisoned in the Château d'If, had a great
shock of hair above a rugged, pock-marked face.   Mme de Staël,
impressed by that aspect of significant strength, felt hope for the
political future.   But Mme de Montmorin, wife of the Foreign
Minister, who was with her, told her that she was making a great
mistake in applauding this summoning of parliament.

" Terrible calamities will be the result not only for ourselves but
for France," she said.   Prophetic words, since her husband was
killed in the historic September massacres, and she herself and her
eldest son were doomed to perish on the scaffold. . . .

On the following day the opening of the Session. . . .   The King
upon a throne canopied with sombre purple velvet upon which
gleamed the lilies of France. . . . His face was expressionless as he
read his speech, but that of the Queen was noticeably pale ; she was
in deep anxiety about her little dying son. . . .   Around the King
were grouped the Princes of the Blood Royal ; below him sat the
ministry, among whom the figure of Necker was visible.

Barentin, Keeper of the Seals, followed the King.   He spoke for
an hour.   It was left to the judgment of the three Orders to meet
together or separately as they would.   In that pronouncement it
has been said the French Revolution was given birth. . . .

Then Necker, whose mendacious speech with its strings of false
figures occupied no less than three hours.   When he had finished the
weary Assembly broke up.

June came and the poor little Dauphin, a child of eleven, died,
shrunken and wasted from protracted illness. The Commons assumed
the title of the National Assembly, and it seemed as if the struggle
between people and Crown were definitely inaugurated.   Louis
replied by summoning the Royal Session to deal with this divergence
between the three Orders.   The Court, closely guarded, went in
procession to the Assembly.   Necker was absent. . . .

A dramatic episode followed.   The King informed the Commons
that their recent proceedings were invalid since they could not
become law without Royal consent.   He commanded them to disperse.   The Bishops obeyed and were followed by the Nobles.   The
Commons alone refused to stir, and it was Mirabeau who voiced their
implacable decision.

" We are here by the will of the people and only death can dismiss
us ! " A challenge to King and Country that rings across the years. . . .

§

" The last happy day of my young life," Mme de Staël described
that June morning when Necker after an audience with the King

was carried by an excited adoring populace through the streets of Versailles. His name—the name of the Swiss banker—was on every lip. His daughter rejoiced at this signal manifestation of public confidence and worship.

All those voices that shouted my father's name seemed to me like the voices of friends who shared my tender reverence for him. . . .

The plaudits were, however, far from universal, and there were even malicious suggestions that Necker had deliberately staged the scene himself. He was vain and full of self-importance—of *flon-flon* as Napoleon was subsequently to say of him. Still, it cannot be denied that after his audience with the King the deputies crowded to see him in such numbers that his house could hardly contain them. His ascendancy appeared to be at its height when not three weeks later he beheld once more the Writing on the Wall.

This time he was dining at home with his wife and a friend ; the scene peaceful and luxurious, with no hint of disaster. And breaking in abruptly upon this private feast came a letter from the King ordering, not only Necker's departure from Paris, but his departure from France. No sojourning this time at St. Ouen. . . . One does not dally with a peremptory Royal command and within an hour Necker and his wife took the road to Brussels.

The news of his dismissal was received with incredible fury by the people of Paris. He left on July 11 ; on July 14 the Bastille was stormed. Necker heard the news after leaving Brussels from a messenger who told him that Mme de Polignac was in the same town, having fled from Versailles at the urgent entreaty of the Queen.

Two days later Louis wrote a note recalling Necker. There was defeat in this missive. Had he not told him that when matters had calmed down he would give him a proof of his sentiments ? The confidence which the nation reposed in him had induced the King to hasten the moment of his return. He invited him, therefore, to come back as soon as possible and resume his place near him. In leaving he had spoken of his attachment and the proof of that attachment, for which Louis now asked, was the most signal Necker could give him.

Such an invitation with its suggestion of panic was not to be disregarded. Necker returned to Paris where he was greeted with the most fantastic enthusiasm. Shouts of *Vive M. Necker* resounded from streets, windows, house-tops. . . .

But he had to deal with a new and powerful rival—the Commune of Paris. Although it owed its existence in great measure to himself it was now under the sway of a man more powerful and even more unscrupulous than he. This was Mirabeau, who did not hesitate to attack and condemn Necker's attempts to obtain funds. " If he remains in office another month," he said in January, 1790, " the écu will disappear, and you will realize then the mistake of that sublime invention—paper money."

Necker had tried to raise a loan, but in times of great national insecurity this procedure, which always signifies following the line of least resistance in economic matters, is doomed to meet with indifferent response. He called for a voluntary subscription and again the response was feeble. The cries of *Vive M. Necker* seemed but the expression of a surface enthusiasm, it might even be of mob hysteria. And Mirabeau was aware of Necker's traffickings in wheat at a time when the people of Paris were faced with famine. . . .

In October another dramatic and highly significant episode occurred. The mob marched to Versailles and brought the King and Queen and their trembling children to Paris. After seven hours of weary travel, exhausted and unstrung, they reached the Tuileries. . . .

§

Mme de Staël's salon lost nothing of its brilliancy during those years of unrest. Never, she declared, had so much " wit, vitality and intellect " met together. Men flocked to the receptions of the Ambassadress, who, according to Gouverneur Morris, an American observer, had the aspect of a chambermaid. Among her most frequent visitors were Talleyrand, the lame Bishop of Autun and a master of diplomacy ; the Count de Narbonne Lara, reputed son of Louis XV, indulging even then in chimerical dreams of wearing in the future the Crown of France ; Mathieu de Montmorency Laval, in all the beauty of his splendid youth, who had fought under La Fayette in America. All these and many more came to the rue du Bac, and the dark-eyed woman with her roughly modelled masculine features continued assiduously to intrigue against the Royal Family. If Necker is said to have precipitated the French Revolution, he was most ably seconded by his daughter.

In July, 1790, there was a reaction in the King's favour. Mme de Staël watched this new development with some alarm. Louis received Mirabeau in private audience and that demagogue swept aside Necker's schemes for obtaining money.

In August Mme de Staël gave birth to her eldest son, Auguste, and before she had recovered she learned that her parents had fled from Paris amid the loud hootings and execrations of the mob that had once hailed Necker as a saviour. Indeed, it was thought at one time he would hardly have been permitted to reach the frontier alive, so violent was the hostility to which he was exposed.

Mme de Staël followed her father to Coppet in October, 1790. She remained there for eleven months, at the end of which time she became restless and bored and returned to Paris. While there she resumed her old game of intriguing, and this time it was with the intention of obtaining for Narbonne, who for some years had been her lover, the portfolio of Foreign Affairs. This did not succeed but he was made Minister of War. Marie Antoinette remarked with not unjustifiable bitterness that it would indeed redound to the glory of Mme de Staël to have the French army under her command. They had got rid of the Swedish Ambassador, but it was less easy to dispose of his wife.

Mirabeau's death in 1791 altered the situation with tragic completeness. He was planning for the safe removal of the Royal Family at the time of his death. He told Talleyrand, who attended him in those final hours, that with him would perish the "last shreds of monarchy " in France.

The departure was attempted, but owing to some act of imprudence the King was recognized at Varennes and he and his family were brought back to the capital. Rumour said that he was intriguing with Austria to recover his lost authority. Shortly before the massacres of September 2, 1792, he and the Queen with their children were imprisoned in the Temple, from which neither was destined to emerge except to encounter death.

Mme de Staël fled to Coppet bringing word of the massacres. She found Necker engaged upon a defence of the King, in which he subtly suggested that had that monarch followed his advice his imprisonment would not have taken place.

During the following month Mme de Staël gave birth to her second son, Albert, reputed child of Narbonne who had almost lost his life in the September massacres and had now escaped to England. Baron de Staël was hoping to return to his post in Paris, and Necker, to whom was still owing the greater part of the one hundred thousand pounds he had lent to the French Government, was getting slightly weary of paying his son-in-law's debts. This time, yes, he had done so for the sake of the infant Albert, but he plainly showed his daughter this kind of thing couldn't go on. He insisted upon a reconciliation between her and her husband. She must, in short, return to him. . . .

These suggestions did not meet with Germaine de Staël's approval. She had no desire to be reconciled to her husband nor had she the slightest intention of returning to Paris, which, considering the perils

she had undergone during her escape from that city, was scarcely a
matter for surprise. No, she was going to England. All her friends
were there, Narbonne, Talleyrand, de Montmorency and the rest.
The Neckers were at their wits' end. Mme Necker even appealed
to her old lover Gibbon then in Lausanne to reason with her head-
strong daughter. But Gibbon was wary ; he did not wish to mix
himself up in the *pasticcio*, and in January Germaine left for England.

She rented Juniper Hall between Mickleham and Burford Bridge,
and thither flocked that melancholy group of French *émigrés* who
had found their own country less than healthy. They were sad and
depressed, disliking the chilly dampness of an English January,
sighing for the familiar boulevards, the cheerful cafés, the gay
salons. But Mme de Staël was in her element. After all France was
no concern of hers. She was Swiss or Swede, but she was not French.
And France was the country that had ungratefully hustled her father
across the frontier.

She read aloud to these weary men from her own book on Happiness. That sorry group of exiles could hardly have been in a mood
to listen to her, but they were after all enjoying her boundless
hospitality so were not in a position to object. In the rue du Bac
they might have discovered charm in writer and reader, now they
were out of sympathy both with her and her subject. Talleyrand
found her voice monotonous, or as she would have called it *cantilène*.
Deeply preoccupied with the events overseas, fearful of what tragic
destiny might yet overtake their country, they bore the spate of
conversation with a certain heroic endurance. But even Narbonne's
devotion was ebbing. His thoughts too were in Paris, city of confusion and bloodshed. Their world was in ruins and she forced them
to listen while she vivaciously declaimed her own views about
happiness ! . . .

On January 21, 1793, Louis XVI was taken to the guillotine and
executed. Aware of his impending fate, he had on the previous day,
pleaded for three days' reprieve in which to prepare himself for
death. *Pour pouvoir me préparer à paraître devant la présence de
Dieu*, ran that proud pathetic petition written in his fine French
script. It was refused, and at six o'clock on a dark blear January
morning the guard came to fetch him. He addressed the crowd
for the last time, declaring that he died innocent, that he pardoned
his assassins and trusted that his death would prove of use to his
people. And as the fatal knife fell his confessor, Abbé Edgeworth,
cried in a loud voice : " *Fils de Saint Louis, montez au ciel !* . . ."

It was not long before the news which horrified Europe reached

"Our Juniperians," as Mrs. Lock of Norbury Park called them. For the most part their English neighbours looked askance at the group of refugees, nor was it only the English who thus cold-shouldered them. Their own countrymen, the Royalist *émigrés*, subjected them to an even more drastic ostracism, classing them with such men as Danton and Robespierre, and regarding them as implicated in the murder of their King.

Narbonne, himself of Royal blood, reacted to this tacit hostility and became daily more morose and gloomy. Mme de Staël could not but be aware that she was losing her hold over him. Her wit and vivacity could no longer charm him or his companions. The situation was a comfortless one. The King's death had changed the face of the world for them and it seemed but the precursor of even more tragic and sinister happenings. A bitter thought that by reason of their Liberal views they should be classed as Jacobins by their own compatriots. . . . In fact so great was the enmity displayed by the Royalists against the so-called Constitutionalists—whom rightly or wrongly they held responsible for the tragic happenings in France —that they refused either to meet or know them.

Among those living in the neighbourhood was Fanny Burney, the famous author of *Evelina*, who shortly afterwards married Général d'Arblay, a French *émigré*. Although she was then forty-one years of age, her father, Doctor Burney, disapproved of her growing friendship with Mme de Staël, and refused to permit her to accept an invitation to stay with her. He may well have asked himself what her relations were with this little group of men at Juniper Hall, and perhaps too rumours of her adventures had reached his ears. Probably he disapproved of her on moral rather than political grounds. Mme de Staël, who had had her own way since she was twelve, could hardly believe that a woman of over forty could be subjected to such coercive parental discipline. "*Mais est-ce-qu'une femme est en tutelle pour la vie dans ce pays ?*" she demanded indignantly of Mrs. Phillips, Fanny Burney's sister. "*Il me paraît que votre sœur est comme une demoiselle de quartorze ans !*"

§

In May Necker awakened suddenly to the realization of the fact that his daughter was living a highly irregular life at Juniper Hall, and that he was moreover footing the bill. This highly unpleasant reflection stirred him to immediate and drastic action. Germaine took absolutely no notice of his letters of remonstrance, so he resolved to send his nephew and niece to England to deliver his ultimatum in person. From this brief, and it must be supposed hectic visit, there sprang up an intimate but apparently blameless friendship between Mathieu de Montmorency and Albertine Necker de Saussure.

Mme de Staël was informed that she must return to Paris and to her husband. Otherwise there would be no money. And money represented the actual power she wielded over her mournful little group of exiles. Juniper Hall provided them at least with a roof and food, even if the climate and the readings were little to their taste.

She did not, however, go to Paris, indeed there would now have been little object in her doing so, since Sweden had, in common with many other European countries, ruptured diplomatic relations with France after the murder of the King. There was a fresh grouping of the Powers, England and Spain joining Prussia and Austria. In view of these changes Mme de Staël preferred to sojourn in her own country, and returning to Geneva took a house at Nyon, some fourteen miles from that city. Soon afterwards the unwelcome Baron de Staël arrived there, and rather oddly she induced him to use his influence to persuade Narbonne to join them. There was a price on his head, and though of course he could remain at Juniper Hall, it would be extremely unsafe for him to set foot in his own country.

That year the Reign of Terror was soaking France in blood. One night at a London theatre the performance was stopped and the audience informed, to their horror, that Marie Antoinette had been guillotined that morning. Silently they rose and left the house, appalled by the dreadful tragedy.

After more than two months' imprisonment in the Conciergerie, the Queen had been taken to her death. During her confinement in that damp unwholesome cell, harassed with anxiety as to the fate of her young son who had been taken from her, she had practically lost the sight of one eye ; her beautiful hair had turned white. She rose on that fatal morning, put on a new white muslin dress, loosely made, and covered her head with a plain white linen cap which almost concealed her hair. It was a broken woman upon whom the jeering mob showered their insults and imprecations. Only once did she show signs of giving way and that was when the tumbril brought her in sight of the terrible machine, awaiting its victim. . . .

Yet the thirst for blood was not yet satiated. Madame Elizabeth, the King's sister, was to follow her. Manon Roland and Philippe Egalité suffered a like fate. And not only in Paris but throughout France there came the same hideous tale of bloodshed and massacre.

Thanks paradoxically to the good offices of the Baron de Staël and his useful Swedish passports, Narbonne arrived in Switzerland and took up his abode at Nyon. But his gloomy morose temper was even more difficult than it had been at Juniper Hall. Nor did he find his hostess's position any easier than it had been in England. Barthélemy, the French Ambassador to the Swiss Diet, had heard of her plan of returning and was violently opposed to it. Nor had it been a simple matter to obtain leave to settle themselves at Nyon. At Berne it was announced that Baron and Baroness de Staël Holstein had applied for leave to rent a house there, in the neighbourhood of Coppet. They were invited to indicate their reasons for this step and to inform the authorities how long they wished to remain and to mention the number of servants as well as the names of the persons who would live under their roof. Finally, a reluctant permission was accorded, but they must apply for a renewal of it in three months' time.

Mathieu de Montmorency and Jaucourt were there under Swedish names. Narbonne took a Spanish one. Berne, aware of these flimsy subterfuges, tolerated them. It was through the influence of Gibbon appealing to Berne through d'Erlach that Narbonne had arrived at Nyon in safety. It was one of the historian's last acts for he died in January, 1794. A queer, undistinguished, corpulent figure, Germaine decided that had her mother married him she could never have been born of such a union ! . . .

Her melancholy, her dislike of Switzerland increased. The mountains seemed to her like convent grilles shutting her off from the outside world, in which she had once played so brilliant a part. She lived at Nyon in what she called a " hellish peace." Each day brought a fresh list of Robespierre's victims. She was a prey to her mother's melancholy, desiring death. . . .

But she had never been so active despite the vigilance of Berne. She must act, agitate, intrigue. For two years she occupied herself with assisting people to escape from Paris and death. What did it matter to her if the Royalist émigrés at Geneva avoided Coppet, Rolles and Nyon like the plague ? She was assisted by Schweizer of Zürich and it was largely owing to her that Baron de Salis and M. de Luze escaped in 1792, arriving in Switzerland with Swedish passports. She acted, somewhat after the manner of Nurse Cavell, as an agent of escape. Her plan was extremely simple—that was perhaps why it so rarely failed. A Swiss, man or woman, was sent to Paris with a passport containing a description answering roughly to the person whose escape was being arranged. On arrival this emissary would accomplish all the formalities, and then deliver passport and papers to the intending émigré, having already secreted about his or her person a second passport for use on the return journey. You cannot prove that you are not Swiss, Mme de Staël averred, especially when you have a Swiss companion to protect you.

The authorities at Berne still proving so narrow and hostile, Germaine now resolved to go to Zürich. She was not at that time on speaking terms with her parents, who refused to visit her. And she believed that at Zürich she would meet with a greater measure of toleration than at Geneva where she was the subject of much malicious gossip.

In the autumn Mme Necker grew worse. She was suffering from dropsy and her husband took her to Lausanne so that she might be under Tissot. But they were less welcome there than they had been ten years earlier. The French *émigrés* were passionately hostile. Many of " la belle Curchod's " old friends were dead.

Mme de Staël, now reconciled with her parents, arrived at Lausanne for a few days bringing Mathieu de Montmorency in her train. One day she read in the paper that Talleyrand had been expelled from England and had gone to America. This flung her into a state of nervous prostration. " I begin to hate Europe ! " she exclaimed, " My last effort for my friends shall be Zürich."

Seeing that nothing could be done for his wife Necker took her home. Coppet was so close to the frontier that he feared for their own safety ; he therefore applied to be permitted to keep a guard of fifty men there at his own expense. This was refused, and he moved to Beaulieu, which he believed to be less exposed. The agent Venet reported to the police that of the so-called Swedish merchants assembled at Nyon only de Montmorency remained. Narbonne had gone, and it was supposed he had planned to join Talleyrand in America.

Mme de Staël did actually go to Zürich for a short period with Mathieu. There she learned of the death of Danton on the scaffold ; how he had shouted as the tumbril bore him past Robespierre's house : " You will follow me, Robespierre ! " so that the little wizened man within trembled as if shaken by palsy. How he had sung until the knife fell exhorting the executioner to display his head well to the crowd as it was " worth looking at. . . ."

Robespierre, like a more modern dictator, was engaged in a drastic clean-up, destroying those whom he feared. And having accomplished this he turned his attention to the men and women of ill-repute. People of criminal records and tendencies were despatched by hundreds to the guillotine. He was Attila, the Scourge of God, divinely appointed to rid the world of such miscreants. More than a thousand persons perished thus during the three months of his

" Purge of Virtue." History repeats itself with a melancholy and savage monotony. . . .

It was Mme de Staël's moment to return to the place where alone she felt at home. The knife was no longer severing Royal, aristocratic and political heads ; its attention was concentrated upon the underworld of Paris. She left Zürich declaring that her friends in Paris were urging her return, and despite her mother's entreaties she made all her preparations for the journey.

In May, 1794, she went to Lausanne on her way to Paris, but hearing that her mother was dying left immediately for Beaulieu. Actually Mme Necker died the day after her daughter's arrival. Terrified of premature burial her will contained instructions that her body was to be embalmed and placed in spirits of wine in a leaden coffin with a glass lid, so that Necker might derive consolation by gazing upon her features. A macabre testament that suggests her mind had given way before the long series of calamities that life had offered her.

And for three months, until the tomb at Coppet was prepared, Necker did actually contemplate his wife's coffin. Impossible for Mme de Staël, despite her vaunted filial devotion, to remain with him in such circumstances. How could she receive her friends in a house where a corpse did actually—as Emerson later averred—form a solemn ornament ? . . .

§

Robespierre, satiated with the blood of degenerates, now turned his attention once more to persons of exalted rank. Madame du Barry went to the guillotine. So did the Abbé de Montmorency, the young priest-brother of Mathieu who was so stricken with grief and horror that he thenceforward led a life of extreme and even saintly piety. Mme de Staël worked ceaselessly to save her friends, and she did actually assist Mathieu's mother to escape. But there was little hope of appeasing Robespierre, a fanatic who professed to act in the name of religion. The truth was that fear possessed him ; he was haunted by the memory of Danton's sinister prophecy ; he was afraid of friends and allies as well as of enemies. Tallien, Fouché, the Comte de Barras who had reduced the population of Toulon to almost a fourth—he had his eye on them all. Tallien who had been working at Bordeaux under his orders had, however, fallen in love with the beautiful Marquise Thérèse de Fontenay, whose life he had spared. He had brought her with him to Paris, and it was her condemnation that sealed the fate of Robespierre.

When he ascended the Tribune one morning to read out the list

of names of those who were to perish, Tallien learned that that of his
beloved Thérèse was among them. Infuriated he incited rebellion
among those present. Robespierre was surrounded and seized ; he
was carried broken-jawed on the following day to the scaffold. . . .

Tallien's first action was to release the Marquise de Fontenay,
together with Joséphine de Beauharnais, whose husband had already
perished under the guillotine, and who was herself awaiting a like
fate. Who could have foretold that the pretty little Creole with
her blond curls was destined to become Empress of the French ?
Thérèse was known thenceforward as Notre Dame de Thermidor,
on account of the date of Robespierre's fall ; she used to affirm with
pride that it was she who had killed him. . . .

While these tragic happenings were in progress Mme de Staël
renounced her project of going to Paris. She took the Château de
Mézery near Lausanne, where Gibbon had stayed with his friend
M. de Crousaz, Seigneur of Mézery. She was proceeding thither after
taking farewell of her father when an adventure befell her. As she
approached Nyon a young pale-faced reddish-haired man rode up to
her. He had been to Coppet at the instigation of Madame de Charrière, and had failed to find her there. His name was Benjamin
Constant, and he was destined to play an important rôle in her
future life.

Born at Lausanne in 1767 he was a year younger than Germaine.
His father was Jules Constant and his mother Henriette de Chan-
dieu who died shortly after his birth. Benjamin had received what
was in those days an unusually cosmopolitan education, having
studied at Erlangen, Oxford, where, however, he only remained two
months, and Edinburgh. He had early shown a taste for literature,
and as a boy of fifteen had even sat at the feet of " la belle Curchod "
at the famous Friday receptions. He had been appointed Chamber-
lain to Duke Charles of Brunswick, and while acting in that capacity
had married Minna de Cramm, with whom he was so unhappy that he
obtained a divorce from her as soon as possible. In 1794, he was
back in Switzerland, and Mme de Charrière, an intimate friend, more
than thirty years older than himself, told him he must really know
Mme de Staël, against whom he had formed some sort of prejudice.

His early reactions were, however, favourable. He considered her
very energetic, very loquacious, highly imprudent, but good, trusting
and devoted. He was invited to Mézery where he found Narbonne,
Mathieu and his mother, Mme de Montmorency, a historic figure
who had survived the dreadful Reign of Terror, escaping the guillotine by the connivance of Mme de Staël. Mme de la Châtre and

de Jaucourt also formed part of the circle which was occasionally joined by Albertine Necker de Saussure and Mme Rilliet-Huber.

They were perfectly independent of Lausanne society. The Royalist *émigrés* were as ever bitterly hostile in their attitude, and the Swiss Republics were far more sympathetic to the Royalists than to the Constitutionalists. The agent, Venet, noted that the Bernese Government watched these assemblies at Mézery with considerable anxiety.

Mme de Staël was in Montesquiou's opinion a dangerous woman. How did she find time, he enquired bitterly, for so much love, so many dissertations, so much verse ? She wrote and wrote. Her novel *Zulma* appeared that year ; it was said to be the actual history of her liaison with Narbonne and his desertion of her. More than any of her other works did it belong to her soul, she affirmed. It was all about love. It was the story of an unhappy passion. . . .

Constant speedily made himself at home at Mézery. His admiration for Germaine increased by leaps and bounds. Never had he encountered such a marvellous combination of attractive qualities, so much brilliancy, so much wit, such accuracy, such universal benevolence, such untiring courtesy. She was in fact a being apart. They had all misjudged her in saying she could not listen but only talk. She enjoyed the wit of others. . . . The fact was he had fallen in love with her and then, as he failed to elicit the slightest response, he became sombre, gloomy, taciturn. One night he had a kind of nervous seizure. The house was awakened at midnight by piercing shrieks traced to his bedroom. Guests and servants quickly surrounded him. He declared that he was dying and wished to take a final farewell of Mme de Staël. This hysterical outburst was probably due to some subconscious jealousy. It failed to arouse the least sympathy in de Montmorency, who was placidly sitting reading the Confessions of St. Augustine in his room, clad in a dressing-gown of white piqué, when someone came to tell him what had happened. Mathieu was unaffected by the prospect of Constant's approaching demise ; he suggested that he should be thrown out of the window since he had given nothing but trouble ever since he came to the house, and his suicide would bring scandal upon them all, attracting too, what was so eminently undesirable, the renewed attentions of the police at Mézery ! . . .

Mme de Staël went to Benjamin Constant's room and soothed him, giving him her hand to kiss. Secretly, however, she seems to have shared Mathieu's sentiments, for when she returned to her room she washed her hand in eau-de-Cologne and remarked to Madame Rilliet-Huber : " I feel I shall have a physical

c

repugnance to that young man which I shall never be able to conquer ! "

She did however conquer it. . . .

At the moment she was greatly preoccupied with a Swede, Count de Ribbing, who was suspected of having been instrumental in procuring the assassination of Gustavus III of Sweden. This was a particularly tactless affair since her husband, who had gone to Denmark on a diplomatic mission, was trying to exculpate himself from any complicity in the crime and was also anxious to be reinstated as Ambassador under the new régime in France.

It became more and more difficult for Narbonne and de Montmorency to remain at Mézery since Berne had issued a decree that permission to remain in the Canton was not to be renewed in the case of men under fifty years of age. Moreover, de Staël who was now in Paris was clamouring for his wife's return. She decided to go and resolved to take Benjamin Constant with her. His ambitions coincided with her own. She believed that there were yet fields to conquer in France.

§

Necker was at Beaulieu, laid up from the result of a fall. She took leave of him but after her departure he wrote a last letter of wise, anxious advice, entreating her to calm her ambition until she was in a country where she was free to write and say what she chose. Constant must give her lessons in prudence and patience. And she must keep an eye on de Staël's expenditure. Patience . . . patience. " *Adieu, chère Minette ! . . .*"

She had just finished her *Refléxions sur la Paix*, addressed to France and to Pitt, but owing to her father's indisposition she did not show it to him for fear of risking their now amicable relations. But when she did so he forgave her. He hadn't much to lose now ; his old age could comfortably be spent at Coppet ; it was unlikely that he would ever return to play a part in the world of either politics or finance. His daughter's vagaries could do him little harm. But then he had not foreseen the new power that was so soon to arise and dominate France.

De Staël promised to be excessively useful to her as a *point d'appui* at this juncture, for he was so far the only Ambassador representing royalty accredited to the new French Government. A unique position, and it is not surprising that she was eager to share it. She went to Paris in May, 1795, accompanied by Constant, and not as was originally intended by her father's old friend, Meister. Once more she could open her salon, place her pawns on the table, and prepare for that game of intrigue which was life to her.

In Paris, which was still a deserted city, she was able to rent four good rooms for the modest sum of five shillings a month. On the other hand living was fantastically expensive, a dinner costing four pounds and a coat one hundred and twenty pounds. The faces of the people wore a hunted yet defiant look. They were the survivors—but for how long ? Not a single class had escaped the terrible lust for blood that had obsessed Robespierre. To such a generation there could be neither sense of security nor hope for peace.

Mme de Staël was anxious to bring Talleyrand and de Montmorency back to Paris ; she also endeavoured to get her father's name removed from the list of *émigrés*. But her efforts were misunderstood in certain quarters and she was publicly accused of being a Royalist agent. Her husband, who was in the House when Legendre thus denounced her, immediately left it. Her comment was characteristic : " The ignorant shout for liberty, but only the enlightened can give it to them ! "

Only in fact herself and Necker, despite his increasing years and weight, his melancholy absorption in his wife's coffin from which Germaine so desired to detach him. . . .

She was in Paris when the Directory was established under five leaders, Barras, Carnot, Lépeaux, Latourneur and Rewbell. There had been a sudden uprising of the populace in October, and Barras, who was in command of the troops, felt unequal to the occasion. Had he not relinquished his task it is possible that the course of history might have been radically changed, but he consigned it to a young Corsican officer of artillery then on half-pay in Paris, and who had first come under his notice at Toulon. The appointment is said to have been suggested originally by Joséphine de Beauharnais.

Napoleon Bonaparte was then twenty-six years of age, but already he had made something of his mark. Two years earlier he had driven the combined English and Spanish fleets from the harbour of Toulon. He was in Paris at the time of the massacre of the Swiss Guard, and also when the September massacres took place. The French, he remarked sagaciously, were " an ancient people out of control."

He gave the mob his famous " whiff of grapeshot " and order was restored.

The Directory was now established and Barras, looking about him for possible enemies, observed the presence of Mme de Staël. He ordered her to leave Paris, quite possibly at Bonaparte's suggestion. The Committee of Public Safety recommended this course, but the

Baron, so dependent upon Necker for funds, obtained her reprieve. She was compelled, however, to close her salon, and in December, in an access of nervousness, left for Coppet. Necker met his cherished Minette at Lausanne. She was accompanied by Constant.

At Coppet she was closely watched by the French police. It was said that the Necker family were friendly with the bitterest enemies of the Republic, one of whom was Mr. Wickham, British Ambassador at Berne. Desportes, a Frenchman living at Geneva in some diplomatic capacity, who was secretly aiming at the annexation to France of the State to which he was accredited, was charged with the surveillance of Mme de Staël. *Mouchards* and spies watched her, and when she met Wickham at Morges, whither he had come from Bâle on purpose to see her, and confided to him her intention of returning to France, it was immediately discovered and reported. Vigilance was redoubled directly Desportes got wind of it. One of her servants was in his pay and opened her letters. An elaborate plot was formed to arrest her at the frontier. But despite their care she discovered it and wrote a letter of indignant protest to Desportes. De Staël was further called upon to demand an apology for the insult offered to his wife. . . .

In June, 1796, she went to see Desportes, telling him that her honour required she should return to France. He counselled patience.

Constant grew weary of the monotonous life at Coppet. It was indeed hardly an existence to satisfy a young ambitious man who wished to have a great career in the world. In the morning they all sat for a couple of hours over their breakfast, while Mme de Staël conversed at great length, arguing with her father and Benjamin. At dinner Necker—who had begun to call himself Baron de Coppet —quarrelled violently with his ancient men-servants. At seven there was a game of whist of the kind which only those who have been privileged to play bridge *en famille* can properly appreciate. This invariably ended in such fierce disputes between Necker and his Minette that they would both fling out of the room in a rage, vowing they would never again play with each other. But on the morrow these trivial dissensions were forgotten and the game was resumed at its usual hour. It was obvious, however, that Mme de Staël's devotion to her father could not survive what Sir Walter Scott has called " the attrition of constant close contact."

So, like his predecessors in her favour, Constant sighed for liberty, for release from that brilliant, egoistic, loquacious personality. Thus he went to Paris, whither at present she dared not follow him. She had, not unnaturally, a horror of prison ; the sight of a gendarme, she was wont to say, deprived her of all courage.

CHATEAU DE COPPET

§

Benjamin Constant returned to Coppet in August and was followed a few days later by the Baron, who had been relieved of his post and was urgently in need of money. Meantime Mme de Staël had written a book : *De l'influence des passions sur le bonheur des individus et des nations.* Few could have been better qualified to write on such a subject.

She now learned that one name was on the lips of everyone in France—that of Napoleon Bonaparte, the young Corsican artillery officer, whose energetic action had quelled the Paris mob. He was now married to Joséphine Beauharnais, who had so narrowly escaped her husband's fate during the Reign of Terror.

The idea of writing to him began to germinate in Mme de Staël's fertile brain. Unfortunately the letter was less than tactful. Joséphine, she averred, was no fit mate for him. He was Scipio and Tancred combined. . . . Bonaparte was furious. He said she must be mad, and how dared she compare his wife thus unfavourably with herself ? Scipio and Tancred . . . such fulsome flattery as that cut no ice with the man who was already dreaming of world power. . . .

Baron de Staël had contracted debts to the tune of £8,000 while in Paris, and he naturally expected Necker to find the money. The banker refused, whereupon de Staël announced his intention of taking his wife and the children to Sweden. The two boys had spent most of their time with Necker and he did not wish to part with them. He paid the money, and the Baron departed to take the waters at Aix-les-Bains.

It was about this time that Goethe sent Mme de Staël a handsomely bound copy of his *Wilhelm Meister.* Knowing no German she was unable to read it, but it served as a pretext later on for introducing herself to that famous personage.

Constant returned to Paris, but early in 1797 he reappeared at Coppet and to everyone's astonishment took Mme de Staël back to France with him. He had obtained leave for her to reside at a distance of eight leagues from Paris, and proposed that she should occupy his house at Hérivaux which he had lately acquired. Necker was powerless to stop her, but he insisted upon keeping the boys with him. " *Quel malheureux vagabondage que tout cela !* " cried the old man.

She remained at Hérivaux until May, when it became necessary for her to go to Paris for her confinement, which must take place under her husband's roof. Deprived of his post, she found him living in great poverty.

In June, 1797, she gave birth to a daughter, Albertine, afterwards

duchesse de Broglie, reputed daughter of Benjamin Constant. Three
days later Montesquiou went to see her and found her still in bed,
but talking and declaiming with her usual energy. There were
seldom less than fifteen persons in the room. She made her usual
quick recovery and then re-opened her salon. It was really almost
as brilliant as in old days. Her ancient allies gathered around her.
Talleyrand limped in, back from his long exile in America, Mathieu,
Constant, even Narbonne were to be seen there. She won over
Barras sufficiently to extract a promise from him that he would
recognize that long-owing debt to Necker.

Through her influence—or so she said—Talleyrand was appointed
Minister of Foreign Affairs. It was like a renewal of old times and
the future seemed to her eager eyes unusually auspicious. Like all
born intriguers she believed that at such moments of apparent
success her fingers could control every pawn on the board. There
was one, however, with whom she had not reckoned, and that was
General Napoleon Bonaparte, fresh from his victories in Italy.

§

On his journey back to France Bonaparte had halted at Coppet
for the ostensible purpose of paying his respects to the aged statesman, and perhaps—who knows ?—of catching a glimpse of his famous
daughter, that dark, plain, brilliant woman who had so gratuitously
offered him her love and compared him to Scipio and Tancred. But
he did not find either father or daughter at Coppet.

Talleyrand, in his quality of Minister of Foreign Affairs, presented
Mme de Staël and Napoleon to each other at a reception in Paris.
She saw for the first time that pale face with its visionary grey eyes,
the classic outline of brow and nose, the compressed mouth, the
dark hair falling limply upon the forehead. A small thin man, yet
one whose name was on every lip and whose destiny she desired to
share. Between them what could they not do ? But after a conventional reference to Coppet and his regret at not having seen
M. Necker, he turned away.

She was not often at a loss, but she reacted to this indifference
with its faint hint of hostility. He was in love with his wife, with
her " *petit visage créole*," and he could not forget that this woman
had written disparagingly of her. He liked pretty dainty women,
and this one was plain, rather stout, and clumsy. He took her
measure and decided she was dangerous. . . .

And she ? With that penetrating insight that so rarely failed
her she discerned something of the quality of the man and her intense
admiration of him gave place to a sensation of actual fear.

The fear which he inspired can only have been due to the singular influence exerted by his personality upon all who approached him. He was more or less than a man. . . .

And she had known many types of men. Those who were fierce, those who merited respect, those who were clever, brilliant, crafty, ambitious, unscrupulous. But in those strange mesmeric eyes of the little pale Corsican she saw one for whom she might spread her nets in vain.

Far from finding myself more at ease in his company as time went on my fear of him increased. I had a vague conviction that no emotion could influence him. Every time I heard him speak I was struck by his superiority.

Subsequent interviews proved still more unsuccessful, nevertheless it seemed as if she were unable to relinquish her pursuit, her hope of conquering this conqueror. She followed him even to his house, endeavouring to penetrate into his study. He could not see her—he was changing his uniform. Snubs such as these had no effect upon her. At balls, receptions and dinners she observed that whenever his eyes met hers they became blank—it was as if he did not see her.

The Swiss Liberals had appealed to France to be delivered from the rule of the Bernese Oligarchy, and orders were given to the army to protect that country in the name of Liberty. What in this case would happen to the feudal dues from which Necker's money was so largely derived ? This new anxiety formed a very substantial pretext for Mme de Staël to seek an audience with Bonaparte. He listened to her for an hour and with apparent patience, but she saw that " Demosthenes and Cicero combined could not by their eloquence move him one inch in the direction of setting aside his personal interest."

The fact was he needed money for those military enterprises, those schemes of conquest, and he believed that Switzerland could provide him with both money and men. Moreover, it would facilitate his attack upon Italy if his troops could pass through the Pays de Vaud. He had visions of cutting a canal across Egypt so as to make a short sea-route to India. This would give the British Navy additional work to do in the East and render more feasible his life's aim—an attack upon England. " England is the enemy," he was fond of saying.

But Mme de Staël could not look upon this plan indifferently. Switzerland—her own country ! . . . Although she professed to hate its dullness, its prim provincial inhabitants who had criticized and

condemned her, she possessed in common with us all that ineradicable
patriotism, that sensitive race-consciousness, which cannot but
experience resentment at any hint of antagonism and attack. All
that was Swiss in her rose up against his cold, deliberate plans to
invade and perhaps despoil her country. She spoke with emotion
of its beauty, its tranquillity, its simple and laborious people. What
did these mean to the man who said : *There shall be no Alps ?* . . .

Besides he maintained that the state of the Pays de Vaud was
sufficient motive for the entry of the French troops. Were not its
inhabitants under the heel of the Bernese aristocracy ? There could
be no freedom without political rights—a contention which she, with
her notoriously liberal views, could hardly gainsay. Still, she maintained that the Vaudois were free, and that where actual liberty
existed it was unnecessary to obtain it by law or by such means as
the admission of foreign troops. What she really feared was the
sequestration of those feudal dues. She was, in fact, one of those
politicians who prefer to impose liberty upon any country rather
than their own. . . . She would go to Coppet. She would be by
her father's side when the French hosts poured through that quiet
valley. Necker was an old man, stout, rather helpless. It was
possible that his life might be in danger. She left Paris in January,
1798, her departure being accelerated by a hint from the police that
it was considered desirable. She had shown her hand too clearly
in her belief that "men must necessarily be won by truth if it is
presented to them with sufficient force." With her was her baby
Albertine.

§

Général Ménard led the French troops into the Pays de Vaud on
January 27, 1798. Mme de Staël stood on the terrace at Coppet
listening to the rolling of drums, the steady tramp of marching feet,
ever a sinister sound to those who have lived through long years of
warfare.

It was a brilliant day, and the Alps with their silver peaks and
crowns were faithfully reflected in the placid waters of the lake.
Some of the servants went down to a point where they could obtain
a better view of the invaders. Suddenly an officer approached to
the terror of the watchers, but happily he proved to be the bearer
of an assurance of safety to Necker from the French Commander.
In response to this friendly gesture Necker invited the staff to
luncheon.

Geneva was annexed, thus he became automatically a French
subject, and his name was removed from the list of *émigrés*. There

was a hint too that the debt might possibly be repaid, a matter of much more consequence to him. Later he wrote to the Directory, proving his Genevese origin.

Mme de Staël went back to Paris in the following year, leaving again in November at the instigation of the police. Early in 1799 we find her established in a furnished apartment at Geneva where she remained for six weeks, returning to Paris and St. Ouen in April only to be expelled again in July. The unhappy vagabondage, as Necker called it, continued.

Her pen was never so busy as at Geneva or Coppet. She now wrote *Des circonstances actuelles qui peuvent terminer la Révolution et des principes qui doivent fonder la République en France.* It embodied the views of herself and Constant, now a French subject and eager as ever to embark upon a political career. In this pamphlet she revealed, as perhaps never before, the antagonism she felt for the Catholic Church. Republics could only replace monarchies by a change of religion, she held. It had been freely urged in France during the preceding year that Catholicism and democracy were incompatible, therefore how much better it would be for that country to become Protestant and preferably Calvinist ! . . . She had been reared in that bleak and gloomy creed, although it has been said her own Calvinism would have somewhat astonished its founder. She wrote of the " Catholic religion which we wish to destroy." Anyone applying for a public appointment should be compelled, in her opinion, to sign a declaration incompatible with any belief in Catholic dogma. She had perhaps forgotten the ancient but still significant saying : *Qui mange du Pape en meurt. . . .*

Further, she argued, Calvinist pastors were citizens and fathers of families. They took no part in politics in Switzerland, and were therefore unlikely to do so in France. And much more to the same effect. But the time was not ripe for the publication of such a pamphlet, so she set herself to the task of writing *De la Littérature*, completing a chapter every morning. On the previous evening she would discuss the subject with her guests, delivering the argument with her usual rapid and brilliant improvisation, thus there was little left on the morrow except to commit it to paper.

In September she went to Lausanne, returning afterwards to Coppet, but in November despite her father's pathetic entreaties, his assurance that without her " *la vie manque,*" she left for Paris.

§

Bonaparte returned from his campaign in Egypt in the autumn of 1799 and was acclaimed as a hero, even a saviour. In November

he was appointed Commander-in-Chief of all the troops of the 17th
Division of the National Guard. Proclaiming this from a balcony
he made a histrionic appeal to the excited mob beneath his window.
" I rely on your aid. Will you help me ? "

The disaster of Aboukir Bay had paled before the triumph of his
arms at the Battle of the Pyramids. And had he not taken Malta,
carrying away precious relics from St. John's ? He had touched
popular imagination ; it seemed as if he could do whatever he chose.
The *coup d'état* of that same month placed him at the head of the
French Government with the title of First Consul. The Directory
was thus overthrown and the Republic established. It was founded
on liberty and on the system of representation. Had he not said
that self-respect and imagination were alike stimulated when a
man felt he had a share in the government of his country ? It was
in his penetrating perception of mass-consciousness that Bonaparte
excelled. Individuals meant little to him, but he knew how to sway
a crowd. He reviewed the troops and his grasp on the country
tightened.

Mme de Staël was in Paris at the time of the *coup d'état*, having
been met on arrival by Constant, who quickly put her *au fait* with
the political situation. She reopened her salon. She professed the
most passionate admiration for the hero. " You are all under a
spell," Necker wrote from Coppet. " I congratulate you on your joy
and on his glory."

The ministers thronged to her house as in the old days when she
was Swedish Ambassadress. Perhaps it was even more attractive
now that the ambiguous figure of de Staël was no longer there.
Talleyrand came, and that sinister sleuth-hound Fouché, the ex-
Oratorian, now once more Minister of Police. Amid that throng of
celebrities several members of the numerous Bonaparte family—
raised to an improbable eminence by the meteoric career of their
brother—were to be seen. Joseph, the eldest, tall, handsome,
clever, who had lately returned from a mission to the Pope, and was
in course of time to occupy two successive thrones ; Elise, afterwards Grand Duchess of Tuscany. Perhaps even one might glimpse
Pauline, afterwards Princess Borghese, then the wife of Général
Leclerc, nineteen years of age and beautiful beyond dreams. . . .
Louis, afterwards King of Holland, not yet married to Hortense
Beauharnais, Bonaparte's stepdaughter. The First Consul did not
forget his family, when he rose to power, but on the other hand they
must not forget that they too had to obey. . . .

Mme de Staël, unaffected by Necker's cynical comments, spoke of
the hero to his relations with the most fervid admiration. Her

remarks were repeated, as indeed she intended, but the great man remained unmoved.

All the time she was aware of his dislike. In his presence she was tongue-tied, a new experience, and felt stupid as a goose. He hated political women—and then she was too fat ! . . . And always, always, when his eyes met hers, they held that peculiar blank look, at once devastating and baffling.

Then she began to criticize, and that was fatal. Joseph went to see her on purpose to remonstrate with her about this new attitude. His brother, he said, had found fault with her. " Why," he had enquired, " does she not attach herself to my Government ? What does she want ? The payment of her father's deposit ? I will order it. His residence in Paris ? I will permit it. But what does the woman *want* ? "

She answered it was less a question of what she wanted than of what she thought. If this retort ever reached his ears she said he would ignore it, since the one person he could never understand was the perfectly honest and truthful one.

The only motive that could have forced her to surrender to that powerful will was her love of Paris, for the society it held. There she was in her element, and she was less pursued by that dread of boredom—*le fantôme de l'ennui* as she called it. Bonaparte had an instinctive flair for the weaknesses and imperfections of others ; he played on them so as to compel their surrender. He was aware that Mme de Staël, brought up in Paris from her earliest youth, would do almost anything rather than forgo her life there.

She held a reception one night at which Lucien Bonaparte was present as was also Constant. The latter told her that her salon was then filled with people who pleased her, but that if he spoke it would be empty on the morrow. " One must obey one's convictions," she replied recklessly. Excitement, the brilliant success of the evening had rendered her less than cautious, but she confessed later that she would not have thus repudiated Constant's advice had she foreseen what suffering such refusal would cause her.

And indeed, it was as he prophesied. She sent out invitations to a number of people and by five o'clock she had received ten letters of excuse. The blow was severe. People blamed her. Bonaparte had so far shown little tyranny ; many who had lost their fortunes during the Revolution were hoping he would restore them and recall their exiled relations to France. And those who had little to hope for believed that he was saving their country from the kind of anarchy they had experienced during the Reign of Terror.

Many of her friends showed Mme de Staël quite clearly that they wree unprepared to forgo the favour of the First Consul for her sake.

He rebuked his elder brother Joseph publicly, for going to see her, and for many weeks he did not set foot within her doors, his example being followed by three-fourths of her friends. Some of them told her they did not dare to come. Fouché kept watch on her house, and he was a man who inspired fear. Bonaparte told him that he could arrest men but he could not arrest ideas, and it was ideas which emanated from Mme de Staël's salon. . . .

§

In 1800, Madame de Staël published her book, *De la Littérature*, and its success restored her to the favour of society. There was no mention in it of the First Consul, but she expressed her own liberal sentiments with considerable vigour. At that time the Press was not muzzled ; censorship was confined to newspapers and was not extended to books which were scarcely read at all by the masses, and circulated only among educated persons.

Bonaparte was occupied at that time with weightier matters than the sentiments of Mme de Staël ; he was in fact planning his Italian campaign. The spring found him on his way thither. He passed Geneva and expressed a wish to see Necker, who complied more from a desire to render a service to his daughter than from any other motive. Bonaparte received him with the greatest civility and spoke of his projects with that frankness which was deliberate rather than spontaneous. The worthy banker was not impressed by the hero of France. He found nothing extraordinary in his conversation, and actually refrained from mentioning the debt, still unpaid after so many years, because he was only anxious to propitiate him in regard to his daughter. Thus he ventured to tell him that since the First Consul was pleased to surround himself with illustrious names he should also encourage talent as a decoration to power. The First Consul answered with civility and the result of the interview was to procure for Mme de Staël a renewed permission to reside in France for the present. It was the last time Necker's hand was thus stretched protectively over his daughter, and had she only learned to be cautious in her speech all might have gone well with her.

But that was, alas, the one thing she was unable to do.

Of course she must be on the spot to see the French Army pour across the peaceful landscape of the Pays de Vaud. She therefore returned to Coppet in the summer, and watched the troops march through that beautiful scene which the ramparts of the Alps, she thought, should surely have protected from such invasion. The

summer nights, the serene and starry skies made her ashamed of her
anxiety, but she could not calm the agitation that possessed her.
She hoped and prayed for the defeat of Bonaparte, yet she dared
not express such a sentiment, although it represented for her the sole
chance of release from tyranny.

M. d'Eymar, prefect of the Léman, remembering the days when
he had shared her dreams of liberty, sent her constant messages
reporting on the progress of the French in Italy, and she dared not
reveal to him that she received what he considered good news in
quite a contrary spirit.

For two hours it was believed that the Battle of Marengo was lost.
During that time of suspense Bonaparte rode slowly about in front
of his troops, pensive, his head bowed, facing disaster with courage,
making no effort, but awaiting destiny with stoical fatalism. Then
the tide turned and the battle was won. An armistice entirely dis-
advantageous to Austria ensued. The Peace of Lunéville signed in
the following February robbed them, however, only of Venice.

Now Bonaparte formed an alliance with the Emperor Paul I who
had rendered him incalculable service by abandoning Austria at a
moment when her struggles promised to be crowned with success.
He persuaded him that the peace of Europe would be secured for
centuries if the two great Empires of the East and West could enter
into an alliance. Paul, who had an enthusiasm for Bonaparte
resembling that of his father for Frederic II, believed him.

Bonaparte was in favour of pacifying Switzerland, traditional land
of mercenaries. Deprived alike of an army and a national budget,
he foresaw that it would become tragically dependent upon France,
which was exactly what he wanted. Had any of the Powers interested themselves in the fate of Switzerland ?—he demanded. He
had enforced recognition of the Helvetian Republic at the Peace of
Lunéville. England had refused . . . but Switzerland was no concern of England's. . . .

§

Mme de Staël spent much of that year at Coppet superintending
the education of her children. Religion was to form a definite part
of it, but they were to have a complete and frank knowledge of life.
She engaged a young Protestant pastor, Gerlach, to teach the boys
German, and after his death, some two years later, his post was
filled at the recommendation of Goethe by Augustus William
Schlegel, who obtained a certain ascendancy over his employer.

Auguste, who was then only ten, seemed to her quite a young
man ; already he was attending college at Geneva where he gained

prizes. Her little girl, Albertine, was, she said, very charming.
Albert . . . but even then the wild unruly Albert was beginning to
cause her trouble.

On one occasion a friend wrote to her asking her to recommend a
tutor for her son and enumerating the various qualifications and
attainments it was desirable that he should possess. Her answer
was witty and characteristic. *My dear, when I find your man I shall
marry him ! . . .*"

She remained at Coppet till the end of the year, announcing that
she was occupied with her father and children, and also with writing
a novel, *Delphine*.

Baron de Staël, who for some time past had been agitating for a
legal separation from the wife who had not only been so notoriously
unfaithful to him, but had also punctually and irremediably queered
his diplomatic pitch, now succeeded in obtaining it. The suit had
been begun when he was still Swedish Ambassador, and when it was
really impossible for him to have a wife under his roof who was not
only being watched by the police but had on more than one occasion
been requested to leave France.

When she returned to Paris in the winter of 1800-1801, before the
Peace of Lunéville, she established herself in the rue de Grenelle.
One night when she was entertaining friends she heard a loud
detonation. They thought it was simple gun-practice, but later
heard that a bomb had been thrown at Bonaparte as he was on his
way to the Opera.

All that winter she saw nothing either of him or of Talleyrand,
who as Minister of Foreign Affairs could hardly compromise himself
by going to her house. But many distinguished foreigners on their
way through Paris, as well as members of the Diplomatic Corps,
attended her receptions. She regarded this cosmopolitan atmosphere
as something of a protection since she sensed the increasing hostility
of the First Consul. He acknowledged that people who visited her
thought less of him after so doing. He rebuked the Prince of Orange
for dining with her, and openly disapproved of so many foreigners
visiting her.

In May, she was back at Coppet, but returned to Paris in the
autumn. There she discovered her husband in a pitiable state of
sickness and poverty. Rarely did she bear malice, this was one of
the " big " characteristics of her complex nature, and she did not
do so now. There was much that was kindly and maternal in her,
and Constant was not far wrong when he accredited her in the early
days of their friendship with " universal benevolence." Thus, it is
not surprising to learn that she immediately went to her husband's

assistance, nursing him devotedly night and day, and doing all she could to alleviate his sufferings.

In May, when her own return to Coppet was due, she resolved to take him with her, but when they reached Poligny he had another stroke and within three days was dead. He was the last to be buried in the old cemetery at Coppet, which has now been destroyed.

Mme de Staël stayed with her father for the remainder of that summer. During that year—1802—*Delphine* was published. The novel made a considerable stir and was very widely read, but it was destined to have dismal repercussions upon the life of its author gazing tranquilly upon her lake. For in it she boldly championed the very things to which Bonaparte was openly opposed. Protestantism, when he was negotiating the Concordat with the Pope. England, whose conquest he was planning, although the Treaty of Amiens had been signed in March and the rush of English to the Continent that summer had been quite unprecedented. The right to free love at a moment when he wished to reimpose upon France the Catholic religion, with its definite doctrines concerning the indissolubility of marriage, the sanctity of the family. Small wonder that it was condemned as " immoral " by the French Press, and she was warned that it would be unwise for her to return to Paris. Let her go to England, Bonaparte said, since she admired that country and its Constitution so passionately ! . . .

With death in her soul, as she expressed it, she resigned herself to the melancholy prospect of spending the winter at Coppet.

Bonaparte had been still further exasperated by Necker's book on *Liberty*. Many things were causing him deep anxiety at that time, and he wanted no enemies about him. The assassination of the Emperor Paul had shattered the alliance which was to have secured the peace of Europe for centuries. Once more he turned his eyes towards the white cliffs of England, so tantalizingly visible from the heights above Boulogne. . . .

The rush of English to the Continent was rudely arrested in the summer of 1803 when war was declared upon England. Many of those who were travelling on the Continent were stopped and interned. Among these was Lord Beverley, father of eleven children, who was returning from Italy with his wife and daughters. He languished for ten years in provincial cities. Another was Lovell Edgeworth, a brother of Maria, who was arrested on his way home from Geneva and remained at Verdun among the *détenus* until 1814. The iron hand of the little pale man whom Maria Edgeworth had seen riding on a white Spanish horse at a review in Paris, was making itself felt throughout Europe. . . .

Mme de Staël had renounced all hope of ever being associated with that world power. No longer did she deem him " the most fearless warrior, the deepest thinker, the most amazing genius the world had ever known." The long struggle between them, which was only terminated by his fall, had begun, and was to continue through the next eleven years.

§

Rashly, considering all the circumstances, Mme de Staël returned to France in the autumn of 1803, when she believed that Bonaparte was far too much occupied with military matters to think of her. She rented a house at Mafliers, some ten leagues from Paris, where she had as neighbours Constant and the beautiful Juliette Récamier. It was Madame de Genlis, a rival novelist, who betrayed her presence, telling Bonaparte that the road between Paris and Mafliers was crowded with the carriages of her visitors. Promptly he gave the order for her exile. She heard that a gendarme was on his way to deliver it, and took refuge in the house of a friend. By night she lay awake listening for the approach of the mounted police, by day she exerted herself to entertain her hosts. She wrote piteous letters to Joseph Bonaparte, begging him to intercede for her with his brother. All she asked was a retreat ten leagues from Paris, since she felt that if she were exiled now it would be for ever. He and Lucien did what they could, but it was of no avail.

Mme Récamier invited her to stay with her at St. Brice, a couple of leagues from Paris. She accepted, never dreaming that her presence could injure a woman so detached from public life and politics. From thence she addressed a letter to Bonaparte himself, saying that while at Mafliers she had been told it was his intention to send gendarmes to arrest her. Such an action would inevitably break her good old father's heart. " Citizen Consul," she added, " let me beg you to pause before you inflict such misery upon a defenceless soul."

Reassured by his silence she returned to Mafliers. One day she was at table with some friends when she saw a mounted figure in grey approaching the house. Another moment and he stopped before the grille and rang the bell. She was convinced that her hour had struck. He asked to see her ; she received him in the garden. He was, he said, in command of the gendarmerie at Versailles, but had been warned not to wear uniform for fear of alarming her. He brought a letter signed by Bonaparte ordering her to go to a distance of forty leagues from Paris within twenty-four hours. Haughtily she told him such notice doubtless sufficed for conscripts, but it was not enough for a woman with children. She suggested accompanying him to Paris where she proposed to remain for three days in order to make preparations for her journey. This was permitted and he drove thither with her and her children.

On the way she stopped at St. Brice to tell Madame Récamier of this fresh blow. Général Junot was there, and out of devotion to his hostess promised to do all in his power to intercede for her. Arrived in Paris she stayed at a house which she had recently rented but never occupied ; the publication of *Delphine* had effectually put a stop to that and to her dream of holding a salon there, whither all the distinguished foreigners, the brilliant and spiritually-minded men who had been in Paris just before the war broke out, would flock as of old to her standard.

Every day a gendarme would appear, entreating her to depart, and every day she demanded a further reprieve. Her friends rallied round her ; she gave dinner parties ; at times, forgetful of the fate that overshadowed her, they were almost gay. They could even jest about the punctual appearance of the gendarme, telling her it reminded them of the days of the Terror when the gendarmes came thus to fetch their victims. . . .

The prospect of exile was like death to her, she said. Had not great men of all ages succumbed to that anguish ? People, she maintained, showed more courage on the scaffold than when faced with banishment from their own country. And perpetual banishment was ever one of the harshest penalties of the law. Yet she was more favourably placed than many—she had her father's house at Coppet ready to welcome her.

Once more Joseph Bonaparte attempted to plead for her. His wife, a woman of " great sweetness and simplicity," invited her to stay with them at Mortefontaine where she remained for three days. Although her host and hostess were kindness itself, the presence of Government officials rendered the atmosphere disagreeably hostile. She had her son Auguste with her and spent long hours in the beautiful gardens of which Joseph was so proud.

She was undecided whether to go to Coppet, where she was so well known and where the humiliation of her banishment would provoke malicious gossip, or to Germany where she had been assured of a warm welcome. Ultimately she decided upon the latter course, but greatly to her subsequent regret since she was thus prevented from seeing her father again alive. Joseph Bonaparte gave her excellent letters of introduction, and she started for Germany with Constant and her two children. As he adored Paris she was not unmindful of the sacrifice he was making in accompanying her.

D

§

Travelling, Mme de Staël observed in her novel *Corinne*, is the
saddest of all pleasures. To traverse unknown lands, to listen to
languages of which you understand nothing, to see human beings
who have neither lot in your past nor your future, is to confront
solitude and isolation without repose or dignity. Further, to arrive
in a place where there is none to welcome you is little conducive to
self-respect. Germany offered her at that time all those disadvantages
and her journey was also attended by other calamities.

She stayed for a couple of weeks at Metz and then proceeded
to Frankfort where Albertine, who was then only five years old, fell
dangerously ill. Mme de Staël was at her wits' end. She knew no
one in the place ; she could speak no German ; the doctor she
called in knew very little French. However, after some days of
terrible anxiety the child recovered, and when she was convalescent
they went on to Weimar where something of courage returned to
Germaine as she contemplated the wealth of intellect that lay beyond
France ! . . .

Her chief reason in going there was to see Goethe and Schiller
whom she " stormed with cannonades of talk." She did not, however,
see Goethe on her arrival, for he was absent at Jena, although he
civilly intimated he would be delighted to receive her there. Schiller
had perhaps presented a slightly formidable portrait of her to
Goethe. He said she was the " most talkative, the most combative,
the most gesticulative of all living creatures he had ever seen,"
adding, however, that she was also the most cultivated and gifted.
" She insists," he said, " on explaining everything, understanding
everything, measuring everything. She admits of no darkness, of
nothing incommensurable, and where her torch throws no light there
nothing can exist. . . . For what we call poetry she has no sense ;
she can only appreciate what is passionate, rhetorical, universal.
She does not prize what is false, but does not always perceive what
is true."

The Duchess Amalia of Saxe-Weimar was fascinated by her.
And early in 1804 Goethe went to Weimar and received her on several
occasions, sometimes alone, sometimes in company. He was cold
and formal to her because quite recently two women had published
the letters they had received from Rousseau, and Mme de Staël
told him frankly she intended to print his conversation.

Her opinion of him was eminently favourable. He was, she
averred, " *un homme d'un esprit prodigieux. En conversation quand
on le sait faire parler il est admirable.*" But he never talked to her

intimately, although sometimes, under the influence of champagne, he was brilliant. . . . She left Weimar on February 29 greatly to the relief of both poets.

Then Berlin where the King┐received her kindly. Yet to her surprise that spring she met many of the former partisans of the French Revolution who did not perceive that Bonaparte was a more bitter enemy of its principles than the ancient European aristocracy.

§

One morning she was told that Prince Louis Ferdinand was below on horseback and wished to speak to her. Hurriedly she went down. He brought the tragic news that the Duc D'Enghien had been seized on Baden territory, handed over to a military court-martial, and shot twenty-four hours after his arrival in France. The last representative of the House of Condé, he was then thirty-two years of age, and it is said had been in no way implicated in the recent Royalist movement, plotted by Pichegru and Moreau, to reinstate the Bourbons.

Despite her hatred of Bonaparte Mme de Staël could hardly believe the news, even when she read the sentence of death against the said Louis d'Enghien in the *Moniteur*. How could any European monarch consent to an alliance with Bonaparte after such a crime ? There must surely be some spiritual sanctuary whither his empire could never penetrate. . . .

Fouché summed it up in his famous phrase : " It is worse than a crime—it is a blunder." Bonaparte asked a senator what was being said about it. He replied that the people were very deeply distressed. " That does not surprise me," Bonaparte remarked. " A House that has reigned so long can always command interest."

In the last letter he ever wrote to his daughter, Necker expressed his extreme indignation at the act. Shortly after the receipt of this missive came the news that he was desperately ill. The messenger concealed the fact of his death from Mme de Staël and it was only at Weimar that she learned the truth. The remainder of her journey was passed in profound, even excessive grief.

Constant went to meet her. At Zürich Mme de Necker-Saussure with little Albert de Staël was awaiting her. Mme Rilliet-Huber met her at Coppet. They told her Necker's last thoughts had been for her. He loved God, he said ; he was going to meet his dear wife. But no one must blame his daughter for her absence. He had wished it, and the father's heart was the best judge. Forgotten were the years when he had played a great and even tragic rôle in the world of affairs, his triumph at Versailles, his last flight to Coppet. Minette —Minette—so lovable, so imprudent, was his one thought. . . .

The tomb he had built for his wife stood close to the walls of the park, surrounded by a plantation. The small mausoleum of black marble contained a deep marble tank divided in two. In one half the body of Mme Necker, still perfectly conserved in the spirits of wine wherein it floated, was visible. Her husband was now consigned to the vacant part, where he also floated in spirits of wine. The doors of the tomb were then closed and the outer walls bricked up. All Coppet was present in tears at these rites.

Just before his death, Necker had, with trembling hand, written a letter to Bonaparte imploring mercy for his daughter, and assuring him that she had had no hand in his book on *Liberty*, for the publication of which he now blamed himself bitterly.

Bonaparte, unmoved by the appeal, flung the letter down. Mme de Staël might well regret her father, he said scornfully, there was never a more commonplace man " with his *flon-flon*, self-importance and columns of figures."

The First Consul was occupied then with far weightier matters for the time was approaching when he was to assume the title and rôle of Emperor. " They may laugh at my new dynasty now," he said, " but in five years' time it will be the oldest in Europe."

What concern was it of his if people muttered that it was the blood of d'Enghien that had baptized this new dynasty ? . . .

§

Necker left his daughter £150,000, which in those days represented a considerable fortune. The money he had lent to the French Government had not yet been repaid, but even without this Mme de Staël, now owner of Coppet, found herself at his death a very wealthy woman.

It was said that despite her grief Coppet now resembled an hotel. Constant was there, grumbling like a spoilt child ; Schlegel addressed his hostess with alternate sarcasm and severity. Someone called her " *la trop célèbre.*" In her deep mourning, with considerable parade of woe, she entertained freely while preparing her father's manuscripts for the press, and examining her own finances which were in chaos.

She wrote *Du caractère de M. Necker et sa vie privée.* Constant affirmed that she was more self-revealed in this book than in any other. She drew her own portrait while purporting to draw that of her father. Her enthusiastic admiration of him, her grief at his death, were alike exaggerated. There were no spots upon that blameless personality, as she now called upon the world to see. Forgotten were those bitter days when he had declined to supply

her with any more money, thus enforcing her departure from Juniper
Hall ; forgotten was the time when he expressed his displeasure by
refusing to visit her at Nyon ; forgotten too were those stormy scenes
at " family whist." . . .

Having performed this filial duty she resolved to go to Italy.
Joseph as usual supplied letters of introduction. At Milan, on her
way to Rome, she met the poet, Vincenzo Monti, whom she added
to the long list of her admirers. But she did not care for the Italians
nor was she greatly impressed by the scenery. She always said she
would not go to her window to look at the Bay of Naples, whereas
she would travel leagues to meet an intelligent person.

At Venice, on her way back, she encountered an Austrian officer
of Irish descent, Maurice O'Donnell de Tirconnell, who is supposed
to have been the original of Oswald, the hero of *Corinne*. It may be
mentioned that Mme de Staël is said to have lived her books before
writing them, and the interminable conversations at Paris, Coppet
and elsewhere provided her with the dialogue.

She was now thirty-eight years old and had grown very stout.
Maurice was only twenty-five, nevertheless, she fell in love with him
and invited him to stay at Coppet. They shared a bitter hatred of
Napoleon. They only spent five days together, nevertheless the
impression this melancholy young man made upon her was profound
and lasting.

Napoleon, planning a descent upon the English coast, wrote to
Fouché saying that if that jade Mme de Staël ventured within a
hundred and twenty miles of Paris, she would be arrested. There
must be no intriguing within his gates for the hour was a desperate
one. Within two months of that letter the French Fleet encountered
the disaster of Trafalgar, which effectually destroyed all Napoleon's
dreams of conquering England. But on land he defeated the allied
Austrian and Russian forces and assured his troops that the English
would be compelled in consequence to make peace.

In the following year, 1806, Mme de Staël succumbed to that
nostalgia for France which from time to time assailed her. She
wished to send Auguste to the Ecole Polytechnique in Paris so she
settled herself at the Château de Vincelles at Auxerre. It was outside
the limits set by Napoleon so that she deemed herself safe from
arrest, although he had clearly demonstrated his desire that she should
remain at Coppet.

Auxerre soon proved to be too far from the capital ; she must
therefore go to Rouen where she could receive daily news of the
happenings in Paris. She was in a highly nervous state and took
opium. She had scenes with Constant, " vile, horrible, senseless "

as he described them. " Either she is mad or I am mad. How will
it end ? "

Now she finished *Corinne*. She was always the heroine, beautiful,
fatal, brilliant and attractive, of her own novels. Ouida and Marie
Corelli were both in the direct descent from her. Their lovely
virtuous intellectual women were portraits of themselves as they
wished to appear before the world. Mme de Staël was however far
ahead of those rivals ; she was more learned and had a wider outlook,
a more penetrating insight. In *Corinne* she wrote explicitly of her
life in Rome, and if there is too much of the guide-book for modern
readers in its pages, it does provide an excellent picture of early
nineteenth-century life in the Eternal City.

The Emperor regarded such writings as tendentious, even dangerous. She extolled the English, their country, their Constitution
and customs, to the detriment of anything France had to offer. The
book expressed views that were in exact opposition to his own, and
of course everyone was reading it. She must be forbidden to write
even fiction since she used it as a vehicle for the expression of
her political aims and antipathies. Hardly had *Corinne* appeared
than she received an order to leave France immediately. Bad citizens,
Napoleon said, were not to be given the opportunity of disturbing
the peace of his capital during his absence. " That wicked intriguer
had better take care. Send her back to her lake ! Have not these
Genevese done us enough harm ? My decision is that she is never
to leave Geneva."

Clever she might be, but she could never learn wisdom. Had she
known how to keep silence and refrain at least from publishing what
she wrote, she might have continued to reside unmolested in France.
But she could do neither, and she never seems to have fully envisaged the relentless will, the ruthless power of Napoleon. Again
and again she would fling a defiant challenge in his face, and he was
not the man to deal lightly with an enemy, man or woman. Broken-
hearted at this fresh manifestation of his implacable hostility, she
returned to Coppet.

Once more the perpetual visitors. Meister was there, Schlegel with
his brother Frederic, Constant with his adorable ways of a spoilt
child, the Châteaubriands.

Why did she not marry Constant now that she was free ?—his
relations had begun to ask themselves. Rosalie Constant, his cousin,
who had always been devoted to him, approached her frankly on
the subject. Why must she, despite so many admirable qualities,
continue to disappoint them ? " Oh, how I could have loved you
had you married Benjamin and he had found happiness with you ! "

But Constant at that time had returned to an old Brunswick love, Charlotte, who was about to divorce her second husband Dutertre. In the meantime he went to Coppet and there were terrible scenes. Even her children regarded him as a monster to cause their mother such sufferings. Rosalie frankly told Mme de Staël that she should have married him the moment she was free. Benjamin was unhappy, undecided. . . .

She went to Lausanne, staying a month at Montagny with Juliette Récamier and other guests. Thither came Prince Augustus of Prussia, who fell in love with the beautiful Juliette. He was a prisoner of war interned in Switzerland. They amused themselves with theatricals, playing *Andromaque*. Mme de Staël took the part of Hermione and Constant that of Pyrrhus. Never, said Rosalie Constant, had Hermione been played so naturally and with such passion ! When Mme de Staël went back to Coppet Benjamin promised to follow her.

He failed to appear. She sent horses, carriages, servants, to fetch him. " I am going to Coppet," he announced tragically. His relations, especially Rosalie, counselled an immediate marriage or a complete rupture. Mme de Staël refused to consider either. There were renewed scenes after his arrival at Coppet, and although there was a reconciliation he rose early and rode back to Lausanne, having covered the distance in two hours and a half. He arrived dropping from fatigue. Mme de Staël appeared not long afterwards and carried him off. Rosalie vowed she would never see her again. . . .

He escaped at the end of November and met Charlotte at Besançon, marrying her in the following year during Mme de Staël's absence in Vienna and Germany. He did not inform his Swiss relations of his marriage nor did he tell Germaine that it had taken place until they met at Sécheron in the following year, when he introduced the two women to each other.

He was greatly in Mme de Staël's debt, but she refused to accept the money when he offered it. They signed a document agreeing that it should be repaid after his death, either to her or her heirs.

§

Mme de Staël returned to Coppet in the summer of 1808, and with the memories of her recent travels in Austria and Germany still fresh in her mind, wrote her book *De l'Allemagne*. And as everything English had been extolled in *Corinne*, so all that was German was represented as perfect in this new venture.

Mme Récamier was with her ; Mme Vigée-Lebrun, who painted her portrait as Corinne holding a harp ; Schlegel, the children. To outward view an innocent and harmonious party ; the ambiguous, brilliant, yet withal childish figure of Constant absent.

It charmed " *la trop célèbre* " to hear that her novels, especially *Corinne*, were influencing men against the policy of Napoleon, although she must have foreseen this would involve an even more stringent exile from the one country where she felt at home and happy. And already the Emperor's sleuth-hounds were on her track. Her friendship with a German called Gentz had been discovered, their correspondence was in Napoleon's hands. He believed her to be intriguing against him not only in Germany but in England. The police were commanded to keep watch on all her movements, to note too the names of those who visited her at Coppet. More friends fell away, fearing to be compromised.

While in Vienna she had renewed her friendship with the young Austrian officer, Maurice O'Donnell, who had introduced her to his friends and notably to his kinsman, the Prince de Ligne. Sometimes he had aroused her jealousy by paying too marked attentions to the young Princesse Flore de Ligne ; there was a scene and she reproached him bitterly.

Now a terrible blow fell upon her. Undoubtedly he had recovered from his infatuation for this plain stout woman so many years older than himself, but in any case a letter reached her in which he definitely broke off all relations. Her fury knew no bounds. She wrote the most violent and tempestuous letters, but the young man stood firm. Perhaps he was actuated by some motive of self-interest, for Napoleon was now turning his eyes towards Austria.

His marriage to Joséphine Beauharnais, which had taken place in 1796, had been happy in its first beginnings, although she was six years older than himself and the mother of two children. But no heir had been born of the union and Napoleon wished to establish his dynasty. It was in 1809 that he took steps to have his marriage annulled. Indeed, that it had ever been a marriage has been questioned since the ceremony was performed by a schismatic priest and therefore invalid. Be that as it may, Joséphine, who had always obeyed him, retired in favour of this Royal rival, the niece of Marie Antoinette, the last Queen of France. Napoleon felt that through the Archduchess Marie-Louise, something of royalty would surely descend upon him.

Their marriage took place early in 1810, and shortly afterwards Mme de Staël resolved to return to France, M. le Ray, an old friend and client of Necker's who was now in America, lent her his château at Chaumont-sur-Loire. On his return to France she moved to an estate at Fossé, placed at her disposal by the owner, M. de Salaberry.

They made much music. Mme Récamier was there, and sang to them in her sweet voice. There was a young Italian who had been engaged to give lessons to Albertine on the harp. Constant was there, and Augustus William Schlegel, her son's German tutor. And beneath the windows the peasants would crowd nightly to listen to this " colony of troubadours." Such a life, so innocent, so apart from politics, so solitary yet devoted to the arts, could surely arouse the suspicions of no one ! . . .

Napoleon was, however, asking himself the old question : " What does the woman *want* ? . . ."

Often they sang a favourite air composed by the Queen of Holland, the unhappy Hortense, daughter of Joséphine Beauharnais, whom Napoleon had married to his brother Louis for purely political motives. Over her he exercised an imperial rather than a paternal tyranny, and was furious when he heard on one occasion that she had left France with her children, ordering them to return immediately. She was very unhappy in her marriage and music was a resource to her. Her best-known song is *Partant pour la Syrie*, but the one which pleased the little colony of troubadours at Fossé was *Fais ce que dois, advienne que pourra*.

After dinner they would all sit round a green table and write letters to each other instead of talking. This amusement proved so enthralling that they would hurry away from the table in order to resume it, and if strangers appeared to interrupt their *petite poste*, as they called it, they were deeply annoyed. Nor did the unwelcome visitors regard it too sympathetically. A pedantic and high-brow means of passing the time ! . . .

One day a young man called to take Albertine for a walk in the woods. His one passion was for hunting so it was unlikely that he would appreciate this unusual diversion. Perhaps too he was suspicious, for when Mme Récamier wrote a letter to him in her delicate script so as to try and draw him into the charmed circle, he refused point-blank to accept it. He could not possibly read it by that light, he said. And although they laughed a trifle acidly they reflected that not many letters from that hand could have shared a similar fate.

Mme de Staël became bolder. She went to the Opera House at Blois to hear a performance of *Cenerentola*, then a novelty which had met with an enthusiastic success. When she emerged she found herself surrounded by a crowd anxious to catch a glimpse of the famous woman. The Minister of Police wrote to inform the Prefect of Loir-et-Cher that she was " surrounded by a court." " That is true," she retorted, " but it isn't one that power has given me."

On September 23 she corrected the last proofs of *De l'Allemagne*

which she said had taken her six years to write. She made a list
of a hundred people to whom she wished copies to be sent, both in
France and other countries. She confessed that her object in writing
it was to bring new ideas to the notice of France ; she believed the
French would discover in it a language they no longer spoke. The
language of liberty ? . . . It was perhaps the most defiant challenge
she had ever flung in Napoleon's face.

But she had no fears. She had been informed that the Censor
had authorized its publication.

She went to stay on the estate of Mathieu de Montmorency five
leagues from Blois. The house was situated in the middle of a forest
almost on the site of the Battle of Fretteval, fought between Philip
Augustus and Richard Cœur de Lion. While there she felt unusually
calm and at peace. Mathieu, who, since his brother's death on the
guillotine, had concentrated all his attention upon religion, endeavoured to help Mme de Staël to save her soul. But his efforts
were abruptly frustrated for driving in the vast plains of Vendôme
they lost their way completely. It was midnight when they suddenly
encountered a young man on horseback who, perceiving their plight,
offered to escort them to his parents' house which happened,
fortunately, to be near.

There they found themselves surrounded by the luxury of Asia
combined with the elegance of France. The owners had spent many
years in India, and their house was adorned with trophies acquired
during that sojourn.

Alas, in the small hours of the following day M. de Montmorency
received a visit from Auguste de Staël, who gave him a letter for his
mother, begging her to return home at once since trouble had arisen
with the Censor in regard to her book. He had followed her and
like herself had lost his way in those vast plains, but fortunately
had chanced upon the very house where she was being entertained.
Auguste left it to de Montmorency to tell her of this fresh demon-
stration of persecution from the Imperial Police, and hurried back
home in order to place her papers in safety.

Mme de Staël did not read her son's letter immediately, as she was
making a tour of the house and examining the Indian treasures,
but when she was in her carriage on their way back to de Montmorency's house she opened it. Fouché had commanded the ten
thousand copies of her book to be destroyed, and she was ordered
to leave France within three days.

This fresh sorrow struck at her very heart. She had believed
in the success of her book. Had the Censor refused her permission
to publish it she could the more easily have understood the present

action of the police. She had made all the changes they desired, yet in spite of this the book had been destroyed and she was compelled to leave the society of those friends who alone could sustain her courage.

As she approached Fossé she gave her desk, which contained certain notes about the book, to her younger son who climbed over the wall so as to enter the house unperceived at the back. Miss Randali, an Englishwoman who was living with her, came to meet her to tell her what had happened. And from afar she could see the gendarmes who always evoked within her a special terror. . . .

The Prefect demanded her manuscript. She gave him a rough copy, with which he was satisfied. She heard that later he was punished for having shown her a certain consideration. Yet the grief he subsequently felt at the fall of Napoleon hastened his own end.

§

Having seen in the newspapers that American vessels could enter the Channel ports, Mme de Staël hoped that her American passport would permit her to disembark in England. Such a journey would, however, require considerable preparation and she begged the Minister of Police to grant her a few days' reprieve. He replied that her son would probably have already told her there would be no difficulty about her postponing her departure for seven or eight days, but that she must make these suffice as he could not give her longer.

The reason of the order I have given you—he wrote—is not to be sought in the silence you observed regarding the Emperor in your last book ; it would be a mistake to attribute it to that since he could not have found any place in it worthy of him. But your exile is a natural consequence of the line of conduct you have pursued now for several years. It appears to me that the air of this country does not suit you, and we are not yet reduced to seeking examples among the people you admire.

Your last work is not at all French. I myself stopped the printing of it. I regret the loss which the publisher must sustain, but it is not possible for me to permit it to appear.

You are aware, madame, that you were only allowed to leave Coppet because you expressed a wish to go to America. If my predecessor permitted you to remain in the Department of Loir-et-Cher you should not have regarded this privilege as a revocation of those orders already made in regard to you.

I shall instruct M. Corbigny to execute the order I have given him when the delay granted to you shall have expired.

There were polite expressions of regret that she should have thus constrained him to open his correspondence with her so harshly. The letter was signed the Duc de Rovigo. In a significant postscript he mentioned the ports from which she would be permitted to embark, requesting her further to indicate the one upon which she decided. They were L'Orient, La Rochelle, Bordeaux and Rochefort, and from this selection she knew that she was to be prevented from going to England.

Of course the letter infuriated her. Why should she have mentioned the Emperor and his armies in a book that was purely literary? The Minister retorted sharply that it was scarcely possible a person so well known as herself could write a book about Germany, with whom the French had now been at war for several years, without mentioning them. "Not only should the book be destroyed but its author ought to have been imprisoned at Vincennes. . . ."

There was no help for it. This meant war to the knife, and she had no alternative but to return to Coppet.

At Dijon she saw groups of Spanish prisoners emerging to enjoy the sunshine, wearing their tattered cloaks with an air of nobility. At Auxonne English prisoners, who only the night before had helped to extinguish a fire in the town where they were interned. At Besançon more Spaniards. . . . And there too an angelic Frenchwoman, Mlle de Saint-Simon, was voluntarily sharing her father's imprisonment in the fortress.

Upon the mountains that separated France from Switzerland she saw the Château de Joux, where the State prisoners languished in an ice-bound solitude. There Toussaint Louverture, the "Black Consul" transported to that "hell of ice," had perished of cold. Perhaps, she reflected, his cruelties had merited punishment, but the Emperor, who had guaranteed his liberty and his life, should have been the last to inflict it.

But then, was there not a complete absence of all security under the empire of Napoleon? she asked herself. Beneath the rule of other despots existing customs, laws, religion had been observed which even the most tyrannical dared not infringe. Only in France one must either hope or fear all things according as one supported or opposed this man whose dream was the conquest of the human race. . . .

On her arrival at Coppet she saw a rainbow above her father's house. It made her feel almost resigned to her lot. Why not give up writing and find happiness only in her affections? But that would mean sacrificing the talent she possessed.

§

Even at Coppet the iron hand of Napoleon's Government could reach her. The Prefect of Geneva informed her that her two sons were forbidden to set foot in France without the permission of the police. This, she said, was to punish them for having taken their mother's part and shown resentment at the manner in which Napoleon had treated her. Her own misfortunes would thus react heavily upon them at the outset of their career, but they made light of this and all consoled themselves—rather strangely when one remembers the hectic scenes at the whist table—in the contemplation of the deceased Necker ! . . .

The Prefect's next step was to demand the surrender of such proofs of her book as she still retained. The Minister's spies had served him well since his information was perfectly accurate, as she now hastened to tell him. But as her copy was not in Switzerland she could not and would not give it to him. However, she promised him that it should not be published on the Continent, adding that she made no merit of this since what European country would permit the publication of a book banned by the Emperor ?

Soon afterwards the Prefect who was, according to her, one of the most honest and intelligent men in France, was removed from his post, and as people attributed this to his failure in regard to her, all those who desired promotion ceased to visit her. It was simply an example of the old aphorism—that it is a mistake to associate oneself with the unsuccessful or unfortunate.

She had many friends in Geneva who with their heritage of liberty still possessed generous impulses, but at the same time she disliked the thought that she might be compromising those who came to see her.

In March, 1811, another Prefect was appointed. He told her that gifts such as hers were made for the exaltation of the Emperor and that this was a subject worthy of the enthusiasm displayed in *Corinne*. Haughtily she answered that, persecuted as she had been by him, all such praise on her part would necessarily sound like a petition and she was sure that even he would regard it as absurd. The Prefect combated this view of the case, and urged her in her own interests to write something—even if it were only a pamphlet of a few pages—in praise of the Emperor, and thus terminate the penalties from which she was now suffering. Would she not perhaps write a poem on the birth of the King of Rome—the longed-for son of Napoleon and Marie-Louise ? She laughed, and said the subject did not inspire her and she could only express the hope that his nurse would be a good one.

Soon afterwards Albert was ordered a course of waters at Aix-les-Bains, and she arranged to go thither early in May when there was practically no one there. She stayed at a village nearby where she knew no one, but scarcely ten days had passed when the Prefect of Mont Blanc sent a courier ordering her return to Coppet. Apparently he feared that she might leave for England, and although Aix could hardly be said to be near London, gendarmes were sent to the different stages to forbid that any horses should be supplied to her *en route*. Ordinarily she would have laughed at this fresh exhibition of " prefectorial activity " as she called it, but her nerve was broken. *Je mourrais de peur à la vue d'un gendarme*, she confessed, and perhaps visions of the Château de Joux rose before her.

Fresh annoyances greeted her at Geneva. Not only was she forbidden to enter any country now allied to France, but she was even advised not to travel in Switzerland. Two leagues from Coppet were to represent the precise limit of her wanderings. She replied with spirit that being domiciled in Switzerland she could not imagine by what right any French authority could prevent her from travelling in a foreign country. The advice was repeated with a hint of menace, and on the following day she learned that Augustus William Schlegel, who had for eight years acted as tutor to her sons, had been ordered to leave both Geneva and Coppet. He was to be removed in her own interests since his influence was making her anti-French. What had he done ? she enquired indignantly. He had compared the Phèdre of Racine with that of Euripides, giving his preference to the latter. A delicate matter, indeed, Mme de Staël said scornfully, for a Corsican monarch to interest himself in the *nuances* of French literature ! The truth was, she told herself resentfully, Schlegel was exiled because he enlivened her solitude. This was merely the beginning of a plan to imprison her soul by robbing it of all the joys of friendship and intellect.

§

Mme de Staël resolved, nevertheless, to leave Coppet despite these prohibitions and the anguish of tearing herself away from her friends and the ashes of her parents. . . . But the route baffled her. She could no longer depend upon her American passport, and the French Government had now threatened with imprisonment all those who attempted to proceed to England without permission. Her thoughts turned to Sweden—an honourable country, once her own by marriage. But to reach it she must travel through Russia, since all Germany was under French dominion. And to get to Russia she must traverse Bavaria and Austria. Austria was in a state of complete servitude, but she felt she could rely upon its monarch not to give her up even if he were powerless to protect her. She studied the map of Europe even as Napoleon had done, but while his motive had been one of conquest, hers was to discover some means of escape, and like his her objective was Russia.

She must get a passport in order to go there, but the officials might reveal the fact that she had applied for one, and the French Ambassador, hearing of it, would probably order her arrest. She would therefore go to Vienna and from there apply to the Emperor Alexander for a passport. She would have to wait at least six weeks for a reply and that interval must be spent under the protection of a Government that had given an Austrian Archduchess to Napoleon. Could one place any reliance upon it ? . . .

Mathieu de Montmorency, her valued friend of twenty years, wished to visit her. But he was in Paris, and the Emperor had expressed his disapproval of anyone who went to Coppet. Mme de Staël did not take this very seriously ; she could not believe it would be accounted a crime for an old friend to visit an exiled woman. His life was further so completely consecrated to pious works and to family life, and was, moreover, so utterly detached from politics that it seemed impossible he should be penalized. And of what use would it be ? She was continually asking herself that question in regard to Napoleon's conduct, but then she had never reckoned with his immense egoism. . . .

She went to meet de Montmorency at Orbe and proposed they should make a little tour together in Switzerland, returning by way of Fribourg in order to see the convent of Trappist nuns in the Val-Sainte. The juxtaposition of Mme de Staël who possessed what Bagehot called the gift of continuous conversation, and the Trappist nuns who preserve perpetual silence, presents a certain comic element, but then she rarely displayed any sense of humour.

They arrived at the said convent in torrents of rain, only to learn no one could be received there. Nothing daunted—for little, except perhaps the sight of a gendarme, really deterred her—she rang the bell and presently a nun peeped from behind the grille and asked her what she wanted. She was what is called among cloistered nuns a *tourière*—one who can interview strangers and even leave the convent on errands.

" I wish to see the interior of your convent," Mme de Staël answered.

" You cannot do that."

" But I'm very wet—I want to dry myself."

The nun touched a spring opening a door into a room where Mme de Staël was able to sit down and rest although she saw no one. The nun had vanished from her post of observation and presently she grew impatient and rang the bell again. The *tourière* from behind the grille told her that no woman had ever been received in the convent unless she had come with the purpose of embracing the religious life.

"How can I know if I want to stay unless I am permitted to see the house?" demanded Mme de Staël.

"It would be useless for you to do so—I am certain you have no vocation for our life," replied the nun. With these words she closed the shutter of the grille.

Mme de Staël was once more left alone, but she was at a loss to imagine what indication she could have given as to her worldly character. Was it her vivacious way of talking—so different from that of the nun herself? How was it possible for her to distinguish those who came out of mere curiosity from those who desired to enter that life of silence and prayer? It never occurred to her that the spate of words must have sufficed to satisfy the nun that she had little vocation for the Trappist life.

After hearing vespers sung in the chapel she came to the conclusion that austere and serious temperaments, rather than religious enthusiasm, led the nuns to embrace that life.

On their return Mathieu de Montmorency stayed for a few days at Coppet, and after announcing his arrival there received by return of post his own sentence of exile. When Mme de Staël was informed of this, she gave vent to shrieks of anguish. Never had heart been so near to despair! He, deeply imbued with religious calm, invited her to follow his example of resignation. While she was still in this hysterical state she received a letter from Mme Récamier announcing a visit on her way to Aix-les-Bains. She would arrive in two days. Something must be done to stop her. This beloved and beautiful friend must not expose herself to the risk of exile. Mme de Staël sent a courier to urge her not to come. But Mme Récamier declared she could not pass beneath the very windows of Coppet without halting there for at least a few hours. She remained till the following day, when she went on to stay with some relations. But it was enough. Moved by a generous and compassionate impulse she had gone to see her friend, therefore, she too must be punished by exile. The misfortunes which Juliette had already undergone made this break-up of her home additionally painful. Separated from all her friends she was doomed to spend month after month in a little provincial town. Birth and virtue were attacked in de Montmorency; beauty in Mme Récamier, and in Mme de Staël herself at least some little reputation for talent. But Napoleon, she said bitterly, only recognized two classes of men; those who served him and those

who preferred their independence.　No one must have any will
but his. . . .

§

"Mme de Staël," pronounced the Prefect of Geneva, "has made
an agreeable life in her own home.　Her friends as well as foreigners
visit her at Coppet.　The Emperor will certainly not allow that."

Mathieu's family intervened and prevailed upon him to leave the
"sad cause of his exile."　He departed on August 31, 1811.

It was intimated officially that those who had anything to hope
or fear from the French Government would do well not to go to
Coppet.　There was a report that a guard of police would be stationed
at the entrance of the avenue to stop her visitors.　A friend warned
her that if she remained there she would suffer the fate of Mary
Queen of Scots—nineteen years of imprisonment and then the final
catastrophe.　Mme de Staël had seen too many heads fall in her
time to deem this an impossibility.　But then on the other hand the
Prefect had warned her if she went to Vienna or Berlin she would
be recalled, and that if she made any preparations for the journey
these would at once be known.　Did he not know all that went on
in her house ?　Events, she remarked, proved him a fool at the game
of spying. . . .

In 1811, she had made the acquaintance of a very young man,
Giovanni de Rocca, of Italian-Swiss birth, handsome, well-born and
a poet.　He had lost a leg in the Peninsular War.　They fell in love
with each other, and perhaps to escape from the phantom of boredom
that for ever assailed her, they entered into a contract of marriage
which was later confirmed by a religious ceremony.　He was twenty-
three, and thus only a couple of years older than her own son,
Auguste.　She was then forty-five.　The marriage was kept an
absolute secret even from those of her immediate entourage, since
she did not wish Napoleon to know that she had changed her name.
Moreover, Giovanni de Rocca was still a Lieutenant of the French
Hussars and on the active list despite his wounds and frail health,
thus there was always the fear that if the truth were known he
would be arrested.　He, on the other hand, wished to proclaim their
marriage to the whole world.

He was violently jealous of her and one night when Constant
had supper with them at Geneva, he went up to him afterwards and
told him that his attentions to her were so displeasing to him that
he—Rocca—wished to fight a duel with him.

Probably few except Schlegel and Miss Randall were aware of
the truth.　The birth of a son to Mme de Staël in April, 1812, was

rigorously hushed up, and the baby was smuggled out of the house and taken to Longirod, where he was baptized on May 11. The register contains the following entry :

Louis Alphonse, fils de Théodore Giles de Boston en Amérique et de Henriette, née Preston, son épouse, né le 7ᵉ Avril 1812 a été présenté au St. Baptême à Longirod le 11ᵉ mai suivant par Louis Jurine, professeur à l'Académie de Genève.

Jurine was, in fact, the doctor who attended her. Lest anyone should suspect the truth Mme de Staël reappeared in less than two weeks. She looked desperately ill ; she was thin, her face was livid. There was a span of twenty-five years between her first child and her last.

A letter from the Emperor Alexander of Russia stimulated her desire to travel. France was preparing for war against Russia, which made her all the more eager to visit that country. But the journey was a formidable one for a woman of forty-six in bad health. When it came to the point her nerve failed her. Her physical strength seemed unequal to the task she would have put upon it. Her imagination conjured up all kinds of terrors. Prison if she were arrested ; capture by bandits if she were forced to travel across Turkey in a last desperate effort to reach England. And then the long sea-voyage if she should decide to go there, fraught with perils for herself and Albertine ! . . .

Her son Albert had already begun to cause her considerable anxiety. He had a fiery temper, was impatient of discipline, and was rough almost to coarseness. Once, when as a boy, he was taken before the judge for galloping down the Grand' rue at Geneva and fined for the exploit, he took out his purse and offered double the amount, calmly saying he intended to repeat the offence at the first opportunity. Perhaps the life at Coppet was scarcely a desirable one for an impressionable, adolescent youth. There were no rules or regulations, no fixed hours except for meals. To talk was the only duty, and one of the guests referred to it as the Tower of Babel.

Finally, Mme de Staël decided to start for England on May 15. But on the eve of that day it was as if all strength and courage forsook her, and she told herself that the morbid terror to which she was now a prey must surely be the precursor of some evil destiny. She roamed about the park at Coppet in a fresh access of nervous restlessness. How could she leave the mausoleum where her parents were entombed ? This was purely sentimental on her part, for she had never got on with her mother and could not surely have forgotten the stormy scenes with Necker. Nevertheless, she passed a whole hour in prayer before the iron gates that guarded all that was mortal of those two noble beings, and growing calmer assured herself that it was necessary for her to depart. She invoked the name of Necker whom she described as that Fénelon of politics ! . . .

She really did leave about a week later, driving off at two in the afternoon and announcing to the servants that she would be back in time for dinner. She and Albertine carried only fans, and the few things they would require during the first days of absence were carefully stowed in the pockets of Auguste and Rocca. As they passed down the avenue—it might be for the last time—she nearly fainted. But Auguste took her hand and said : " Mother, think you are going to England." The word revived her old energy.

When they had proceeded a certain distance she sent one of the servants back to say she would return on the morrow, and they pursued their way to Berne where Schlegel was to meet them. Auguste was to be left behind at Berne. She looked at him in anguish, remembering she must part from him. In features and character she assured herself he resembled Necker. Again her courage failed her. How could she leave Switzerland, so tranquil, still so beautiful, the people still free even if they had forfeited their political independence ? But she had taken no irremediable step ; there was still time to return. . . .

Other fears assailed her. Once beyond the frontier would she ever be allowed to go back to Coppet ? Yet if she permitted this opportunity to slip she might never again have a chance of escaping.

At some unspecified point Rocca, possibly for purposes of safety, had left the little party in order to return to Geneva. On arrival at Berne Auguste was deputed to obtain the passports that were necessary to enable them to enter Austria. He was a young man of pleasing manners and address, with a good deal of his mother's charm, and he applied immediately to the Austrian Minister who supplied the desired documents without delay. Thus after ten years of persecution from a man whom Mme de Staël described as " less French than herself," she left her country and entered the Tyrol, beginning that long and often painful odyssey in her endeavour to escape from her foe.

§

Their departure became known and on June 4, 1812, the Prefect of Léman wrote a letter to Professor Marc Auguste Pictet, Inspector-General of the University at Geneva, in which he informed him that a flight had taken place in the vicinity—that of a widow who wished to shield her child from shame. Her destination was unknown, but Miss Frances Randall, who was, he said, assuredly no angel, but who had assisted at the flight without participating in it, informed him that she had gone to the baths of Schinznach. But it was generally believed that she had quitted the banks of " your beautiful lake " for those of the foggy Thames. He himself had only heard of the flight two days after it occurred. Events were being watched with impatience. He feared that the friend, Schlegel, the probable instigator of the mad enterprise, had in this case counselled an act of great folly. But if no harm came of it it would at least be a happy release for Geneva. . . .

I am at a loss to conceive why he should have thus cast aspersions on the character of poor Miss Randall, a most faithful and loyal friend who combined the rôle of governess to Albertine with that of devoted companion to Mme de Staël. She was absolutely reliable and identified herself with all her employer's interests, noting the movements of the gendarmes and covering up her ultimate flight with considerable skill. Englishwomen in all ages have thus become devoted to their foreign employers and have often made for themselves a special niche in their lives and homes. And Miss Randall certainly displayed courage in staying behind at Coppet to " face the music," and submit to the interrogation of the French police.

In the meantime de Rocca returned to Geneva to bid his father farewell before leaving to rejoin Mme de Staël in Austria.

Albert left Coppet on May 27 with the servants and luggage. He was to meet his mother at Melk.

As she was still in weak health and highly nervous, it was found impossible for her to travel at night, so the journey was slow. A shock awaited them at Salzburg, for on arrival the manager of the inn went up to Schlegel and told him that a French courier had been enquiring for a lady and a young girl who were expected from Innsbrück in a carriage, and was to return later to ascertain if there had been any news of them. Mme de Staël turned pale with terror. Schlegel further learned that the man came from Munich ; he had gone to the frontier but having misssed them there had thus come on ahead to await them.

She resolved to leave Albertine with Schlegel and go alone into the town, entering the first house where the people seemed to her to have kindly faces and begging them to shelter her. Schlegel would say he was going to join her in Austria whither she intended to make her way, disguised as a peasant. Happily there was no need for her to put this fantastic plan into execution for the courier appeared and proved to be no other than Rocca himself. He had assumed the rôle of a French agent in order to profit by the alarm inspired by such a functionary and thus facilitate his own journey. Mme de Staël's terror was changed, she assures us, to a tender emotion of security and gratitude. . . .

On their way to Vienna the party stayed at the famous Benedictine Abbey at Melk, built upon a hill whence once Napoleon had gazed down upon the winding Danube, and admired the landscape so soon to be devastated by his troops. It was there Mme de Staël awaited the arrival of Albert with her servants and luggage.

The economic condition of Austria at that time must closely have resembled that which it presented more than a century later. The value of the paper money had enormously depreciated, and the uncertainty attendant upon all industrial and financial operations affected every class. Mme de Staël was not a banker's daughter for nothing, and she observed sagaciously that nothing demoralizes a people so much as perpetual fluctuations in the value of money. In such circumstances the temptation to speculate is so great that everyone practically becomes a money-changer, and instead of working for their bread, men prefer to enrich themselves by cunning. While she was in Vienna a man was executed for making false notes just at a moment when the old ones were being recalled. He cried for mercy, declaring it was not he who had robbed, but the State.

Misfortunes had crowded upon the country, Mme de Staël re- marked just as she might have done to-day, less as a result of the late war than as that of the late peace, another and dreary example of the sordid monotony with which history repeats itself. But that was, in her view, part of Napoleon's method—to reduce a country ·with which he had made peace to such a miserable condition that almost any change was acceptable. Having given both money and men to help him, it seemed to the ruined inhabitants that to be allied to him could not add anything to their sum of misery. And the Government was now allied to that of France by reason of the Emperor's marriage.

The little party reached Vienna barely two weeks after their departure from Coppet. Two hours after their arrival the Russian Ambassador sent a courier to the Emperor Alexander to ask for passports for them, assuring Mme de Staël that she would receive them in about three weeks and that in the meantime she could remain in Vienna without fear of consequences. The Court was at Dresden, where all the German princes had assembled to do homage to Napoleon, now bent upon that Russian campaign which was to end in such signal disaster. He was especially cordial, she learned, to the Emperor Francis, saying he had no wish to diminish the power of Austria since he preferred that his father-in-law should be an important prince. " Also," he added, " I have greater faith in the old dynasties than in the new. Has not General Bernadotte taken part in making peace with England ? " (It was then about two years since he had assisted that filibuster to assume the crown of Sweden.)

England . . . England . . . it was ever the thought of that island lying so safely beyond his attacking armies that haunted him. Twice had he seen the French Fleet destroyed by Nelson, whose death seemed to have robbed it of none of its puissance. " It has always been the same since Crécy," he is said to have murmured wearily after the defeat of Waterloo.

§

After a brief interlude of complete peace, instructions were sent to the Chief of Police to keep watch upon Mme de Staël. Spies were placed at her door to note all her movements. She was also informed that it might be several months before she could obtain her passport for Russia and by that time war would probably have broken out, rendering it impossible for her to go there at all. Europe seemed to her then like a vast network formed by Napoleon to entrap the traveller at every step. And she could remember the time when it was easy to pass freely from one country to another. . . .

Ultimately she left Vienna without waiting for the passport, begging one of her friends to follow with it as soon as it arrived. She had now only Albert, Albertine and Schlegel with her. At Brünn there was trouble about the passports, and she asked permission for her son to return to Vienna to obtain the necessary documents. She was brusquely informed that he, as little as herself, would be permitted to go back one single league. Everyone she encountered betrayed the same fear of being compromised, aware that to incur Napoleon's wrath signified either exile, imprisonment or death. . . .

The Governor of Moravia told her she must cross Galicia as quickly as possible, and that she must not remain more than twenty-four hours at Lanzut, the property of Princess Lubomirska, with whose nephew and niece she was acquainted.

Pursued, as she tells us, by this phantom of tyranny, she entered Galicia, nor were the people she encountered there of a kind to give her much confidence in the future of the human race. But then the Austrians, she declared, had not the gift of making themselves beloved by those they had conquered. Had they not forbidden the Carnival to take place when they first possessed themselves of Venice ? . . .

Sometimes they met religious processions, men and women following a Crucifix and chanting psalms as they went, their faces imbued with a profound sadness. When they received a gift of food they would raise their eyes to heaven as if reluctant to believe themselves worthy of such benefits. . . .

At last the passports arrived, and she imagined she would now be able to spend several days at Lanzut and renew acquaintance with Prince Henry Lubomirska and his wife, whom she had known at Geneva. She wished to stay there a couple of days and then pursue her journey, since on all sides she heard the rumour that war had been declared between France and Russia.

However, on arriving at the place where their passports were examined, these hopes were dashed to the ground. Her son as usual went to obtain the *visas*, and as he was absent so long she sent Schlegel to see what had happened. Both returned accompanied by a man. Albert, who had lost his temper, told her the commandant had said that she could only remain eight hours at Lanzut and that a *commissaire* was to accompany her thither to ensure that this order was obeyed. Albert had protested in vain that after her long journey she would require more than eight hours' rest.

M. de Rocca, travelling under another name as a precaution, now came to meet her, full of joy and confidence and little suspecting that she was being closely followed by a police officer. Pale with terror she made a warning gesture to him to retire and a kindly Pole helped him to escape. But this untoward incident brought on such a violent attack of nerves that she was compelled to alight from her carriage and lie down by the roadside.

At last her *berlin* rolled into the courtyard of Lanzut while the commissioner followed in a *calèche*. Prince Henry came out to meet her and alarmed at her pallor inquired what was the matter. She explained the presence of the ambiguous guest who had been forced upon him.

After dinner the police-officer approached Albert and in a soft voice which she detested the more on account of the cruel words he uttered, informed him that he had orders to spend the night in Mme de Staël's room so as to ensure her speaking to no one, but that out of regard for her he would not do so.

"You'd better not do so for your own sake as well as hers," Albert retorted, "for if you put your foot inside her room I shall throw you out of the window."

However, the man was so royally entertained by the Prince's secretary that Mme de Staël believed she could have safely spent several hours longer at Lanzut, and had time to wander in the beautiful garden with its sub-tropical plants, and go over the house which had given shelter to so many persecuted *émigrés*.

The *commissaire* accompanied her to the limits of the circle over which his supervision extended, and at every halt she saw that grenadiers were stationed to see that she did not linger on her way. But at Léopold she was kindly received and given a passport which enabled her to enter Russia.

§

Russia had never been regarded as a free country by the rest of Europe, but Napoleon's iron hand weighed so heavily upon the others that to enter it seemed to Mme de Staël like breathing the air of a Republic. When the gates were opened to allow her to pass into Russia she resolved never again to set foot in a country that was under the sway of Napoleon.

Already the French armies had penetrated deeply into that land, yet the foreign traveller could move about freely without let or hindrance. None of their little party knew a word of Russian and the language they spoke was French—that of the enemy who was now devastating their empire. However, they fell in with a German doctor who offered to act as interpreter, otherwise they would indeed have merited the epithet of " deaf mutes " which the Russians were wont to bestow upon those who were unable to speak their language.

At Volhynie she stayed with a Polish noble who warned her to hurry on as the French were marching on the place and might be there within a week. She found that as a whole the Poles preferred the Russians to the Austrians.

The Russian Minister of Police, M. de Balasheff, had been sent to Wilna to ascertain the reason of Napoleon's aggressive action and to make a formal protest against his invasion of Russian territory. The Emperor Alexander had done all in his power to preserve peace and had made innumerable sacrifices to that end. He was accused of having broken the Treaty of Tilsit, whereas according to Mme de Staël he had kept it only too faithfully.

" Do you think I care for those Jacobins of Poles ? " Napoleon retorted disdainfully. And in front of M. de Balasheff, he asked one of his generals whether he knew Moscow and what sort of a place it was. " More like a big village than a capital," the officer replied. " And how many churches are there ? " " About sixteen hundred." " Impossible now when people are no longer at all religious ! " Napoleon exclaimed. " Pardon, sire—the Russians and the Spaniards are still so. . . ."

The French armies made such rapid progress that Mme de Staël was actually afraid of encountering them on the road to Moscow. A strange destiny, she thought, that forced her thus to escape from the French among whom she had been born, and who had carried her father in triumph shoulder-high through the streets of Versailles! Even the thought of Necker could not give her courage now, and she tried to calm herself by composing a poem on Richard Cœur de Lion, which she hoped one day to write if life and strength were spared to her.

Fears and uncertainties beset her. It was the proximity of Napoleon that caused her a thousand terrors. Should she go to Odessa and from thence to Constantinople? Her companions dissuaded her from such a course, assuring her that she could post more rapidly than the dreaded army and they continued their journey to Kiev.

The Russians, Mme de Staël observed, never passed a church without crossing themselves. Their immense beards gave them a religious aspect. They wore for the most part a long blue robe, girdled with a red sash. The women had a slightly Oriental appearance and were fond of bright colours. She grew to admire the Russian costume so much that she disliked to see the people dressed as other Europeans.

She found much to admire in the Orthodox Church; she thought the ceremonies beautiful and the music marvellous. And whatever might be their religious differences the people were united in the bonds of fraternal patriotism from the Don to the Neva. She noted that for the most part their priests were married and that few were of gentle birth. She thought the religion more capable of captivating the imagination than of regulating the conduct. The minarets reminded her more of the Turkish or Arab mosques; there was little sign of the sentiment which had inspired the Gothic architecture of France and Germany, the art of Italy.

At Kiev she visited the Catacombs which recalled to her those of Rome, and was hospitably entertained by the Governor. The people resembled rather those of the South and East than of the North. She could find little that was European except in the Court customs which resembled each other in all countries. And the character of the people was Oriental, especially in that fatalism which enabled them to endure the sufferings of war, the rigours of their harsh climate with a certain contempt for the physical sufferings of the one and the obstacles offered by the other. In short, she felt herself at the gates of the East. . . .

Nine hundred versts separated Kiev from Moscow, but the drivers urged their horses with kindly words till they seemed to go like the wind. The country was, however, so monotonous with its sandy steppes, its scattered villages, its wooden houses all built on precisely the same pattern, that she felt as if they were making no progress at all.

Presently horses became much rarer, they had been seized for purposes of transport. What if she were to encounter delay just when it was most necessary to hasten ? And as at each halt there was rarely a room she could enter, she trembled to think that the French Army might suddenly descend upon her, rendering her situation at once tragic and absurd. . . .

It was like passing through a deserted country. No birds broke the silence of those vast steppes. Luxury was impossible, and even to live on the modest scale of a French peasant would entail an immense expenditure. No vegetables were grown, and fruit and flowers only under glass. What the English called " comfort " was unknown. Everywhere man had to struggle against the rigours of climate, the barrenness of steppe and forest. The great land-owners would show a magnificent hospitality to strangers while often lacking the necessities of life. Exterior pomp rather than personal comfort was their ambition. But ordinary dimensions were not applicable to them ; they thought in gigantic terms. . . .

§

At last the gilded cupolas of Moscow came in sight across the wide plain. At the final halt before entering the city some peasants, picturesquely attired, danced, and, at her request, sang to her. There was, she said, a mixture of indolence and vivacity in that strange Russian dance.

She remembered that someone had said Moscow was more like a province than a city. Diversity of race and costume was everywhere visible. Guides approached her with eager enquiries. Would she go to the Tartars' quarter and buy Cashmere shawls ? Had she seen the Chinese city ? Europe and Asia seemed to meet there. But there was more liberty than at St. Petersburg. . . .

She visited the Kremlin, where but a few days previously the Emperor Alexander had mounted the steps to bless his people and to promise them he would defend his empire at all costs. And they had responded nobly with gifts of men and money. Count de Mononoff raised a regiment in which he himself would only serve as a second lieutenant. Countess Orloff gave a quarter of her revenues. And as Mme de Staël drove past sumptuous palaces she was told that the possessor of one had given a thousand serfs to the State, another two hundred. She shrank from the expression of " giving " men, but discovered they were eager to be so given. When a Russian became a soldier he shaved his beard and from that moment was free. She rejoiced in the liberty, but regretted the long picturesque beard ! . . .

Diderot had said the Russians were rotten before they were ripe. Nothing so false, she observed ; they seemed to her more violent than corrupt.

She dined with Count Rostopschin, who had been Minister of Foreign Affairs under Napoleon's ancient ally, Paul I. To arrive at his house, which was in the middle of Moscow, she had to cross a lake and a wood. The Count subsequently set fire to his abode with his own hands at the approach of the French Army. He was to blame, she felt, for so long concealing the ill news about the war ; he lacked the " admirable straightforwardness " of the English which made them acknowledge the reverses they sustained with as much frankness as they proclaimed their victories. But how could the Russians attain to such moral perfection which was the result of a free Constitution ?

Between Moscow and Petersburg there was nothing but sand and stretches of marshland. When rain fell the soil was blackened and the road was lost to view. Petersburg itself was built upon a marsh ; even the marble buildings rested upon stakes, but when looking upon those superb edifices she forgot their fragile foundations. But her first act was to thank God that the city was a port. She saw the Union Jack floating upon a ship in the river and felt that if the worst happened she could confide her fate to the ocean.

Whereas in Moscow she had met men of science and letters, she found that in Petersburg nearly all the professors were Germans. Young men only entered the University in order to join the army more rapidly. The spirit of the people was entirely military. Administration, economics, public instruction, were brought to them from other countries. They were devoted to literature, but unhappily made the mistake of imitating that of France, whereas she felt they ought to have based their studies on the Greeks rather than the Latins. She found the people unreliable in the ordinary affairs of life ; they were more capable of dissimulation than of reflection. And it seemed to her they were a Southern people, condemned to live in the North.

Their patient acceptance of hardship always impressed her. Coachmen would wait for hours outside in the bitterest winter weather without a word of complaint. They would even sleep in the snow beneath the carriages. Servants would sleep on the stairs, sometimes enveloped in down quilts, sometimes standing upright leaning their heads against the wall. They would yield themselves as readily to profound slumber as to incredible fatigues.

Luxury reigned in the great houses. There were plants and flowers from the South, perfumes from the East, divans from Asia, great greenhouses where fruits of all countries ripened, yet just beyond some of these luxurious abodes stretched the barren regions of steppe and swamp.

While she observed and criticized and preached her gospel of liberty, her interlocutors were not always so indulgent in their judgments. People were eager to meet her for her name was celebrated throughout Europe, but they came away disappointed. She was too fat, and she dressed in a manner that was little suited to either her age or her figure. She talked too much among a people who liked to hear the sound of their own voices.

She went to the Orloffs on the very day peace with England was declared. It was a Sunday and their gardens were open to the public. The band played *God save the King*. When Orloff informed the assembled crowd that there was peace with England they made the Sign of the Cross and thanked God the seas were once more free to them.

Still, when all was said and done, Petersburg was not Paris. Despite the brilliant atmosphere one learned nothing there ; one could not develop one's faculties. Pleasant and amiable as it was the conversation never sounded the depths of thought. . . .

§

The Empress Elizabeth seemed to Mme de Staël like the guardian-angel of Russia. She was reserved in manner and yet Mme de Staël listened to her with a certain emotion. Such a combination of virtue and power had long been a stranger to her ! . .

But her chief object in going to Petersburg was to see the Tsar, and he did not disappoint her. He spoke to her as freely as the English statesmen she had met had done. Nor did he conceal from her his regret at his old friendship with Napoleon. His ancestor had experienced a like enthusiasm for Frederick II. Still, it had not been without certain practical results since it had enabled him to procure an intimate knowledge of Napoleon's true character. Had he not told him once that it was his policy to antagonize his ministers and generals, so that they would complain to him about one another, and that he deliberately fostered an atmosphere of jealousy among those about him by showing partiality to one man one day, and to another the next, so that no one could ever feel sure of his favour ?

Mme de Staël was convinced of the Tsar's good faith in the matter. Never, surely, would he make an ignoble peace with Napoleon as the German princes had done. A noble soul would not permit itself to be duped a second time by the same person. When he expressed regret that he was not a great soldier, she flattered him by saying that a sovereign was a rarer thing than a captain.

She was once more in her element. Russia, the home of intrigue, offered a limitless scope for her ability in that direction. But she had found her match in the Tsar. He hid his cunning beneath a disguise of extreme frankness, and he was in no wise deceived by her flatteries. " Sire," she told him, " your character is your Empire's Constitution and your conscience is its guarantee." He replied ambiguously : " If that were so I should never be anything but a happy accident." She believed that this noble phrase was the first of its kind ever uttered by an absolute monarch.

What she could tell him and what he really wished to know, was more about Bernadotte, who two years earlier had become King of Sweden. The Tsar was on the point of leaving for Abo to meet him there in order to ensure his neutrality upon which so far he had felt unable to depend. On his return Mme de Staël saw him once more and then went to Stockholm to watch the progress of affairs herself. Russia had taken Finland from Sweden, but as the price of her neutrality now offered her Norway.

She left Russia at the end of September and was seen off by a number of important personages—Sir Robert Wilson, Stein, the British Minister Lord Tirconnel, Admiral Bentinck, the Spanish envoy and Alexis de Noailles, who had escaped from the tyranny of France and shared her hatred of Napoleon.

Embarking at Abo for Stockholm, all her old terrors assailed her since she had an especial fear of the sea. Everyone assured her of the safety of the passage, but after the cruel vicissitudes she had endured during that long persecution, she could put no confidence in her own fate. Schlegel observing her terror used an odd method of distracting her from it by pointing out the prison near Abo where the unfortunate King of Sweden, Eric XIV, had been immured. " If you were imprisoned there," he said, " imagine how you would long for this voyage which now terrifies you so much."

The first few days were pleasant enough ; her fears were stilled. They passed the Island of Aland where peace had been signed between Peter I and Charles XII, and hoped to arrive at Stockholm on the following day. But a contrary wind sprang up forcing them to anchor close to a rocky island, and for a time the ship was in actual danger. When they arrived at Stockholm it was to learn of

Napoleon's victory on the Borodino on September 12, and of the burning of Moscow. She could not tell that the hour of defeat had nevertheless sounded for him. During the retreat in that icy winter weather practically the whole of his armies perished upon those frozen steppes.

Mme de Staël's visit to Stockholm was fruitful on more than one count. She used all her arts of political intrigue, all her powers of loquacious persuasion, to secure the allegiance of Bernadotte to the Russian cause. It was true he had been robbed of Finland, but then had not Alexander promised him Norway as the price of his neutrality? Bernadotte, even without the assistance of Mme de Staël, must have perceived the expediency of going into the fray on the side of the victor. For despite the Battle of Borodino, the taking of the smoking ashes of Moscow, the French Army had been utterly lost in that disastrous winter retreat, one of the most poignant as it is one of the most tragic episodes in the history of war.

Not only were her machinations successful as regarded Russia, but she secured appointments for both Albert and Schlegel. Her son was placed most advantageously as Bernadotte's *aide-de-camp* while the tutor received the post of secretary. Auguste de Staël then joined his mother in Sweden and she tarried there for a few months in order to write her book, *Dix années d'exil.* The narrative ends abruptly at the somewhat disastrous voyage from Abo.

While at Stockholm she went through a ceremony of marriage with Giovanni Rocca, whom, however, she never in her lifetime acknowledged publicly as her husband, possibly believing she might lose prestige if it were known that she had married a man young enough to be her son.

All the time her restless, active brain was busy with projects for the future. Supposing Napoleon fell, for instance, would it not be well to place Bernadotte upon the throne of France ? A return of the Bourbon dynasty was in her eyes highly undesirable, but she felt she could rule Bernadotte ; already he had listened and obeyed. And he had taken the troublesome Albert, whose irregular life had for some time past cost her the greatest anxiety, off her hands. Albert had, as she said, *pris le mouvement de travers.* . . . It was what might have been expected of the unstable Narbonne's son. . . .

§

June found her in London with Auguste, Albertine and Rocca, who was generally supposed to be her lover and always appeared like other guests with his hat and stick. She preferred this to any acknowledgment of the truth.

Her thoughts had long turned to England, the home, as she believed, of true liberty, and to the English character she had admired so much—at a distance.

London " did her proud." She was invited everywhere, she met all the celebrated persons—and they were many—of that day. People crowded to see this famous woman who was the enemy of their own arch-foe, Napoleon. Yet a hint of dissatisfaction creeps into her letters. " The crowds are so great, the women so many. . . ."

She was received by the Queen, the Prince Regent, the Duchess of York. She dined out constantly, and was seen yawning over *Falstaff* at Covent Garden. People were invited to meet her, but the ceaseless eloquence confused and disconcerted them. Her talk persisted despite interruptions, of which she took no notice. Then she began to criticize saying that the untravelled English had little to say for themselves, and seemed to belong more to Albertine's generation than to her own. Albertine. . . . Was it possible that the mother was to share her own mother's fate and become jealous of the daughter, as had happened thirty years before in Paris, when the beautiful Mme Necker had watched her admirers drifting from her side, attracted by the impudent vivacity of the young, intelligent Germaine ? Albertine—whom someone wittily nicknamed *La Libertine*, although her conduct was exemplary—was then fifteen years of age and pretty and attractive. She could dance a Russian saraband with great vigour, force and expression, according to Byron's testimony. In short, she was beginning to become a problem. It may be too that she was more easily able to assimilate the manners of the gay younger set than her mother who disliked what she termed their " *ton moqueur*." Mme de Staël had her gospel to preach, and the frivolous English youth of the day had little desire to hear it.

Croker reported that her ugliness " was not even of the intellectual sort." He said that " her features were coarse and the ordinary expression rather vulgar. She had an ugly mouth and one or two irregularly prominent teeth." But he admitted that her eyes were dark and expressive, and that when she declaimed, as she nearly always did, one forgot her plainness.

John Louis Malet from Geneva, who had been for some years naturalized in England, was even less flattering. She was of middle height, he said, inclining to stoutness ; she had fine large dark eyes, a bad colour, dark hair ill-arranged. She was not at all well-dressed, and her neck and shoulders were far too bare for a woman of her age, nor were they beautiful. Still, the arms and eyes were very mobile and the voice harmonious and agreeable. . . .

She and Maria Edgeworth were the lions of 1813, Byron noted, just as he himself had been the lion of the previous year. But Maria Edgeworth paled a little before ·her more brilliant and famous foreign rival. She had been dazzled by *Corinne*. And Mme de Staël appreciated her " with a difference." Really, she said, Miss Edgeworth was worthy of enthusiasm, *mais elle se perd dans votre triste utilité.*

On the other hand Mme de Staël had no appreciation of that incomparable artist, Jane Austen. Sir James Mackintosh, the Scottish philosopher, who literally sat at her feet, paying her the most fulsome compliments and speaking to no one else when she was in the room, lent her one of the novels. It was probably *Sense and Sensibility* published in 1811, although it might have been *Pride and Prejudice* which appeared during the year of her visit. She returned it saying that it was *vulgaire*—quite the last word we should now apply to that delicàte and unique talent.

Her political opinions were not always acceptable, since she was passionately opposed to any return of the Bourbons which was exactly what England hoped for. All Tories were in her opinion stupid, luxurious and proud, while all Whigs were intelligent and wonderful. She must have been astonished at the lack of personal enmity that existed in London between the great political parties.

The climate did not suit her too well ; she grew thin and melancholy. Rocca too was ill ; the first symptoms of tuberculosis manifested themselves at that time.

She wrote many letters to Constant and Schlegel, both of whom showed a lamentable disposition to indifference now that she was safely across the seas. When her book, *De l'Allemagne*, was sold for fifteen hundred pounds, she wrote to tell Schlegel that he was mentioned in it. She warned him, however, that his French writings would not be acceptable in England. And she wished to send him two hundred pounds—how could this be done ? She reproached him with his silence. Was he too slipping from her ? Was she to subsist on the devotion of Rocca—M. L'Amant, as Byron ironically called him ? The formidable silence of Schlegel aroused within her a kind of jealous fury. There were hints, too, in her letters, that Albert's conduct was unsatisfactory. " Albert is mad . . . make him see reason . . . give him the enclosed letter and tell him I decline to mix myself up in his affairs ! " She begged Schlegel to convey her profound admiration and homage to Bernadotte. As for Albertine she could see no future for her but " the veil."

With Constant the quarrel was more serious. She wrote violent and passionate letters, which must have inspired him with a sense of thankfulness that she was in England. Never, never did a day pass without her experiencing some suffering on his account ! Never did she take out her writing materials without thinking of him. " My father, yourself and Mathieu, share a place in my heart that is for ever closed." Only it was over. Never again could his wonderful intellect cause her any illusion. . . .

Constant had been for some years married to Charlotte, but as if in proof of the old proverb that we always return to our first loves, he could wonder then why he was going to Vienna with her when he had once refused to accompany Mme de Staël thither ! . . .

§

There was a group in London then, headed by Beau Brummel, and known as the Dandies, and these mocking creatures refused to take Mme de Staël seriously. They told her that Lord Alvanley, one of their number, had a fortune of one hundred thousand pounds a year, and rejoiced when she fell into the trap and admired his looks to his face. Here was the very man for Albertine ! . . . It was rather a cruel little joke.

In July she published her *Essay on Suicide* which Byron said would certainly make someone go and shoot himself. Writing to Miss Milbanke—afterwards Lady Byron—he said :

You made sad havoc among " us youth." It is lucky that Mme de Staël has published her anti-suicide at so killing a time. November too ! I have not read it for fear the love of contradiction might lead me to a practical confutation. Do you know her ? I don't ask if you have heard her ?—her tongue is the perpetual motion. . . .

The essay received attention and was well reviewed. In the fol lowing August tragedy descended upon her, for Albert was killed in a duel. He was gambling at Doberan, a Baltic resort of Mecklen- burg-Schwerin whither he had gone with some of Bernadotte's staff, when a quarrel arose between him and another officer in regard to some money. A duel ensued, when the boy's head was practically severed by one of the long Prussian sabres. He was only twenty-one and had inherited much of Narbonne's charm as well as his fatal instability.

Byron wrote to tell Thomas Moore that " Corinne had lost one of the young barons, and was going to write an essay about it."

She did not, however, permit the bereavement to interfere with her social activities. But her one link with Bernadotte was severed, and Schlegel continued to bewilder her with his prolonged and inexplicable silences. She told him in a letter how deeply humiliated she felt when people enquired if she had had any news of him. Even

F

Auguste and Albertine were distressed at his indifference. Oh, if
Albert had only been alive, he and Bernadotte would not thus have
forgotten her ! . . .

Her book *De l'Allemagne* was published in the following spring
by Murray, and the edition was sold out in three days. She urged
Schlegel to come to England and then take her to Germany. Neither
she nor Albertine was happy in England. " Since our separation
and Albert's death I feel isolated." Had she not always believed
that Schlegel had been the one chosen by Necker to close her eyes in
death ? " *I love you in life and in death.*" It was the pitiful letter
of a woman trying to recapture a vanished love. . . .

§

In November Byron was invited to Middleton by Lady Jersey to
meet Mme de Staël. He refused and his comment was ironical. To
travel sixty miles for such a purpose when he had once travelled three
thousand to " get among silent people " ? She " writes octavos and
talks folios," he observed, and he did not answer the many notes
with which she bombarded him. He called her Mme *Stale*, saying
that was how John Bull would probably pronounce her name.

At times she criticized him hotly, yet *au fond* they liked each other,
for both were writers and both were rebels. Once she told him he had
no right to make love since he was totally insensible to *la belle passion*, and had been so all his life. " I am very glad to hear it, but
did not know it before," Byron wrote, for he had been in love with
someone or other almost from childhood. But perhaps he showed her
too plainly that though he admired her intellect he was blind to her
charms. He could only listen to " a pretty or foolish woman," and
she was neither. But he delighted in her books, had read *Corinne*
more than once, and had also enjoyed *De l'Allemagne*, even if the
" cooling stream " people sought in them occasionally proved to be
a mirage.

She was delighted to find herself mentioned in a note at the end
of the *Bride of Abydos* when Byron defends his own line :

The mind, the music breathing from her face . . .

by referring the reader to " an eloquent passage in the latest work of
the first female writer of this, perhaps of any, age, on the analogy
(and the immediate comparison excited by that analogy) between
painting and music, see Vol. III, cap. 10, *De l'Allemagne*."

Of course, she wrote to him at once. How could she find words to
express how deeply she felt the honour of being thus mentioned in
his poem, and such a poem ? For the first time she felt assured that

her name would live.   She wished to talk to him about his poem which
was admired by the whole world.   *" Donnez-moi,"* she wrote, *" quel-
quefois le plaisir de vous voir : il-y-a un proverbe français qui dit
qu'un bonheur ne va jamais sans d'autre."*

And Byron, although he knew perfectly well he was being flattered, enjoyed—as indeed most people would—this ingenuous
adulation.   " Her works are my delight," he told Moore, " and so is
she herself—for half an hour. . . .   I admire her abilities, but really
her society is overwhelming—an avalanche that buries one in glittering nonsense—all snow and sophistry."

It piqued her, however, that he would not go and see her.   But
would he not accept her dinners ?   " For after all what is the use of
living at the same time as yourself if one is never to see you ? "

Byron disliked the tone of her conversation—it was all about either
herself or himself and neither subject interested him.   He thought
Rocca remarkably handsome, and quoted someone's spiteful remark
that " he was the only proof of her good taste."

Mme de Staël, on her side, told " Monk " Lewis that Byron was
affected and sat at table with his eyes shut or at least half-shut.
" Monk " Lewis, being a friend of Byron's and a malicious gossip,
was careful to repeat this and it had the very natural effect of disturbing him.   " I must cure myself if it is true."   He only wished his
attention had been drawn to the trick sooner, as he was unconscious
of it.   Still he would like to have heard the " Amœbæan eclogue "
between her and Lewis, both " obstinate, clever, odd, garrulous and
shrill."

Mme de Staël stayed that autumn at Brocket Hall with Lady
Caroline Lamb, and the visit does not appear to have been a success.
She was little accustomed to rising early, and when in Paris would
receive her morning callers sitting up in bed with the famous turban
surmounting the dark coarse curls.   But at Brocket, breakfast was
served at eight o'clock, dinner at four, tea at eight, and everyone
went to bed at ten.

Never in her life could she have had to submit to such a régime
as that, nor was she of an age or figure to participate in the amusements of the other guests.   They rode, hunted and bathed, and it was
observed that she had no particular predilection either for fresh air,
water or soap.

Mme de Staël tried to like us—wrote Lady Caroline—but I am convinced she found us all much too mortal for her taste.

Nor had she, according to that same critic, learned such simple
social rules as to speak the truth and never to repeat in one company

what she had heard in another. Devoured by an insatiable curiosity she showed a disposition to meddle in the *tracasseries* of people whom she hardly knew. She went so far as to question Lady Caroline about her rupture with Byron, an offence that was very properly resented. She merely answered that while blaming him for his conduct towards herself, " he was and ever would be very dear to her."

Impossible that Lady Caroline, fifteen years younger, an enchanting elfin creature, slim as a boy, with her crop of golden curls and brilliant smile, her charming little *retroussé* face with its hint of puzzled sadness, could have much in common with the famous Swiss sibyl, elderly, stout, loquacious, to whom England had opened its hospitable doors.

Mme de Staël went to Bowood to stay with Lord Lansdowne, and here an unfortunate episode occurred. She wished greatly to meet the poet-parson, Mr. Bowles, whom Byron called the " sonneteer," and he was invited to dinner. On the way he had a fall from his horse and sprained his shoulder. On arrival he told them of the mishap and Mme de Staël congratulated him upon his courage in continuing the journey. " Oh, ma'am," was his answer, " say no more, for I would have done a great deal more to see so great a curiosity ! " During the blank, dismayed silence that ensued, Mme de Staël's face was a study, and for once she was shocked into a speechless surprise. Lord Lansdowne explained to her that he was only a simple country parson. " I can see he is only a simple curé," was her reply, " but he has no common sense even if he is a great poet ! "

She needed something beyond all this generous hospitality— Schlegel . . . " But the winds make a prison of this beautiful island where I wait for news of you." England had taught her one thing—that he was " incomparable."

Few people, however, held this view of the vain, self-important Prussian she had thus taken to her heart. He was the laughingstock of Coppet and even her children disliked him. Byron relates that when asked if he did not consider Canova a marvellous sculptor, he replied : " Ah, but you should see my bust by Tiecke ! "

Auguste and Albertine were admittedly bored and had not much to say for themselves. So unlike Albert, who had the " flair," mourned his mother.

Byron was a spectator of the little scene when the Irish wit Curran was presented to Mme de Staël, and was able to enjoy it.

It was the grand confluence between the Rhône and the Saône—he wrote—and they were both so d——d ugly that I could not help wondering how the best intellects of France and Ireland could have taken up respectively such residences.

§

The long years of exile were drawing to a close. In April, 1814, Napoleon was forced to abdicate, and Louis XVIII succeeded to the throne of France. Napoleon was sent to Elba, and there was thus nothing to prevent Mme de Staël's return to France.

The little party landed at Calais in May, 1814, and it seemed to her she was entering a strange world. Nothing but foreign troops—for the most part wearing Prussian uniforms—met her gaze. . . .

Strange rumours concerning the captive at Elba reached Paris. Maréchal Bertrand, who had followed him into exile, was said to have returned, announcing his insanity. At another time there was a report that his life had been attempted. It even occurred to Mme de Staël that she might go to Elba to comfort her ancient enemy !

She opened her salon, this time in the rue Royale. This must have been the supreme moment of her career. Someone wittily remarked there were now three powers in Europe, England, Russia and Mme de Staël. Newer celebrities mingled with the old allies who gathered around her. Talleyrand, Mathieu, even Fouché came to her receptions that were frequented also by the heroes of the hour—the Tsar Alexander, the Emperor Francis, Frederick William of Prussia, Bernadotte and Wellington. King Louis was kindly but cautious. Constant returned to his old allegiance, yet he would do nothing to help her to recover Necker's money which was now badly needed as a dowry for Albertine. Nor would he waive the agreement as to the repayment of his own debt to her. It was not a convenient moment. . . . " What a man who injures the child as greatly as he injured the mother ! " she exclaimed. " What a man ! " Constant, retaliating, threatened to publish her letters to him. " How worthy of you ! When you come to die, the thought of your past life will make you shudder," she wrote. He was the most cruel, the most indelicate man in the whole world. . . .

Her lawyer in Lausanne told her that Constant was liable for the debt, as the agreement they had mutually signed was against the law of the country. By that time, however, Waterloo had changed the face of Europe, and she was again clamouring for the repayment of Necker's money.

But although she had parted many times from Constant in a rage, he was necessary to her ; perhaps he had really been dearer to her than all the others. And it was he who watched over her when she was lying dead in Paris. . . .

But even now, when all was comparatively smooth and happy, her

fame established, her popularity greater than ever, she could not
desist from her old game of intrigue. She began to exchange letters
with Murat, King of Naples, who had married Napoleon's sister.
They were intercepted, and she received a cold and cutting communication telling her that the King had read the correspondence
and that she might write and receive what letters she pleased, she
might go and come as she wished, since no importance was attached
to anything she might do or say. The Government was not interested
in her schemes and had no desire to interfere with them.

Politically, therefore, she was no longer considered of any importance. She was not even worthy of that persecution which had lent
such a terrifying zest to life. She went back to Coppet that summer
feeling lonely and miserable. " John "—as she called Rocca—was
very ill; the climate of England had developed his tendency to
tuberculosis. She admitted to Mathieu that she was desperately
anxious about him. Once more the abyss of despair opened before
her feet. . . .

Still, despite agitation, despair and other violent emotions, the
windows of Coppet were flung wide and once more the courtyard
resounded to the arrival of carriages and horses. And she was
delighted to exhibit her pretty Albertine to an admiring Geneva. The
girl enjoyed the walks and rides, the simple country life. But the
stay lasted barely three months, for in September Mme de Staël was
at Clichy, near Paris. She received many famous people; Lord
Wellington dined with her; she supped with the Duke of Orleans.
But on the other hand " John " was very ill; Constant, aloof and
bitter; Auguste, who only wasted his time in Paris, was on the point
of departure.

In the autumn Albertine became engaged to the Duc de Broglie.
He was twenty-nine years old and had little money; it became more
than ever necessary for Mme de Staël to recover Necker's loan in order
to provide her daughter with a *dot* since Constant either could not,
or would not, help her in the matter.

Six months passed, and on March 6, 1815, there came the—to her—
appalling news that Napoleon had escaped from Elba and had landed
on the coast of Provence. She fled to Coppet, deeply preoccupied
with the thought of Constant who, she feared, might now suffer for
the violent things he had written against Napoleon.

France rallied to the side of her ancient hero. But he had grown
fat in exile; there was noticeable at times a strange apathy; he
had lost his grip. And his political opinions had changed. He
intended to abolish the censorship. He would do all in his power to
hasten Albertine's marriage. He invited Constant, deeply implicated

in the adventure of the Hundred Days, to assist him in drawing up his new Constitution. It was wittily nicknamed *le Benjamin*.

§

Even after the defeat of Waterloo and the disappearance of her old enemy to the rock of St. Helena where six years later he was to die in great agony, Mme de Staël did not return to Paris. It was deemed desirable that Rocca should winter in a mild climate and she took him to Pisa accompanied by Albertine. Early in 1816, Louis XVIII repaid the famous loan, although without interest, thus facilitating the girl's marriage to the Duc de Broglie. But fresh difficulties arose since she was a Protestant and he a Catholic. An appeal to Rome for a dispensation had to be made before the ceremony could take place.

De Broglie left Paris in January with Auguste and after a brief halt at Coppet they went to Pisa. The marriage was celebrated on the 20th of that month and soon afterwards Mme de Staël took Rocca to Florence. He had been worse since the cold weather set in and now looked a dying man. There was much kindness of heart and real benevolence in her complex nature and she tended her young frail husband with maternal care and solicitude.

At Florence she saw the Countess of Albany and the Grand Duke of Tuscany. Auguste and de Broglie went to Rome for Holy Week. The marriage, she said, was a success though by no means an ideal love. There was a lack of passion in de Broglie which did not escape her. Schlegel who was with her had fallen in love with a German lady, and was consequently " insupportable." They stayed in Florence till the end of May and then returned to Coppet.

It was the year of Byron's separation from his wife when he left England never to return. That summer he was staying at the Villa Diodati, near Geneva, and was a constant visitor at Coppet. When he first went there in July, he felt uncertain of his reception, since so many of his friends in England had deserted him after the separation. But Mme de Staël received him with the utmost kindness and he was always grateful to her for befriending him at that desolate time.

She was fifty and he twenty-eight, so she was perhaps in a position to take him to task. " You should not have warred with the world," she told him, " it will not do—it is always too strong for any individual. I myself tried it in early life, but it will not do."

However, as Byron pointed out with considerable truth, it was the world that had begun the war against him.

She exercised a certain influence over him since she actually persuaded him to write a letter in which he expressed a willingness, even a wish to be reconciled to his wife. But it was of no avail.

At Coppet he met Bonstettin, an elderly man of letters. Schlegel, he mentioned, was in great form and Madame as " brilliant as ever." She was at her best in her own house, he declared, " in any other person's you wished her gone and in her own again."

Rocca was there looking desperately ill and spoke little. Byron, however, aroused his anger one day by abusing the people of Geneva ; he turned to him furiously and said : " Eh ! milord, pourquoi donc venez-vous fourrer parmi ces honnêtes gens ? "

There was an antipathy between Byron and Schlegel. Although Byron was studiously polite to the self-important Prussian he absolutely refused to flatter him even though Albertine begged him to do so. All the other guests at Coppet laughed at Schlegel behind his back. And on his side he disliked Byron and later planned to write a book about and against him. The air must have been slightly sultry at Coppet that summer. . . .

Albertine, however, won Byron's praise. He remarked that " nothing was more pleasing than to see the development of the domestic affections in a very young woman."

Mme de Staël lent him Lady Caroline Lamb's *Glenarvon*, telling him " wonderful and grievous things of it." He lent her the *Antiquary* which she had expressed a desire to read. And perhaps out of gratitude he penned a tribute which delighted her :

> Rousseau, Voltaire, our Gibbon, and de Stael
> Léman ! These names are worthy of thy shore. . . .

When his own *Don Juan* was criticized as immoral he said he did not believe it would do a girl half so much harm as to read the writings of Mme de Staël. There was in what he termed her " sentimental anatomy," as well as in that of Rousseau, something that was " more formidable than any quantity of verse, because they sapped the principles by reasoning upon the passions."

From Venice in the Spring of the following year, he wrote to his publisher Murray, urging him to close with Mme de Staël, for her book *Considérations sur la Révolution Française*, which Auguste had offered him, for the sum of four thousand pounds. It was, he affirmed, her best book and would prove permanently historical. Although he had not read it himself, Bonstettin had told him it was *very great*. But the negotiations had not been completed when her death occurred and the book was subsequently published by another house.

§

Early in October, 1816, Albertine left for Paris with her husband.

On the 10th of that month Mme de Staël and Rocca made a declaration before the pastor, saying that they had been bound by a reciprocal promise to marry in 1811, that this promise had been made in a most solemn manner and should have been fulfilled a few weeks later had it not been for the persecution of Napoleon, her own exile and other reasons. They further declared that of this union had been born a male child on April 7, 1812, that he had been duly baptized at Longirod, receiving the names of Louis Alphonse and that they recognized him as theirs. This union was now consecrated by a religious ceremony, but was to remain a secret for the present. Miss Frances Randall was Mme de Staël's witness, and the judge, Charles Jean Louis Rocca, was witness for " John."

On October 16 they left for France, from which she was destined never to return alive. She opened her apartment in the rue Royale, and the old life, with its brilliant parties and receptions, began once more. But she confessed to feeling ill and tired, and planned to return to Coppet after the birth of Albertine's child.

Then came the catastrophe. She collapsed one night at a reception given by the Duc Décazes. She tried to cling to Rocca's hand but found herself powerless to do so. She was paralysed in both hands and feet. A clot of blood had produced the seizure.

They took her back to the rue Royale and later moved her to a house in the rue Neuve des Mathurins where there was a garden. But henceforth she was doomed to see life from a wheeled chair, unable to write, unable to move of herself, this brilliant woman of only fifty-one. She was as helpless as her new-born granddaughter. . . .

They gave her opium. She could sense the progress of the paralysis. She was very patient, very gentle. She prayed. . . . Sometimes she would say : " My father is waiting for me on the other shore." Miss Randall nursed her with the most unflagging devotion. She was surrounded by love and care.

Her children exhausted the medical knowledge of Paris. Doctor after doctor was called in. The Duc de Broglie, no less than his wife, sought help in every likely or unlikely quarter. Not one could honestly say there was any ground for hope, and all alike condemned any thought of taking her to Coppet, for which she now longed with a devouring nostalgia. The lake, the Alps pencilled against the sky ; her own trees, her flowers. . . .

Jurine came from Geneva to see her ; he could only alleviate the bed-sores from which she was suffering, for which he used the strange and painful remedy of mustard. . . .

On July 12, she was wheeled into the garden. On the following day she was less well and was confined to her room. Visitors came and went, but her languor was pronounced. She fretted over "John," believing him worse, fearing he might die. As he was not well enough to come and see her, she caused herself to be carried to his room. That day he was in bed, visibly perishing. "I have told them to light a fire in your room to-night," she told him, "it is so very cold." But Paris was sweltering in the dog-days; it was she who was cold with the chill of approaching death.

"I have always been the same," she gasped. "I have loved God, my father and Liberty. . . ."

She died at sunrise on July 14. It was the twenty-eighth anniversary of the storming of the Bastille, the full and sinister importance of which episode was now clear to all the world. It led through successive stages to the Revolution, the murder of King and Queen, the Reign of Terror, Napoleon. . . .

All that night Constant watched beside the dead woman. Byron was in Venice when he heard the news with true sorrow. "She would have made a great man," he said. Perhaps there could scarcely be a better epitaph. . . .

§

On July 26, 1817, a funeral carriage rolled into the courtyard of Coppet, escorted by Auguste, bowed with grief, and Schlegel. Already the Duc and Duchesse de Broglie with their baby girl, Rocca and Miss Randall were there; they came out a sorrowful group to receive all that remained of Mme de Staël.

The little mausoleum with its portico fashioned like a Greek temple had been closed since Necker's burial. It was overhung with trees and a high wall had been built around it. Necker had presented it to the Commune of Coppet at a nominal rent so as to preserve it from destruction. The façade was decorated with a bas-relief by Canova representing Mme de Staël weeping at the tomb of her parents, while her father, ascending to join her mother, held out his hand to her in a last farewell.

De Broglie engaged a single workman to make a hole in the wall. In the midst of the tomb within stood the deep marble tank still half full of spirits of wine in which the bodies of the dead couple floated side by side covered with a red mantle which veiled the face of Mme Necker. The features of her husband were perfectly preserved. . . .

On July 28 Albertine and Frances Randall knelt side by side before the coffin within the house while the pastor pronounced a discourse. Rocca was too ill and broken-hearted to leave his room, and the Duchess retired to her own apartments while the

melancholy cortège was formed. It was followed by Auguste and
De Broglie, who alone of the mourners entered the mausoleum while
the four men who carried the coffin followed them. They placed it
on the ground at the foot of the marble basin. The outer walls
were then bricked up never to be reopened. . . .

§

The will was read, and in it Mme de Staël announced her marriage
to Albert Jean de Rocca, which, owing to the disparity in years
and for various other reasons political and private, had been kept a
secret. But she acknowledged Louis Alphonse de Rocca as the
legitimate son of this union so that he might be admitted to his
full rights.

She left " John " 82,000 Swiss livres, the sum of a thousand louis
in English funds, and the properties of Gaville and Bel-Hôtel, which
they had purchased together. To Louis Alphonse de Rocca she left
408,000 Swiss livres, making especial provision for the payment of
this in case her other children should predecease her and the question
of his legitimacy arise. Should they survive her she had no fear ; she
could trust them to recognize him as her son.

The rest of her fortune was divided between Auguste and Albertine,
the former to receive three-fifteenths more than his sister, because he
would inherit Coppet which was a source of expense rather than of
revenue. Albertine had thus twelve hundred thousand francs including her dowry, while Auguste had fifteen hundred thousand and so
in proportion as to the residue after the other bequests were paid.
She further said they would not find the fortune Necker had left
her in any way diminished ; she had always administered it with the
greatest care.

To Auguste and Schlegel was entrusted the task of editing and
publishing her manuscripts, of which the profits were to be distributed
as follows : up to the sum of five hundred louis to Schlegel and the
remainder to her son who was also to edit the works of the late
Necker.

To the Duc de Broglie she left a thousand écus so that he might
purchase a souvenir of her who had a deep respect for his character
and full confidence in the happiness he would bestow upon her
daughter. There were also other bequests to Mme Necker de Saussure and even to Mme Rilliet-Huber, which she little deserved seeing
that she had deserted her during Napoleon's persecution on hearing
that one of her correspondents had been thrown into Vincennes.
To Mme Necker de Saussure, always a faithful and loyal cousin, she
also bequeathed the portrait by Mme Vigée-Lebrun, now in the

museum at Geneva. Miss Randall, her faithful and good friend, was left a life annuity of 1,400 francs or 60 louis, but Mme de Staël had also dictated instructions shortly before her death to the effect that she was to receive at once the sum of 12,000 francs. Rocca, too, was given at the same time 20,000 francs with permission to take his son wherever he wished. Schlegel was remembered beyond his deserts, for he received an annuity of 3,000 French francs with permission to retain his apartment at Coppet " which would always be honoured by his presence "—an arrangement which must have been particularly objectionable to both Auguste and Albertine who disliked him very much.

§

On the day following the reading of the will, Auguste de Staël set forth upon a filial mission. His destination was Arbonne, and on July 31 he reached Longirod, where he visited the frail, sickly, but beautiful child, Louis Alphonse de Rocca, and took him home. When some three years later Maria Edgeworth visited Coppet she was shown over the house by Auguste and Miss Randall, and was impressed by the reverent silence of the young man when he entered his mother's apartments. With them was Alphonse whom she described as a " pleasing, gentle-looking, ivory-pale boy with dark blue eyes." He did not resemble his mother. . . .

Auguste and Albertine acknowledged him as their brother, and also obtained the recognition of the authorities in respect to his birth and legitimacy. Later that same year Rocca took him to the South of France, and after his own death at Hyères in January, 1818, the boy returned to Coppet, where he was brought up by Albertine exactly as if he had been her own son. Despite the frail physique he inherited from his father, he grew up and at the age of twenty-two married a daughter of Count Rambuteau. He died eight years later.

Auguste, passionately devoted to the memory of his famous mother, lost no time in editing her complete works. An accomplished linguist he lived chiefly between Paris and Coppet, but spent also some time in England. He published his Lettres sur l'Angleterre in 1825, and a year later married Mlle Adelaide Vernet, daughter of a Genevan magistrate. Their happiness was short-lived, since he died suddenly in 1827, and his posthumous son survived only two years. His widow continued to live at Coppet until her death in 1876.

Albertine died in 1838, broken-hearted, it is said, at the death of her youngest daughter, a girl of fifteen. Her second daughter married in 1836 the Comte d'Haussonville, whose descendants still possess the beautiful property of Coppet. . . .

Jane Austen

JANE AUSTEN

§

JANE AUSTEN was born at Steventon in Hampshire, where her father was vicar, on December 16, 1775, and was privately baptized on the following day. There were already four sons so that a second girl was welcome, and Mr. George Austen, in announcing the event, wrote as follows :

> We have now another girl, a present plaything for her sister Cassy, and a future companion. She is to be Jenny, and it seems to me as if she will be as like Harry as Cassy is to Neddy.

She was the seventh child of a family of eight, and the younger of the two daughters. By the superstitious it is sometimes held that a specially fortunate destiny awaits the seventh child, and if to have amused and enlivened people across the lapse of a century and a quarter can be thus designated, Jane Austen did certainly fulfil it in a most enviable degree and as no other prose writer of her epoch has possibly done.

Although born nine years later than her famous foreign contemporary, Germaine de Staël, she survived her but four days. The two women never saw each other, for when Jane was invited to meet her in London she declined the honour.

They lived and wrote at the same time, but while with the one we breathe the air of glittering political salons, hot with passion and intrigue, the other transports us to the cool quiet English landscape, its simple, leisurely village life, its charming domestic interiors, quite remote from the game of politics and with only an occasional reference—even in her letters—to the wars which affected two of her brothers so closely.

Jane's ancestry is interesting since the Austens were one of the families of Kentish clothiers who, settling in that county early in the seventeenth century, became possessed of wealth and lands in the Weald through that now forgotten manufacture. Such families were known as the Gray Coats of Kent, and the Austens still retain on their livery the facings of that peculiar whitish-blue known as

Kentish grey, which also served for those of the Militia of that county.

These riches had, however, escaped Jane's father, who was very early left an orphan and was adopted and educated by an uncle who sent him to Tonbridge School and thence to St. John's College, Oxford, where he held a Smyth scholarship. He returned to Tonbridge later as second master, but in 1758 was given the preferments of Deane and Steventon in Hampshire, the one in the gift of Mr. Francis Austen, his benefactor, and the other in that of Mr. Knight, of Godmersham, near Canterbury, and Chawton Manor near Alton, who had married a cousin of his. The two villages were not far apart and possessed between them but three hundred inhabitants, so that his duties were by no means onerous, and he was able to take pupils to supplement his income.

George Austen's wife was the youngest daughter of the Rev. Thomas Leigh, brother of Theophilus Leigh, a well-known Master of Balliol.

They were of the family of the Leighs of Adlestrop in Gloucestershire, of whom the Leighs of Stoneleigh were a younger branch and to whose property they ultimately succeeded. Originally they came from Cheshire where their ancestors had been settled since the time of the Conquest. Mrs. Austen's paternal grandmother, Mary Brydges, daughter of Lord Chandos, Ambassador to Turkey, and sister of the first Duke of Chandos, married Theophilus Leigh of Adlestrop in 1698. One of the family, Sir Thomas Leigh, was Lord Mayor of London at the time of Queen Elizabeth's Coronation in 1557. But they were passionate adherents of the Stuart cause, a devotion which Jane inherited, and in the brief and absurd *History of England* which she wrote as a young girl she evinced her own hearty dislike of Elizabeth and her ministers.

The George Austens lived at Deane for the first seven years of their married life, and four sons were born to them there. In 1771 —the year of the birth of their fourth son Henry—they moved to Steventon, where Cassandra, Francis, Jane and Charles were born, and where they remained until Mr. Austen's retirement thirty years later.

James, the eldest son, was born in 1765, and was thus ten years older than Jane. Like his father he became a clergyman, a usual proceeding in those days when there was a living in the family. He married first Anne Mathew who was five years his senior and by whom he had a daughter Anna, afterwards Mrs. Lefroy. His second wife was Mary Lloyd whom he married less than two years after the death of his first. Their son James, late in life, wrote a memoir

JANE AUSTEN

of his aunt, and their daughter Caroline frequently figures in Jane Austen's later letters, but we also know from her that her sister-in-law was " not a liberal-minded woman."

The second son, George, was not even mentioned in the original and invaluable memoir written by Mr. James Edward Austen-Leigh, the only son of James and the youngest member of the family to be present at his aunt's funeral. Indeed, very little is known of George, except that he had fits and was mentally undeveloped and lived to be sixty-one years old. It is possible that his very existence was unknown to his brothers and sisters, since in those days the family skeleton was rigorously consigned to the cupboard.

The third son, Edward, was the most fortunate of all the Austens despite his somewhat delicate health, since he was adopted at an early age by Mr. Francis Knight, who had married his father's cousin, and who, having no children of his own, treated him exactly as if he were his son leaving him the fine properties of Godmersham and Chawton Manor—that beautiful Elizabethan house of which glimpses can be seen through the trees as one passes along the Portsmouth road. As a youth he went on the Grand Tour, visiting France, Italy and Germany. At the age of twenty-four he married Elizabeth Bridges, daughter of Sir Brook Bridges, and had six sons and five daughters. She died in 1808, shortly after her eleventh child was born. Their eldest girl, Fanny, was an especial favourite with Jane Austen—almost another sister she used to say. She eventually married Sir Edward Knatchbull and lived to be nearly ninety years old. Her son became the first Lord Brabourne, the author of many delightful fairy tales for children.

The Fourth son, Henry, was Jane's favourite brother. He was over six feet in height and extremely good-looking, and perhaps—for an Austen—a little wayward. Refusing to be a clergyman he entered the Oxford Militia, and was made captain and adjutant some years later. On his retirement he became a banker and in course of time Receiver-General, but in 1816, he was adjudged bankrupt through the failure of an Alton bank. That same year he became a clergyman, although he was then forty-five, and was for many years perpetual curate of Bentley, Hampshire.

At the age of twenty-six he had married his cousin, Eliza de Feuillide, whose first husband, Jean Capotte, Comte de Feuillide, had perished under the guillotine during the Reign of Terror. She was ten years older than Henry. Owing to her French connections Jane Austen saw a good deal of cosmopolitan society at their house in Sloane Street. Eliza had had a son by her first marriage who died at the age of five.

G

The family disapproved of the marriage, but it turned out quite happily. Eliza was pretty and charming and full of vivacity. She was the daughter of Mr. Austen's only sister, Mrs. Hancock, whose husband had sought his fortune in India where he was an intimate friend of Warren Hastings who stood godfather to his child. Eliza went to Paris to be educated and there met the Comte de Feuillide who possessed extensive properties in Guyenne. Their marriage took place in 1781 and all went well until the Revolution broke out. Then they came to England and stayed for a time at Steventon. On hearing that if he did not return to France he would be regarded as an *émigré* and his lands confiscated, Comte de Feuillide went back alone, but on some perfectly trivial pretext, such as his having turned a few acres of arable land into pasturage, his life was forefeited and Eliza took up her abode in England.

She brought a strangely exotic element into the quiet rectory of Steventon. Fond of acting, she organized private theatricals in the great barn, and two of the Austen brothers fell in love with her— James, during his brief period of widowerhood, and Henry, who married her against the wishes of his family, who considered the disparity of ten years between their ages too great. Jane was little more than twenty at the time, but she was already at work on *First Impressions*—as she originally called *Pride and Prejudice*—and she was keenly observant of all that went on around her.

Eliza died in 1813 and about seven years later, when he was nearly fifty, Henry married Eleanor Jackson. He left no children.

The two youngest sons, Francis and Charles, entered the Navy, for the Austens had no prejudice against that Service, although if one is to judge from Jane's work they held very strongly antagonistic views towards the Army, and one might also gather were slightly ashamed of Henry's very moderate connection with it. Both these younger sons distinguished themselves. Francis lived to be ninety-one years old ; he was made a G.C.B. and Queen Victoria appointed him Admiral of the Fleet. He died in 1865. His first wife was Mary Gibson, and when he was sixty-three, and had been a widower for some years, he married Martha Lloyd, sister of James Austen's wife and an intimate friend of both Cassandra and Jane. Like his brother, Edward, he had eleven children.

Charles, the youngest of the family, died of cholera in Burmah, where he was still serving at the age of seventy-three. Indeed, with the exception of Jane, they were a long-lived family. Such flame-like spirits as hers rarely attain longevity.

Of Cassandra, her beloved sister, some three years older than herself and her lifelong friend, it is scarcely necessary at present to speak; so intimately was she bound up in her existence. They were very close sisters, always sharing a room and imparting their few and innocent secrets and ambitions to each other. In Cassandra Jane had a model for the perfect elder sister, whose qualities may have been revealed in Jane Bennet and Elinor Dashwood.

§

Steventon Parsonage, long since destroyed, stood in a valley surrounded by a park-like land of meadows shaded by splendid elm-trees. It was quite a commodious house containing three sitting-rooms, seven bedrooms and three attics, and was situated in a pleasant garden. It had nothing of the bleak aspect of Haworth Parsonage, with its barren treeless surroundings, its melancholy view of the overfull churchyard. *Wuthering Heights* could never have emanated from Steventon, nor *Pride and Prejudice* from Haworth.

It was the somewhat barbarous custom of those days to place infants of about ten months old with some respectable but poor family in the village for a year. In this way it was supposed they would be more constantly in the open air, although—unless things have changed very much—all fresh air must have been most rigorously excluded at night. It was a favourite means of facilitating that sinister process of " hardening " children, which perhaps accounts for the many cases of early decline that characterize the memoirs of that epoch. After this dour period the infants returned to their homes, but, to our modern notions, the plan seems fraught with peril considering the highly important part played by early influences in the moral and physical development of the child.

Jane's education began sooner than was really necessary, because when Cassandra went to school at the age of nine it was found impossible to separate the little sisters. Jane would have been lost without her beloved companion and infinitely preferred the alternative of school. They went first to Oxford, where a Mrs. Cawley, widow of the Principal of Brasenose College, received a few pupils, and where their cousin, Jane Cooper, a girl slightly older than themselves, was being educated. But Mrs. Cawley moved soon afterwards to Southampton and here disaster fell upon the little group. It was, perhaps, from her unpleasant memories of those early days that Jane always disliked the place, and indeed wrote ungracefully later of its " stinking fish."

While there the two little Austen girls fell ill with typhoid—or as it was then called putrid—fever. Mrs. Cawley seems to have taken this quite calmly, for she did not even tell Mrs. Austen, but little Jane Cooper, evidently alarmed at the condition of her cousins,

wrote to inform her. Both Mrs. Austen and Mrs. Cooper hastened
to Southampton, armed with a remedy which is said to have saved
Jane's life. But a very severe illness of that kind could not but
leave its impression both mentally and physically upon a sensitive
child of seven. The sequel too was disastrous; for Mrs. Cooper, on
leaving, went to Bath and succumbed shortly afterwards to the same
malady.

When fully recovered, the Austen girls were sent to a more
ambitious school kept by a Mrs. Latournelle at Reading. One of
her subsequent pupils was Mary Martha Butt, afterwards Mrs.
Sherwood, the author of the *Fairchild Family* and *Little Henry and
his Bearer*. Indeed, the former book, published in 1818, was actually
contemporaneous with *Persuasion*, however difficult it must be
for us now to believe that these two novels, differing so widely in
aim and sympathy, could have seen the light at the same time.

It is, however, greatly to Mrs. Latournelle's credit that her school
should have produced two such famous pupils. Mary Butt and
Jane Austen were born in the same year, but while the former
married and spent much of her life in India, dying in 1851, Jane
passed her briefer span wholly in England, now at Steventon, now
at Bath, now at Chawton, with interludes of Southampton and
London, and those prolonged visits to her brother's house, Godmersham Park.

It is certain that Jane had known no such home-life as that so
relentlessly depicted in the *Fairchild Family*. Mr. George Austen
seems to have been a most kind and indulgent father judging from
his wise affectionate letters to his sailor sons, while Mrs. Austen was
always more or less of an invalid needing the most solicitous care
on the part of her daughters. Catherine Morland's father in *Northanger Abbey* may afford us as close a glimpse as we are likely to obtain
of Mr. Austen.

Her father was a clergyman without being neglected or poor . . . he
had a considerable independence besides two good livings, and he was not
in the least addicted to locking up his daughters.

I imagine there was as little coercion as possible at Steventon.
The children were all—with the exception of the poor absentee
George—healthy and handsome, high-spirited, devoted to each other
and to their parents. That Jane was aware of the revolt of youth
which so early disintegrated Shelley's life, causing him to be expelled
from Oxford, and also from his own home at the age of nineteen,
is fully divulged in her admirable comedy, *Love and Friendship*,
written probably before she was fifteen.

" But do you think my Father will ever be reconciled to this imprudent connection ? " (said Augusta).

" Augusta," (replied the noble youth) " I thought you had a better opinion of me than to imagine I would so abjectly degrade myself as to consider my Father's Concurrence in any of my affairs either of Consequence or Concern to me. Tell me, Augusta, tell me with sincerity, did you ever know me consult his inclinations or follow his Advice in the least trifling Particular since the age of fifteen ? "

" Edward," (replied she) " you are surely too diffident in your own praise. Since you were fifteen only ! My dear Brother, since you were five years old I entirely acquit you of ever having willingly contributed to the satisfaction of your Father."

No girl who had experienced such parental severity as so largely prevailed in those days could have written that sparkling satirical passage. It may have been that she had her brother Henry in mind, for perhaps less than any of them did he attempt to conform to the wishes of his parents.

The life at Steventon could never have been dull with such a large family of sons and daughters besides the pupils who were being prepared for the Universities. When they were first married Mr. and Mrs. Austen accepted the charge of the little son of Warren Hastings, probably at the instigation of Mrs. Hancock, but greatly to their grief, he died at a very early age of putrid sore throat or diphtheria. They also had for a time under their care Lord Lymington, the five-years-old son of Lord Portsmouth, but, as their own family increased, it became more convenient for them to receive youths who had left school.

§

Comtesse de Feuillide had heard that her cousins, Cassandra and Jane, were two of the prettiest girls in England, so it is hardly surprising to find that one of the aforesaid pupils, Thomas Fowle, son of Mr. Thomas Fowle, Vicar of Kintbury, fell in love with Cassandra in 1795, after he had left Steventon and been ordained. It was considered imprudent for them to marry before he had a living and he went to the West Indies as chaplain to Lord Craven's regiment. He died two years later of yellow fever at San Domingo, leaving Cassandra £1,000.

Jane had a great friend, Mrs. Lefroy, daughter of Sir Egerton Brydges and wife of the Rev. Isaac Lefroy, Vicar of Ashe, who was one of the first to discern in her those outstanding qualities of wit and intelligence of which her novels give such abundant proof. That Jane unfortunately permitted herself to be influenced by this lady, so many years her senior, is hardly to be doubted ; the rough outline of the story is used in the last novel she finished, her little masterpiece *Persuasion*. Whatever of bitterness she may once have felt had long passed away ; Mrs. Lefroy was dead ; there were few who would remember that frustrated romance which had taken place twenty years earlier.

Mr. Lefroy had a nephew, Tom, who came to stay at Ashe, and evidently fell in love with Jane. They danced together at the Basingstoke ball, and from a letter to Cassandra it is clear that she confidently expected him to propose to her and that she intended to accept him, despite the white coat he insisted upon wearing, out of admiration for *Tom Jones*.

On January 9, 1796, Jane wrote to her sister for her birthday, mentioning that Tom had celebrated his on the previous day.

You scold me much in the nice long letter which I have just this moment received from you that I am almost afraid to tell you how my Irish friend and I behaved. Imagine to yourself everything most profligate and shocking in the way of dancing and sitting down together. I *can* expose myself however only *once more* because he leaves the country soon after next Friday, on which day we *are* to have a dance at Ashe after all. He is a very gentleman-like, good-looking, pleasant young man I assure you. But as to our having ever met except at the last three balls I cannot say much, for he is so excessively laughed at about me at Ashe that he is ashamed of coming to Steventon, and ran away when we called on Mrs. Lefroy a few days ago.

But even as she wrote the above letter, she was interrupted by a visit from the young man and his cousin George. When she again took up her pen she said she meant to confine herself in future to Mr. Tom Lefroy, " for whom I don't care sixpence." And on the very day of the ball she wrote thus :

At length the day has come when I am to flirt my last with T. L. and when you receive this it will be over. My tears flow as I write at the melancholy idea.

The ball at Ashe took place, everything was beautifully done, the greenhouse was illuminated, the supper excellent. But there was no proposal, and on the following day the young man left the neighbourhood. He was only nineteen, being two years younger than Jane, so that at best it must have meant a long engagement, and Mrs. Lefroy was undoubtedly averse to the idea since she sent him away after three weeks " that no more mischief might be done." As an old man he confessed his love for Jane Austen, admitting, however, that it was only a boy's love. With him it was certainly not serious, and some years later he married. He lived to be Chief Justice of Ireland. The fact that he was the nephew of her greatest friend may have imbued him with a kind of reflected glamour, but it is evident that Jane felt his defection acutely. More than two years later she wrote to Cassandra about a visit she had received from Mrs. Lefroy :

" with whom, in spite of interruptions both from my father and James, I was enough alone to hear all that was interesting, which you will easily credit when I tell you that of her nephew she said nothing at all and of her friend very little. She did not once mention the name of the former to *me* and I was too proud to make any enquiries ; but on my father's afterwards asking where he was I learnt that he was gone back to London on his way to Ireland where he is called to the Bar and means to practise."

Mrs. Lefroy had then recently returned from Bath, and on this occasion she also showed Jane a letter she had received from the said friend, a Mr. Blackall, Fellow of Emmanuel College, Cambridge, to whom she had written on behalf of a nephew of Mrs. Russell.

I am very sorry—wrote Mr. Blackall—to hear of Mrs. Austen's illness. It would give me particular pleasure to have an opportunity of improving my acquaintance with that family—with a hope of creating to myself a nearer interest. But at present I cannot indulge in any expectation of it.

This, Jane commented, was rational enough ; there was less love and more sense in it than had hitherto appeared.

Mrs. Lefroy,—she added—made no remarks on the letter nor did she say anything about him as relative to me. Perhaps she thinks she has said too much already.

But I think if anyone ever touched her heart it was Lefroy, and perhaps she had him in mind when she wrote that poignant passage in *Persuasion*, where Anne Elliot suddenly reveals what is in her heart to Captain Harville in the presence of the man she loves.

I should deserve utter contempt if I dared to suppose that true attach-ment and constancy were known only by woman. No, I believe you capable of everything great and good in your married lives. I believe you equal to every important exertion, and to every domestic forbearance so long as—if I may be allowed the expression—so long as you have an object. I mean while the woman you love lives and lives for you. All the privilege I claim for my own sex (it is not a very enviable one ; you need not covet it) is that of loving longest when existence or when hope is gone.

Rarely did Jane Austen reveal such emotional passion as in that profoundly dramatic scene. Frederick Wentworth, repudiated more than eight years earlier at the instigation of Anne's friend, Lady Russell, and still not daring to approach her, listens to that speech and writes the famous letter to Anne, a device which Mrs. Humphry Ward adopted in *Marcella*.

I can listen no longer in silence. I must speak to you by such means as are within my reach. You pierce my soul. I am half agony, half hope. Tell me not that I am too late, that such precious feelings are gone for ever. I offer myself to you again with a heart even more your own than when you almost broke it eight and a half years ago. Dare not say that a man forgets sooner than a woman, that his love has an earlier death. I have loved none but you . . .

We may regret that Jane Austen did not retain some of the passages in the suppressed chapter.

Still, a little nearer and her hand taken and pressed ; and " Anne, my own dear Anne ! " bursting forth in all the fullness of exquisite feeling,—and all suspense and indecision were over. They were reunited. They were restored to all that had been lost. . . .

It was as yet too soon for Jane to contemplate Mr. Blackall's suit with any enthusiasm. Mrs. Lefroy might send one lover about his business, but she could not force a second, however eligible, upon her, especially one whom Jane described later as a " piece of noisy perfection." On hearing of his engagement many years afterwards to a Miss Lewis, she even expressed a hope that the lady was of a silent turn, rather ignorant but willing to learn, fond of cold veal pies, green tea in the afternoon and a green window-blind at night. She must have discerned a disposition on Mr. Blackall's part to improve her and quite naturally resented it.

Other shadowy romances are recorded but on slender evidence. There was, for instance, the meeting between the Austen sisters and a charming young man one summer at some unspecified place in the West. He was very agreeable and good-looking and was said, according to Caroline Austen, to resemble a young engineer, Mr. Henry Edridge, whom they met much later at Newtown. Agreeable and good-looking, he made a profound impression upon Jane, and a warm attachment sprang up between them. Whether there was an engagement we shall perhaps never know, but he died very shortly afterwards.

Matrimony was much discussed at that time, for on the last day of 1797 Henry married Eliza de Feuillide after, it is said, two years' resistance on the part of the lady. Early in the century, after the Peace of Amiens, they visited France together and then he retired from the Militia and settled in London as a banker and Army agent. Nearly all Jane's experience of London life—which, however, she used so sparingly in her novels—was acquired during those long visits to Sloane Street and Hans Place both before and after Henry was left a widower. Always a kind and helpful brother, he both believed in and admired her work, and dealt with both publishers and printers when the time came for the novels to appear.

Despite the frustration of her early love affair, which I am inclined to believe left a more permanent impression upon her than most of her biographers are disposed to allow, Jane's intimacy with Mrs. Lefroy at Ashe continued, and it is to that lady's brother, Sir Egerton Brydges, who frequently saw her there that we owe the following description of Jane in the bloom of her girlhood.

When I knew Jane Austen I never suspected that she was an authoress ; but my eyes told me that she was fair and handsome, slight and elegant, but with cheeks a little too full.

This, however, does not altogether coincide with the description given by Mr. James Edward Austen-Leigh, who wrote the first Memoir of his aunt in his old age :

In person she was very attractive ; her figure was rather tall and slender, her step light and firm, and her whole appearance expressive of health and animation. In complexion she was a clear brunette with a rich colour ; she had full round cheeks with mouth and nose small but well-formed, bright hazel eyes and brown hair forming natural curls round her face. If not so regularly handsome as her sister yet her countenance had a peculiar charm of its own to the eyes of most beholders. She was never seen, either morning or evening, without a cap ; I believe that she and her sister were generally thought to have taken to the garb of middle age earlier than their years or looks required ; and that though remarkably neat in their dress as in all their ways, they were scarcely sufficiently regardful of the fashionable or the becoming.

Still it was the age of caps, and Fanny Knight, Edward's eldest child, wore them as quite a young girl, and Jane always made a point of buying the newest models during her visits to London. From her letters we may gather that the said caps were worn out driving as well as in the house, and that for balls and other evening festivities they were extremely ornate. Nearly all women in those days wore some kind of head-dress, and at the parties given by the Regent at Carlton House enormous feathers of different colours decorated their hair so that the rooms presented a sea of nodding plumes. And then there was the famous turban of Mme de Staël worn also when she received her morning visitors in her bedroom.

§

Jane Austen's young life was both pleasant and in a sense gay. With so many brothers married she had no lack of interests, and her youth was by no means the dull and monotonous one which many of her biographers have portrayed. There were visits to her cousins at Bath, to the Leighs at Adlestrop and Stoneleigh, to Edward, first at Rowling and then at Godmersham, as well as to Henry and

Eliza in London, and visits were protracted in those days, often lasting a couple of months or more. The delightful letters to Cassandra, which begin in 1796, form an almost complete picture of Jane's girlhood and womanhood. It is true there are long blanks when the sisters were either together at Steventon or Cassandra considered it more judicious to destroy the correspondence. We have thus no allusions to the death of Tom Fowle in 1797, but there is an amusing letter from Jane written to her sister, then staying with his parents at Kintbury, just after the young man's departure.

I am very glad to find from Mary that Mr. and Mrs. Fowle are pleased with you. I hope you will continue to give satisfaction. How impertinent you are to write to me about Tom, as if I had not had opportunities of hearing from him myself ! The last *letter* I received from him was dated Friday, 8th, and he told me that if the wind should be favourable on Sunday, which it proved to be, they were to sail from Falmouth on that day. By this time, therefore, they are at Barbadoes, I suppose.

These letters to her sister reveal a perfectly spontaneous sense of humour and are full of vivacity, as when she writes thus from Rowling :

Mr. Children's two sons are both going to be married, John and George. They are to have one wife between them : a Miss Holwell, who belongs to the Black Hole of Calcutta.

Her father, Governor Holwell, had been one of the survivors of that grim tragedy of which he published an account in 1758.

All through August and September, 1796, Jane remained at Rowling. Frank was also there, waiting for a ship, and in the meantime amusing himself by turning. It was arranged that she should travel to London with him when he left, as he disapproved of her going alone in the stage-coach.

He was a year older than Jane, coming between her and Cassandra. One of the handsomest of the Austens, he was educated at the Royal Naval Academy, Portsmouth, where boys were received between the ages of twelve and fifteen, since even then it was considered desirable to begin their training for that life as early as possible. He left the Academy at the age of fourteen and went to the East Indies as a volunteer in the *Perseverance*, remaining there for four years as midshipman in the *Crown*, and subsequently in the *Minerva*. Nothing could have been wiser and more judicious than the letter his father sent him just before his departure, and it gives us a pleasant insight into both their characters. He told him that the friendship of his Commander and the other officers would be more readily won by a respectful behaviour and prompt obedience to orders.

Good humour, an inclination to oblige and the carefully avoiding every appearance of selfishness will infallibly secure you the regard of your own mess and of all your equals.

Prudence, he continued, would teach him the proper disposal of his time and the management of his money. He urged him also to make himself as useful as possible, carefully studying everything connected with his profession. So far he had been singularly fortunate in making friends, and had borne a high character during his time at the Academy. He was to draw on his father for what money he required and must keep an account of all he spent and was never to risk any of it by " gaming."

Both Francis and Charles were very handsome, with dark hair, and eyes set under level, dark brows, and both had the straight nose and well-cut features of the Austens.

Frank left Rowling suddenly in September having been appointed to the *Triton*, a frigate recently launched, and Jane was unable to accompany him to London as she had not had time to ascertain whether her friends the Pearsons, who were to put her up, had yet returned.

For if the Pearsons were not at home—she wrote to Cassandra—I should inevitably fall a sacrifice to the arts of some fat woman who would make me drunk with small beer.

This made it necessary for her to wait until Edward went to London himself.

My father will be so good as to fetch home his prodigal daughter from Town I hope, unless he wishes me to walk the Hospitals, Enter at the Temple or mount Guard at St. James's.

§

In addition to these visits to her brothers, Jane early became acquainted with Bath since her uncle Mr. Leigh-Perrot, brother of Mrs. Austen, had a house in the Paragon in that city. He had married a rich woman, and had also been left a property which entailed his adding the name of Perrot to his own.

But there were naturally long intervals at Steventon and it was there that Jane, at an early age, began the series of novels which have made her name for ever famous. It is generally believed that *Pride and Prejudice*, one of the most sparkling and complete of them all, was begun before she was twenty-one in the autumn of 1796. It was finished by November of the following year, and her nephew, Mr. James Edward Austen-Leigh, quotes a letter which her father wrote to the publisher Cadell.

Sir,—I have in my possession a manuscript novel comprising 3 vols., about the length of Miss Burney's " Evelina." As I am well aware of what consequence it is that a work of this sort should make its first appearance under a respectable name, I apply to you. I shall be much obliged therefore if you will inform me whether you choose to be concerned in it, what will be the expense of publishing it at the author's risk, and what you will venture to advance for the property of it, if on perusal it is approved of. Should you give me any encouragement I will send you the work.

I am, Sir, your humble Servant,

George Austen.

November 1, 1797.

Steventon, near Overton, Hants.

Some of Jane's biographers have from this fallen into the error of concluding that Cadell refused *Pride and Prejudice*, after reading it, but he did no such thing. He never saw the precious manuscript ; he did not in fact " choose to be concerned in it " or otherwise offer the slightest encouragement to the author. He declined the honour of examining it by return of post.

Nineteen years had passed since Fanny Burney had stormed London with her *Evelina or the History of a Young Lady's Entrance into the World*. It was published anonymously, for in those days and for more than eighty years afterwards, there was a curious, almost inexplicable, prejudice against the career of novel-writing for women. Many of our most famous women novelists of the nineteenth century preferred to adopt noms-de-plume rather than reveal their identity. Currer, Ellis and Acton Bell concealed the immortal name of Brontë ; Marian Evans, perhaps wisely since she disliked to be thus known after her association with Lewes, adopted the more definitely masculine pseudonym of George Eliot. It is on record that many manuscripts of that epoch were destroyed by irate mothers as well as by stern husbands. I have an idea it was considered not quite " nice " for a woman, whatever her age, to disclose any intimate knowledge of human nature or passion. And there was another more practical reason. Both the parents and husbands of those days were strenuously opposed to their womenkind having any money at all of their own. It would only make them independent, and that was the very last thing they could wish for them. At any rate this peculiar prejudice lasted far into the nineteenth century, and even in the 'fifties when Charlotte Yonge published the *Heir of Redclyffe* with its impossibly immaculate hero Guy Morville—under her own name it must be confessed—she was compelled to devote the very considerable sum it earned for her to charity. She had then reached the age of thirty and might have been expected to have some say in the matter, but it was evidently not quite " the thing " for a gently-born woman to earn money for her own use.

A writer possessing a sense of his own powers is rarely deterred by a single rebuff of the kind, and judging by the spontaneity of her work—afterwards so carefully polished and " lop't and crop't," as she expressed it—writing must have been as natural to Jane as eating and sleeping. She proceeded to write *Sense and Sensibility*, of which the first draft was in the form of letters, to which she was attracted by *Clarissa Harlowe* and *Evelina*. But it was a form of which the public was growing weary, and *Elinor and Marianne* later became *Sense and Sensibility*. Hardly had it been finished, and with still no prospect of publication, when Jane wrote *Northanger Abbey*, of which the early scenes were laid in Bath.

Nor were these first books the work of a prentice-hand. Jane had been writing since she was fifteen, perhaps even earlier, since we know that she solemnly advised her niece not to begin too young, saying that she herself always wished she had read more and written less at that age.

In those days of rare and difficult travelling, of few active amusements and recreations in which women could take part unless they were rich enough to afford horses, physical exercise was necessarily largely confined to walking. Lawn tennis and golf were unknown in the English countryside; the mild croquet of a later date had not so far invaded the decorous lawns of parsonages. In bad weather Cassandra and Jane must have been thrown upon their own resources, and reading was the chief of these, just as, thirty years later, it was to be the principal recreation at Haworth Parsonage. But Steventon was far more adequately supplied with new books than remote Haworth. There were clubs to which people in the neighbourhood subscribed, and among which the latest novels were freely circulated. And, even as at Haworth, reading was but a step to writing. Only here Jane had no rival except in the prologues contributed by James to the plays they performed under the vivacious ægis of Eliza de Feuillide, whose mind was still occupied with the problem as to whether she should marry Henry or not. . . . Moreover the atmosphere of the Parsonage was an intellectual and cultivated one. Mr. Austen, an ex-schoolmaster and ex-Don, was a first-rate classical scholar ; the sons were highly educated, the daughters agreeable and cultured, with a knowledge of French, Italian, drawing and music.

Beginning young, as most fiction writers do, practising the art till it became the polished, witty, perfect thing it was, Jane seems to have sought no solitude for the exercise of her gift, the development of her genius. Her little mahogany desk, still faithfully preserved, was placed on the parlour table round which the other members of the family sat sewing or reading. Their talk was not interrupted, and Jane even joined in it. How she contrived under such conditions to concentrate upon those very human creatures of her imagination it would indeed be hard for the modern author, who as a rule seeks solitude at any price, to comprehend. But, it was not till a few months before the end that she let any complaint escape her.

In Cassandra's absence she did the housekeeping, for Mrs. Austen by then had retired from any active participation in the management of the parsonage. And here Jane exhibits a certain humorously pessimistic outlook. Of a new laundress she wrote :

She does not look as if anything she touched would ever be clean, but who knows ?

She acquired fresh ideas about food at her brother's house where living was naturally upon a higher scale, and, when possible, introduced them at Steventon. Speaking of her housekeeping she wrote :

I think it my peculiar excellence and for this reason. I always take care to provide such things as please my own appetite which I consider as the chief merit in housekeeping. I have had some ragout veal, and I mean to have some haricot mutton to-morrow. . . . I am very fond of experimental housekeeping, such as having an ox-cheek now and then ; I shall have one next week, and I mean to have some little dumplings put into it that I may fancy myself at Godmersham.

During Cassandra's absence at Godmersham in November, 1798, James's only son was born—the James Edward Austen-Leigh, author of the Memoir. But Mary was never a favourite with her sister-in-law, and when she saw her a week or two later, Jane complained that she was not sufficiently tidy.

She has no dressing-gown to sit up in ; her curtains are all too thin, and things are not in that comfort and style about her which are necessary to make such a situation an enviable one.

Mr. Austen constantly exchanged notes about live-stock with his son Edward, sending him a message to the effect that he had given twenty-five shillings apiece for his sheep, and wished for some of his son's pigs. Lord Bolton had had pigsties of " a most elegant construction " built for his, and visited them every morning as soon as he rose. This suggestion of " brighter pigsties " strikes quite a modern note. . . .

Already, at twenty-three, Jane was making herself some caps to wear in the evening which would save her the trouble of doing her hair. Her long hair was braided and out of sight, and the short curled naturally over her forehead.

A new library was started about this time by a Mrs. Martin to
which Mrs. Austen subscribed. Mrs. Martin explained it was not
only intended for novels, but for general literature, and Jane, who
had strong views on this subject, as we know from *Northanger Abbey*,
added in her letter to her sister :

She might have spared this pretension to *our* family who are great novel
readers and not ashamed of being so.

Glimpses of that simple home life are given in these intimate letters.
Dinner at Steventon was at half-past three and tea at half-past six,
although later hours were then beginning to be fashionable elsewhere. " I fear you will despise us," Jane added. And in the evening
Mr. Austen would read Cowper aloud to them, " to which I listen
when I can."

And there was to be a ball, but she feared there would be no one
worth dancing with.

People get so horridly poor and economical in this part of the world
that I have no patience with them. Kent is the only place for happiness.
Everybody is rich there ;—I must do similar justice however to the
Windsor neighbourhood.

She stayed with the Bigg-Withers at Manydown for the said ball
which was only attended by thirty-one people, of whom eleven were
ladies, including five unmarried ones. She and Catherine Bigg (afterwards Mrs. Hill) teased a Mr. Calland into dancing with them.

I was very glad to see him again after so long a separation, and he was
altogether rather the genius and flirt of the evening.

Jane danced all the twenty dances, and her black cap was openly
admired by Mrs. Lefroy. This mild gaiety was not, however, to be
compared with a ball which Cassandra attended about that time at
Ashford, and at which she had supper with the Prince (Prince
William of Gloucester). The extraordinary menu of this feast has been
preserved. Beginning with salmon, trout and soles, soup makes an
appearance about half-way down, while goose winds up the repast
following baskets of pastry and custards !

It was about this time that Mr. Austen appealed to Admiral
Gambier on behalf of Charles, who wished to serve in a frigate, since
they were usually more successful in capturing " prizes " than other
ships. He was duly appointed to the *Tamar*.

Frank Austen, now with Lord St. Vincent in the Mediterranean,
was appointed to a sloop, the *Peterel*, in December of that same year.

Jane was invited to Lady Dorchester's ball, Mrs. Lefroy having
previously warned her that she was to receive an invitation. She
danced less than usual, remarking sagaciously that " one's con-

sequence, you know, varies so much at times without any particular reason." Still, she sat down two dances rather than endure Lord Bolton's eldest son as a partner, since he danced "too ill to be endured." Jane was fond of introducing ballroom scenes into her novels ; she was particularly happy in describing them, for they played an important part in her own life. No such frivolities occur in the Brontë novels, indeed it is not on record that those three sad-faced girls ever even learned to dance.

Charles was at home that winter and was much admired, Mrs. Lefroy considering him even handsomer than Henry. He left home in January, 1799, hearing that the *Tamar* was then in the Downs. To Jane he was always "our own particular little brother," a source of constant pride and admiration. We can trace a resemblance in him to the William Price of *Mansfield Park*.

§

In May of that same year, Jane accompanied her mother, Edward, Eliza and their two elder children to Bath. Edward had been ill and was to take a course of the waters. They stopped at Devizes on the way, partaking of an excellent dinner, asparagus, lobster and cheese-cakes figuring on the menu. (Jane always took the keenest interest in food.) On their arrival at Bath they stopped at the Paragon to enquire for Mr. Leigh-Perrot, meeting on the way an acquaintance who proved to be Doctor Hall, "and Doctor Hall in such very deep mourning that either his mother or his wife or himself must be dead."

Throughout her letters we find such delicious items as this :

Dr. Gardiner was married yesterday to Mrs. Percy and her three daughters.

They remained in Bath until the end of June, Edward benefiting greatly by the treatment. Once Jane walked up Beacon Hill and across the fields to Charlcombe, "sweetly situated in a little green valley, as a village with such a name ought to be." She was accompanied on this occasion by Miss North and a Mr. Gould. The latter walked home with her and of course he must be described in a thumbnail sketch to Cassandra : "A very young man who had just gone to Oxford, wore spectacles, and had heard that *Evelina* was written by Doctor Johnson ! "

After their return to Steventon there were fewer letters until Cassandra went to stay at Godmersham with Edward. Then there was an account of a ball which Jane enjoyed.

Lady Portsmouth had got a different dress on, and Lady Bolton is much improved by a wig.

Then there was a dinner at Ashe Park where Jane made the discovery that to " sit in idleness over a good fire in a well-proportioned room was a luxurious sensation." Sometimes they talked and sometimes they sat in silence.

I said two or three amusing things and Mr. Holder made a few infamous puns.

Her sister-in-law Mary, who was with her, found it very dull, but Jane was too brilliant ever to be bored.

A few items of her letters to Cassandra before they left Steventon deserve to be quoted.

" Mrs Powlett was at once expensively and nakedly dressed."
" Mrs. John Lyford is so much pleased with the state of widowhood as to be going to put in for being a widow again."
" So Lady Bridges—in the delicate language of Coulson Wallop—is *in for it*."

But even then a tragic change was impending. In 1800 Mr. Austen decided to resign the livings of Steventon and Deane in favour of his son James. Jane was staying at Ibthorp with the Lloyds and did not hear the ill-tidings till her return home, when it is recorded that she actually fainted. Not often did the brilliant, high-spirited girl exhibit such sensibility, a proof of the intense shock she had sustained. All her memories were bound up in Steventon ; it was there she had spent her happy youth ; she had many friends in the neighbourhood and it held the associations of twenty-five years. It meant, too, that she must leave the one woman who, with the exception of Cassandra, ever enjoyed her warm and intimate friendship. Mrs. Lefroy may have been injudicious—even as Lady Russell in *Persuasion* was injudicious—in separating Jane from her handsome nephew Tom Lefroy ; it may well be that she thus frustrated what might have proved a happy marriage, but she was nevertheless very dear to her.

Nor was the prospect of living in Bath at all attractive to Jane. Country-bred, she disliked cities except for brief sojourns. She needed the quiet countryside for the exercise of her unique gift. . . .

It was undoubtedly for this reason that during her ten years of exile from the fields and lanes of Hampshire, she wrote so little, except for such unfinished fragments as *The Watsons* and *Lady Susan*, books which she never completed. It is quite possible, however, that drafts of some of her other novels were prepared since she worked over her manuscripts with the most meticulous care.

Before leaving Steventon, she wrote to Cassandra giving her news of the two sailor brothers who were then both at sea, Francis in the *Peterel* and Charles in the *Endymion*.

H

Charles, she said, had spent three pleasant days at Lisbon, and they were all very well pleased with their royal passenger—the Duke of Sussex—whom they found " jolly and affable," and who talked of Lady Augusta as his wife and seemed deeply attached to her. Charles wrote the letter when the *Endymion* was becalmed, but he hoped to reach Portsmouth on the following Monday or Tuesday, and though much surprised to hear of the impending move, was resolved to come to Steventon while they were still there.

Despite her distress on first learning her father's decision, Jane soon became outwardly reconciled to her lot and took a keen interest in the future arrangements and plans. Her mother bargained to have no trouble in furnishing the house at Bath, and Jane assured her that Cassandra would take all that off her hands. Mrs. Austen also looked forward to keeping two maids, though so far she had not revealed this ambitious intention to her husband.

I get more and more reconciled to the idea of our removal—Jane wrote—We have lived long enough in this neighbourhood ; the Basingstoke balls are certainly on the decline ; there is something interesting in the bustle of going away, and the prospect of spending future summers by the Sea or in Wales is very delightful. For a time we shall possess many of the advantages which I have often thought of with envy in the wives of Sailors or Soldiers. It must not be generally known that I am not sacrificing a great deal in quitting the Country—or I can expect to inspire no tenderness, no interest, in those we leave behind. . . .

Among those to be thus left were the Bigg-Withers of Manydown Park, where Jane was a frequent visitor. Mr. Lovelace Bigg-Wither had three daughters who did not, however, like his sons, add the name of Wither to that of Bigg. Elizabeth became Mrs. Heathcote ; Catherine, Mrs. Hill ; while the youngest, Alethea, remained unmarried. The second son, Harris, fell in love with Jane and there are many allusions to him in her letters, though this particular fact does not transpire. Six years younger than herself he suffered from delicate health. He asked her to marry him when she was on a visit to Manydown, after the Austens' removal to Bath, and Jane, accepting him overnight, withdrew, it is averred, her consent in the morning, and made a hurried departure from the house in consequence. Harris survived his elder brother Lovelace, and two years after her refusal, married Miss Anne Frith. One may, however, feel a certain regret that Jane never occupied the position of châtelaine at Manydown Park, where she would surely have been in her element. . . .

Before leaving Steventon, Martha Lloyd stayed with them, the girls hoping still that Frank would marry her, a hope which was not to be fulfilled until more than thirty years later.

Jane told her sister about this time that Charles had received thirty pounds as his share of the privateer and expected ten pounds more, " but of what avail is it to take prizes if he lays out the produce in presents to his sisters ? " He bought topaz crosses and gold chains— still faithfully preserved—for Cassandra and Jane. The latter further told her sister that the *Endymion* was under orders to take troops to Egypt, which she should not like at all did she not believe that Charles would be removed from the ship before she sailed. This letter was written in February, 1801, when English troops were on their way thither to oppose Napoleon. Sir Ralph Abercrombie landed at Aboukir and defeated the French on March 8 of that year, compelling them to evacuate Egypt. Thus Jane Austen was drawing on her personal experience when she wrote in *Persuasion* :

She (Anne) gloried in being a sailor's wife, but she must pay the tax of quick alarm for belonging to that profession which is if possible more distinguished in its domestic virtues than in its national importance.

§

In May, 1801, Jane left Steventon with her mother and went to Bath. Cassandra and Mr. Austen were to follow later, and in the meantime the former stayed with her friends the Lloyds near Hurstbourne Tarrant. On arrival Mrs. Austen and her daughter spent some time with the Leigh-Perrots in the Paragon, until a suitable house could be found.

The first view of Bath in fine weather does not answer my expectations ; I think I see more distinctly through rain. The sun was got behind everything, and the appearance of the place from the top of Kingsdown was all vapour, shadow, smoke and confusion.

Mr. Austen remained at Steventon to dispose of most of his furniture, books and stock. Sixty-one guineas for the three cows compensated in some sort for their receiving only eleven for the tables. Eight for Jane's pianoforte was much what she expected, and she was delighted to get ten shillings for her copy of Dodsley's poems, declaring she did not mind how many copies she sold at that price.

Mrs. Leigh-Perrot took her to a ball at the Assembly Rooms which was ill-attended. But Jane was not idle. Her bright, observant eyes watched and noted, and she wrote charming little satirical descriptions with just a hint of malice in them to Cassandra about the people she met and saw. It was there she must have pictured the famous scene in *Persuasion* when Sir Walter Elliot and his eldest daughter stepped forward to greet Lady Dalrymple " with all the eagerness compatible with anxious elegance."

Living was cheap in Bath, and Jane seems to have cherished hopes of inducing Mrs. Lloyd and Martha to move thither. Meat was eightpence a pound, butter one shilling, and cheese ninepence half-penny. On the other hand fish was dear, salmon being sold at two and ninepence the pound, but this was thought to be due to the presence of the Duchess of York in the city. Her departure was expected to make the price more reasonable. . . .

Meanwhile search was made for a suitable house. But many of those handsome stone-built structures in the lower part of the town proved to be damp on closer inspection. And Jane was not at her ease staying with the Leigh-Perrots, who constantly gave card-parties in the evening. Such complaints as these occur in her letters to Cassandra :

I cannot continue to find people agreeable. . . . We are to have a tiny party here to-night : I hate tiny parties—they force one into constant exertion. . . . The Pickfords are in Bath and have called here. She is the most elegant-looking woman I have seen since I left Martha. He is as raffish in his appearance as I would wish every disciple of Godwin to be.

A house was finally taken in Sydney Terrace. Their summers were spent at the seaside, usually at Dawlish or at Teignmouth, but in August, 1804, Jane went to Lyme with which her name must for ever be associated on account of the famous scene of Louisa Musgrove's fall in *Persuasion*. It was from thence she wrote to Cassandra in September of that year :

My dear Cassandra,—I take the first sheet of fine striped paper to thank you for your letter from Weymouth, and express my hopes of your being at Ibthorp before this time. I expect to hear that you reached it yesterday evening being able to get as far as Blandford on Wednesday. Your account of Weymouth contains nothing which strikes me so forcibly as there being no ice in the town. For every other vexation I was in some measure prepared, and particularly your disappointment in not seeing the Royal Family go on board on Tuesday, having already heard from Mr. Crawford that he had seen you in the very act of being too late. But for there being no ice what could prepare me ! You found my letter at Andover, I hope, yesterday and have now for many hours been satisfied that your kind anxiety on my behalf was as much thrown away as kind anxiety usually is.

I continue quite well ; in proof of which I have bathed this morning. It was absolutely necessary that I should have the little fever and indisposition which I had ; it has been all the fashion this week in Lyme. We are quite settled in our lodgings by this time as you may suppose and everything goes on in the usual order. The servants behave very well and make no difficulties, though nothing can exceed the inconvenience of the offices except the general dirtiness of the house and furniture and all its inhabitants. I endeavour as far as I can to supply your place, and be useful and keep things in order. I detect dirt in the water decanters, as fast as I can, and keep everything as it was under your administration.

The ball last night was pleasant, but not full for Thursday. My father staid till half past nine (we went a little after eight) and then walked home with James and a lanthorn, though I believe the lanthorn was not lit, as the moon was up ; but sometimes this lanthorn may be a great convenience to him. My mother and I staid about an hour later. Nobody asked me the first two dances ; the two next I danced with Mr. Crawford, and had I chosen to stay longer might have danced with Mr. Granville, Mrs. Granville's son, whom my dear friend Miss A. introduced to me, or with a new odd-looking man who had been eyeing me for some time, and at last without any introduction asked me if I meant to dance again. I think he must be Irish by his ease, and because I imagine him to belong to the Honble B——'s, the son, and son's wife of an Irish viscount, queer-looking people, just fit to be quality at Lyme.

I called yesterday morning (ought it not in strict propriety to be termed yester-morning ?) on Miss A. and was introduced to her father and mother. Like other young ladies she is considerably genteeler than her parents. Mrs. A. sat darning a pair of stockings the whole of my visit. But do not mention this at home lest a warning should act as an example. We afterwards walked together for an hour on the Cobb ; she is very conversable in a common way ; I do not perceive wit or genius, but she has sense and some degree of taste, and her manners are very engaging. She seems to like people rather too easily.

It will be seen from this letter that Mrs. Austen had relinquished all share in the domestic concerns of the house. Such matters could be safely entrusted to either of her daughters, Jane especially bringing a sort of imagination to the task. We can also discern that Jane was more than apt to be a little on her guard with new acquaintances such as " Miss A " who " liked her too easily." But her quick, observant eyes were even then memorizing scenes and impressions for *Persuasion*, this mental activity enabling her to endure the commonplace chatter of her companion.

She was now twenty-nine years old and could still thoroughly enjoy dancing. That she was extremely attractive with her bright eyes and dark, curly hair, we can gather from her account of the poor man who eyed her for some time before he ventured to approach her, and then apparently met with such short-shrift at her hands.

§

Tragedy was approaching, for if, as the French say, " *un bonheur ne va jamais sans d'autre*," we have a more gloomy adage to the effect that misfortunes rarely come singly. On Jane's twenty-ninth birthday, December 16, 1804, Mrs. Lefroy was killed by a fall from her horse. She had been her girlhood's friend and was extremely dear to her. A clever, cultivated woman herself, she had no doubt encouraged her to write, and four years later, when time had somewhat healed the wound, Jane alluded to that early friendship in a poem she wrote to her memory.

> Can aught enhance such goodness ? Yes, to me
> Her partial favour from my earliest years
> Consummates all : ah, give me but to see
> Her smile of love ! The vision disappears.

Hard upon the death of Mrs. Lefroy came that of Mr. Austen, who died in the following January after a brief illness, of which Jane gave full details in a letter of the same date to her brother Frank. On the Saturday morning he was taken ill, with oppression in the head, fever and trembling, symptoms from which he had previously suffered. The usual remedy of cupping was resorted to, but failed to alleviate him. Towards the evening he seemed better, had a good night, and joined his family at breakfast on the Sunday, even walking about a little with the aid of a stick. This was obviously imprudent since the symptoms of the previous day seemed to indicate some kind of cerebral seizure. But people in those days were hardy ; they were disciplined from their earliest years not to give way, thus they rarely took to their beds till they were actually dying. There was at that time a peculiar dread of sloth and self-indulgence which was both Puritan and Spartan in its origin. . . .

As the day advanced, the fever increased, and Doctor Bowen, who saw Mr. Austen at ten o'clock that night, took a very grave view of the case. He returned at nine o'clock on the following morning and called in another physician. But it was too late and twenty minutes later Mr. Austen died.

> Heavy as the blow is—wrote Jane—we can already feel that a thousand comforts remain to us to soften it. Next to that of the consciousness of his worth and constant preparation for another world, is the remembrance of his having suffered, comparatively speaking, nothing. Being quite insensible of his own state he was spared all the pain of separation, and he went off almost in his sleep. . . . His tenderness as a Father who can do justice to ? My Mother is tolerably well ; she bears up with great fortitude, but I fear her health must suffer under such a shock. The funeral is to be on Saturday at Walcot Church. . . .

It was the very church where his marriage to Cassandra Leigh had taken place nearly forty-one years earlier. At the time of his death he was in his seventy-fourth year.

Very soon afterwards Mrs. Lloyd died at Ibthorp. She was the mother of James Austen's second wife, and of Martha Lloyd who had always been such an intimate friend of both Cassandra and Jane. Indeed Cassandra was staying with them at the time of her death, and was assisting Martha in the task of nursing her.

The Austens remained in the house at Green Park Buildings for another three months, afterwards moving to No. 25 Gay Street. Indeed Mrs. Austen exhibited some reluctance to leave a place where she had so many friends.

They went to Clifton in June, 1806—" with what happy feelings of escape," as Jane subsequently wrote, for she had never felt at home in Bath. She and her mother paid visits to Adlestrop and Stoneleigh Abbey which Mr. Thomas Leigh had just inherited. " The house is larger than I could have supposed," Mrs. Austen told her son James in a letter, " so that its new owner has difficulty in finding his way about." But to Jane it gave one of those intimate glimpses of a large and opulent country house which she used to such good purpose in her novels.

In August she was at Godmersham while Cassandra was staying at no great distance with Lady Bridges at Goodnestone. The sisters had arranged to meet in Canterbury, and Jane warned Cassandra that she was very poor.

It is as well to prepare you for the sight of a Sister sunk in poverty that it may not overcome your spirits ! . . .

Mrs. Austen found herself in very reduced circumstances at her husband's death. She had an income of £210 which included the interest on Cassandra's legacy from Tom Fowle, and began the year 1806 with a balance of only £68. Edward agreed to allow her a hundred a year, while James, Henry and Frank each contributed £50, thus bringing her total annual income up to £460.

It was settled that they should live at Southampton, Frank who was now married, sharing the house with them. The move being accomplished, Jane began to take an interest in the garden. She could not do without a syringa, she said, for the sake of Cowper's line :

> Laburnum rich
> In streaming gold, syringa ivory pure . . .

and aspired also to a laburnum. The border under the terrace was cleared in order that currant and gooseberry-bushes could be planted there, and a place was found " very proper for raspberries."

But Jane was never really happy at the house in Castle Square, Southampton. She pined for the freedom of her old country life. Visitors were frequent, and as in our own day she noticed an improvement in the manners and assurance of the children who stayed with them.

She is a nice open-hearted girl—she wrote of one such little visitor— with all the ready civility which one sees in the best children of the present day—so unlike anything I was myself at her age that I am often all astonishment and shame. What is become of all the shyness in the world? Moral as well as natural diseases disappear in the progress of time, and new ones take their place. Shyness and the sweating sickness have given way to Confidence and Paralytic complaints.

Then with a touch of her old humour she tells Cassandra :

Miss Jackson is married to young Mr. Gunthorpe and is to be very unhappy. He swears, drinks, is cross, jealous, selfish and Brutal.

Her brother James came to stay with them, but the visit was apparently the reverse of successful, since he spent his time walking about the house, banging the doors, and ringing the bell for a glass of water.

During a visit to Godmersham in 1808, a note of dejection is observable. " I am sick of myself and my bad pens." The author was then apparently at work.

§

In 1808 a fresh blow fell upon them. Edward's wife gave birth to her eleventh child in the September of that year and died a couple of weeks later. She had some kind of seizure, and her end came very suddenly while Cassandra was staying at Godmersham. Two of her sons, Edward and George, were at Winchester, and went over to Southampton to stay with their grandmother for the purpose of buying mourning. Jane did her best to amuse them, taking them from Itchen Ferry to Northam and walking home. Both boys rowed part of the way and George, whom she found as engaging as Edward, though in quite a different manner, often reminded her of her own brother Henry. Within doors she kept them constantly amused in a tender effort to induce them to forget their grief. They played bilbocatch, spillikins and cards ; made paper ships, and asked each other riddles and conundrums.

At Godmersham poor Fanny, now promoted to her mother's place, was broken-hearted at her loss, while Lizzie, a child of eight, was described as " sunk in grief."

It was shortly after this event that Edward gave the choice of two cottages to his mother, one being in Kent and the other at Chawton, near Alton. The latter was eagerly accepted ; it would signify a return to their old neighbourhood, a prospect that enchanted Jane. All their friends in Southampton declared that they knew Chawton and described it as a remarkably pretty village. The cottage, which although much altered still stands close to the Portsmouth Road, proved a sufficiently roomy one. In addition to the sitting-rooms there were six bedrooms besides attics and " store places."

The Austens spent the winter at Southampton, and Jane attended a ball there and was distressed that two girls should sit out during two dances, despite the fact that one of them was called *Emma*! This suggests that she was contemplating using that name for one of her heroines, most probably in her charming unfinished sketch, *The Watsons*. She herself danced with a gentleman whose very name she did not know, simply because his black eyes pleased her.

Of Lady Sondes's marriage to a General Montrésor, which took place about that time, she expressed her opinion that everyone had a right to marry once for love, and hoped the said lady would now leave off having bad headaches and " being pathetic."

Before leaving Southampton Jane wrote to Crosbie & Co., the publishers, in respect to a novel entitled *Susan* which had been sold to them six years earlier by a gentleman called Seymour, and for which they had paid ten pounds with the promise of early publication. She could only suppose that the manuscript had been lost, but said she could supply another copy if the said publishers would assure her there should be no further delay, otherwise she would feel herself at liberty to offer it elsewhere. The letter was signed M. A. D. and the address given as Mrs. Ashton Dennis at the Post Office, Southampton.

Crosbie replied that there had been no stipulation as to the date of publication, and if it were produced elsewhere they should stop the sale. However, if the money were refunded they would return the manuscript. This was done although two years had still to elapse before *Sense and Sensibility* was published.

It was supposed originally that this referred to *Northanger Abbey*, said to have been sold by Henry to a bookseller in Bath and recovered after Jane had become famous. But it seems to me far more probable that the manuscript in question was *Lady Susan*, since Jane herself always referred to *Northanger Abbey* as *Catherine*. It is possible that both manuscripts were similarly disposed of, one in Bath and one in London.

§

Jane stayed with Henry and Eliza in Sloane Street while correcting the proofs of *Sense and Sensibility*. She was now thirty-five, and some fifteen years had elapsed since her two earlier books were written. Still, she had never lost heart, and with the prospect of returning to a quiet country life at Chawton she could normally have looked forward to many years of mental activity. Her time in London was not, however, wholly spent in revising proofs for the press. She replenished her wardrobe, spending, as she said, all her own money and some of Cassandra's. Seven shillings a yard was paid for a checked muslin and a guinea for a straw hat. Staying in Sloane Street she could still write of " walking into London."

Eliza gave a dinner followed by a musical party, at which Jane's head-dress was composed of a bugle band and a flower. Mrs. Knatch-bull described her as a " pleasant-looking young woman." The dinner began with a pair of very fine " soals " at half-past five. At the party the guests numbered sixty-six, many more than Eliza had expected, which suggested that " gate-crashing " was not wholly unknown in those days. It lasted till midnight, and during the evening a Captain Simpson told Jane that Charles was bringing the *Cleopatra* home, and was probably already in the Channel, but as he was " certainly in liquor " she did not attach much credence to the information.

Despite these gaieties the book was seldom out of her thoughts. " I can no more forget it than a mother her sucking child," she wrote. Already she told Cassandra she had corrected two sheets, but that only took her as far as Willoughby's first appearance. Thus she had scarcely any hope of its being published before June, although Henry was doing his best to hurry the printers. During his absence from London the proofs were sent to Eliza, so deter-mined was Jane to maintain her anonymity.

She expressed a fear too that both plot and characters might be forestalled in a novel called *Self-Control* by Mary Brunton, which was shortly to appear. This is by no means an uncommon experience with authors ; even in our own day novels with almost identical plots are wont to appear simultaneously. Jane tried, without success, to obtain a copy of *Self-Control* in her anxiety to learn whether it resembled her own book. It must, however, have appeared at much the same time, since both were advertised in the *Edinburgh Review* of November, 1812, where *Sense and Sensibility* was placed in the list just after Maria Edgeworth's *Tales of Fashionable Life*, while other books were *Traits of Nature* by Miss Burney, *I'll Consider of It : a Tale*, and what must surely have been a facetious work called *I Says, Says I*, by Thinks I to Myself. I owe this information to the indefatigable researches of Miss Constance Hill, whose delight-ful book *Jane Austen : Her Homes and Her Friends* is invaluable to the student.

By May the proofs were finished and Jane went to stay with her old friend, Catherine Bigg, now Mrs. Hill, whose husband was an uncle of Southey. Sometimes there were allusions in her letters to the Peninsular War, but as a rule she refrained from any reference to the topics of the day in her correspondence.

Sense and Sensibility was published in October, 1811. Little could it be foretold that a new era of novel-writing was thus inaugurated. Simple yet interesting stories without any heroic adventures, the comedy of country houses, the inimitable and life-like portrayal of everyday characters, all these were faithfully and wittily depicted, giving an insight into the ways and manners of the early nineteenth century, that can surely never be surpassed, to a world growing a little weary of the picaresque romance, the Gothic melodrama, the stories whose sole purpose was to inculcate a moral

The title-page bore only the information that it was By a Lady, this leading to some confusion since the *Morning Chronicle* of November 7 described it as an " extraordinary novel by Lady A——." Fanny Austen mentioned in her *Journal* that Cassandra had written to beg her not to tell anyone that her Aunt Jane was the author.

The book was an immediate success and within eighteen months the whole edition was sold out and, after paying all the expenses, Jane found herself the possessor of £140. But perhaps this pecuniary success was the least of her rewards, since the favourable reception accorded to the book assured its author of public interest in any further work that might issue from her pen. She had broken new ground ; her purpose was to amuse rather than to instruct. Forthwith she proceeded to revise *Pride and Prejudice*—so long a favourite with her own relations, some of whom had read it more than once in manuscript—and prepare it for the press.

§

The year 1812 brought various changes to the Austen family. Mrs. Knight died that year, and Edward, who had long been in possession of the estates of Godmersham and Chawton, now took the name of Knight, which was also adopted by all his children. " I must learn to make a better K," wrote the practical Jane in a letter to Martha Lloyd which was subsequently sold for £1,000. In the same letter, dated November 29, 1812, she mentioned that *Pride and Prejudice* had been sold to Egerton for £110. She would have preferred £150, which she certainly had every right to expect, but sensibly remarked that they could not both be pleased, and the sale would save herself and Henry a good deal of trouble. Martha, who had lived with them since her mother's death, was naturally admitted to the secret.

The copy of her " darling child," as she called that ever-famous novel, reached her in January, 1813, when the success of her first book was thoroughly established. It was " tried out " on Miss

Benn, who was then staying at Chawton Manor—the Great House as Jane called it—and who happened to be dining with them. She was merely told that hearing such a book was about to appear they had asked Henry to send them a copy. To the author's satisfaction she really did seem to admire Elizabeth, and Jane wrote thus to her sister :

> I must confess that I think her as delightful a creature as ever appeared in print, and how I shall be able to tolerate those who do not *like* her at least I do not know.

There are glimpses of both Cassandra and Jane in Jane and Elizabeth Bennet, but it would be idle now to seek for other models. And, indeed, in these days there is little left for a critic to say about the famous novels. They have been subjected to the most minute scrutiny ; the number of shrubberies has been accurately counted, the entire absence of lovers' kisses duly observed. Jane rather resembled Sir Walter Scott in one respect—she preferred to leave the room when her characters began to make love. The nearest approach to a passionate scene is that dramatic but suppressed chapter of *Persuasion* which so failed to satisfy the author that she decided to re-write it.

The original price of *Pride and Prejudice* was eighteen shillings, but Jane resolved that one guinea should be asked for her two next, and one pound eight shillings for her " stupidest of all."

Her niece Fanny's praise was especially gratifying to her. Her approval of Darcy and Elizabeth was enough. " She might hate all the others if she would." And could Cassandra, who was then staying with the Bigg-Withers at Manydown, find out anything about the ancient oath of Bell, Book and Candle ? Surely the ladies who read those enormous quarto volumes that were always to be seen on the table of the breakfast parlour at Manydown must know everything in the world ! " I detest a quarto," Jane added. But someone had applied to her for information on the subject of the said oath and she had been unable to supply it.

In April, 1813, when *Pride and Prejudice* had been before the world for a period of about three months, Henry lost his wife, Eliza. She had been ill for some time and the end was not unexpected. Ten years older than Henry and coming to him with an unusually full experience of the tragedy of life, their marriage seems, nevertheless, to have been a perfectly happy one. The £10,000 given by Warren Hastings to her parents, and settled ultimately upon herself, had enabled the couple to live comfortably as well as to entertain in London. Jane had frequently mingled with the cosmopolitan element to be found at their house, although she never introduced a foreign character into any of her novels.

Henry went down to Chawton after his bereavement, and in the following month took Jane back with him to London. He had moved to rooms in Henrietta Street, Covent Garden, above his bank, and Jane found them in considerable confusion when she arrived. Her brother took her to the exhibition in Spring Gardens, where to her great delight she discovered a portrait of " Mrs. Bingley," although her hope of seeing one of Mrs. Darcy remained ungratified. It is by no means an unusual experience for authors to see in some portrait, or even in some casual passer-by, the similitude of their own imagined creations.

Mrs. Bingley's is exactly herself—size, shaped face, features and sweetness ; there never was a greater likeness. She is dressed in a white gown, with green ornaments, which convinces me of what I had always supposed, that green was a favourite colour with her.

And there was a Miss Burdett who wished to make her acquaintance, evidently a friend of Henry's, who as a handsome widower had plenty of admirers.

I am rather frightened by hearing that she wishes to be introduced to *me*. If I *am* a wild beast I cannot help it. It is not my own fault.

One can only wonder if Miss Burdett had any suspicion of the truth, since Henry was ultimately the first to give away his sister's secret.

That summer proved a happy one for Jane, since Edward and his family spent most of it at Chawton, and thus she was able to see a great deal of her favourite niece, Fanny. Henry too had recovered his spirits, thus confirming her opinion that his was not " a mind for affliction." He was, she said, " too busy, too active and too sanguine."

She had now, as she expressed it, written herself into £250, which only made her long for more. She had something in hand, the something being *Mansfield Park*, by many preferred to all her novels, since it contains the inimitable character of Mrs. Norris, whose parsimony may have owed something to Mrs. James Austen, who, despite an income of £1,100 a year, was continually crying poverty.

The dramatic contrast between the leisurely comfort of Mansfield Park and Fanny Price's rather squalid home at Portsmouth, to which she was banished after her refusal to marry such an eligible *parti* as Henry Crawford, must always remain one of Jane's masterpieces. She asked her brother Frank's permission to use the name of his ship, the *Elephant*, in it, he being then in command of her in the Baltic, assisting in the safe transport of Bernadotte's troops on their way to Russia, which at that time was being attacked by the common enemy, Napoleon.

When Edward returned to Godmersham from Chawton, Jane accompanied him, and this proved to be her last visit, although four years were yet to elapse before her death.

On the way thither they stayed three days in London, spending one evening at the Lyceum Theatre and another at Covent Garden.

It was about this time that Henry, while on a visit to Scotland, heard *Pride and Prejudice* being so enthusiastically praised by Lady Robert Kerr, that in the " warmth of his brotherly vanity and love " he revealed the identity of the author.

I am trying to harden myself—she wrote. After all what a trifle it is in all its bearings to the really important points of one's existence, even in this world. . . .

Indeed, the secret was now so well known that she believed, when *Mansfield Park* was published, she should not even attempt to tell lies about it, but would try to make all the money instead of all the mystery she could out of it. " People shall pay for their know-ledge if I can make them," for she by no means despised what her nephew, Edward Knight, was wont to term " Pewter."

She had never had much money to spend and now she could enjoy the pleasures of generosity. From London she sent some poplin to Cassandra. " Remember that it is a present. Do not refuse me. I am very rich," she wrote.

She enjoyed that last visit to Godmersham, during which Charles arrived with his wife and children. Mrs. Charles Austen was a Miss Palmer, daughter of the Governor of Bermuda, and after her death in 1814, Charles married another sister. If the children, who were then quite small, were too " Palmery " in feature to please their aunt, she nevertheless quickly made friends with them.

As usual there was a good deal of coming and going at the Park, and Jane watched the visitors with unflagging interest. A Mrs. Chapman called with five daughters. " I never saw so plain a family. Five sisters so very plain ! " Still there were compensations since one of them was called Laura and had a double flounce to her dress. Then there was a Mr. Wigram, about five or six and twenty, not ill-looking but not agreeable. " They say his name is Henry. A proof how unequally the gifts of fortune are bestowed."

She did not, however, lose interest in all the domesticities of Chawton and begged to be told when they began the new tea and the white wine. " My present elegancies have not yet made me indifferent to such matters. I am still a cat when I see a mouse."

As she was no longer young she discovered that many privileges were attached to the position of chaperon. " I am put on the sofa near the fire, and can drink as much wine as I like." And Lady Bridges had found her handsomer than she expected, " so you see I am not so very bad as you might think for."

It was about this time that James Austen's elder daughter, Anna, became engaged to Mrs. Lefroy's son, Ben. Jane was not at all enthusiastic about it, considering their tastes far too dissimilar. " She so fond of company and he hating it. This with some queerness of Temper on his side and much unsteadiness on hers, is untoward."

Nor did the engagement prosper at first since Ben refused a curacy because he was unwilling to " take orders " so early, and declared that if Mr. James Austen insisted upon his doing so before his marriage, he would rather give Anna up than become a clergyman against his will. Jane suggested to her sister that it would be an excellent moment for him to go to Chawton " now that we, the formidables, are absent."

They did, however, marry, and Jane visited them at Hendon in the following year. It was to this niece who had been trying her hand at novel-writing that she gave the now famous advice, revealing too something of her own method.

You are now collecting your people delightfully, getting them exactly into such a spot as is the delight of my life ;—3 or 4 families in a Country Village is the very thing to work on, and I hope you will write a great deal more, and make full use of them while they are so favourably arranged.

The name of Rachel was, however, as much as she could bear, though that of Newton Priors was a Nonpareil—" Milton would have given his eyes to have thought of it."

And then she added that Walter Scott had really no business to write novels, especially good ones. " It is not fair—He has Fame and Profit enough as a Poet and should not be taking the bread out of other people's mouths. I do not like him and do not mean to like Waverley if I can help it—but fear I must. . . ."

She spent part of the spring of 1814 with Henry in London, and found him reading the proofs of *Mansfield Park* with great enjoyment. His praise, at once so enthusiastic and authentic, was always dear to Jane. While there she read the *Corsair* which had just taken London by storm. She met a young Mr. Wyndham Knatchbull, son of Sir Edward Knatchbull, who, she thought, would do very well for Fanny. But it was his elder brother, after he became a widower, whom Fanny eventually married in 1820.

By November the first edition of *Mansfield Park* which had been published in May was sold out, and Jane was engaged in writing *Emma*.

§

In the autumn of 1815 Jane was once more staying with Henry who was now living in Hans Place. He was negotiating with Mr. John Murray for the publication of *Emma*, but before anything could be settled he fell ill with high fever. He was bled twice according to the custom of those days and at first seemed to improve.

Murray offered £450 for *Emma*, but wished to have the copyright of *Mansfield Park* and *Sense and Sensibility* included. Henry dictated a letter in reply, Jane acting as his amanuensis, telling him candidly that the sum he offered did not equal the amount his sister had received for " one very moderate edition of *Mansfield Park*."

Henry became much worse, and as his life seemed in danger, Jane summoned her brothers and sister. She nursed him with such assiduous care that it had a detrimental effect upon her own health which from that time appeared to decline.

During his illness Henry was attended by a Mr. Haden, father of Sir Seymour Haden, the famous etcher, and one of the Prince Regent's physicians was also summoned in consultation. It was from this source Jane learned that her novels were so much admired by the Prince that he kept a set in each of his various residences. His librarian, the Rev. Stanier Clarke, called upon her and invited her to go and see the library at Carlton House, intimating too that if she had any other work in preparation she would be permitted to dedicate it to His Royal Highness. This Mr. Clarke was obviously a very foolish man and something of a sycophant, and had not *Pride and Prejudice* been long since published it might easily have been imagined that he had served as a model for Mr. Collins.

This permission, however, stood Jane in good stead when it came to dealing with Murray's rather dilatory printers. She informed her publisher that *Emma* was to be dedicated by Royal permission to the Regent, and this letter brought three sheets and an apology from Roworth, while Mr. Murray himself was " so polite as to be quite overcoming." He lent them books, and by December the printing was so far advanced that Jane was able to write to Mr. Clarke telling him that Murray had promised to send an advance copy to the Prince under cover to him.

The Dedication ran as follows :

To His Royal Highness, the Prince Regent, this Work is By His

Royal Highness's Permission Most respectfully Dedicated by His Royal Highness's Dutiful and Obedient Humble Servant the Author.

In the following March, when Henry had recovered and she herself was back at Chawton, she received the thanks of the Prince through Mr. Clarke who had, as is well known, advised Jane to write a romance about the House of Cobourg, notwithstanding the fact that she had previously written thus to him :

I think I may boast myself to be with all possible vanity the most unlearned and uninformed female who ever dared to be an authoress.

But then did not George Sand much later lament her own ignorance, declaring it was her great sorrow as a novelist ?

§

It was well that Jane was earning money, since financial disaster fell upon her family at that time. A bank at Alton failed and Henry's firm was involved in its ruin. He was declared bankrupt and several of his relations, including Edward Knight and Mr. Leigh-Perrot, lost considerable sums in consequence. Thirteen pounds of the earnings of *Mansfield Park* also disappeared in the general smash.

Jane was thoroughly overdone by her assiduous care of Henry during his long illness, and this fresh disaster had a highly detrimental effect upon her health and nerves. She suffered even more from it than Henry himself, whose sanguine disposition did not permit him to brood over his misfortunes. He immediately decided to become a clergyman, thus fulfilling his father's wish of more than twenty years before, and from which it is suggested he had been deterred by Eliza de Feuillide, who could not envisage herself as the wife of a country parson. At fifty he married a Miss Jackson and after his retirement lived for a time in France—a country he had first visited with Eliza—dying at Tunbridge Wells in 1850.

All through that year—1816—Jane's health was failing. She had much to trouble her for, in addition to Henry's bankruptcy, Edward Knight was involved in an expensive lawsuit to establish his claim to the Godmersham and Chawton estates. In the Spring she accompanied Cassandra, and Mrs. James Austen to Cheltenham, and it was while her sister was again there later in the year that the first note of complaint was sounded in her letters. She was then at work on *Persuasion* and it seemed as if the task combined with that of housekeeping was proving too much for her enfeebled health.

Thank you, my Back has given me scarcely any pain for many days. I have an idea that agitation does it as much harm as fatigue, and that

I

I was ill at the time of your going from the very circumstance of your going. I am nursing myself up into as beautiful a state as I can.

How good Mrs. West could have written such books and collected so many hard words with all her family cares is still more a matter of astonishment ; Composition seems to me Impossible with a head full of Joints of Mutton and doses of Rhubarb.

Still her letters to her nephews and nieces never lacked gaiety and animation, as when she wrote to Edward Austen to give him joy at having left Winchester. His Uncle Henry, she told him, wrote very superior sermons and they must try and get hold of some of them to put into their books. It was fortunate that she had not been to Steventon, and thus could not be accused of having purloined the two chapters of Edward's novel which were missing. " Two strong twigs and a half towards a nest of my own would have been something," although she did not think that a theft of the kind would have been of great use to her.

What should I do with your strong, spirited, manly Sketches full of variety and Glow ? How could I possibly join them on to the little bit (two inches wide) of Ivory on which I work with so fine a Brush as produces little effect after much labour ?

In January, 1817, she was still feeling ill, though convinced that bile was the real cause of her malady. *Persuasion* was now ready for publication, and she told Fanny Knight in a letter that she might like the heroine " as she is almost too good for me." She had then been ill for several weeks, suffering from fever and insomnia, and wrote with something of melancholy :

I must not depend upon ever being very blooming again. Sickness is a dangerous Indulgence at my time of life.

She needed, she said, air and exercise. In March she went for her first ride, Cassandra and her nephew Edward walking beside her. She spoke too of her sister's excellence as a nurse, " so assiduous and unwearied."

But at the end of the month the Austen family sustained a fresh shock which especially affected Jane in her weak state of health. Mrs. Austen's brother, Mr. Leigh-Perrot, from whom they had expectations, died, and when his will was read, it was found that he had bequeathed all his fortune to his wife for her life. She was to enjoy also the life-interest in the large sum he left to James Austen. At her death each surviving child of Mrs. George Austen was to receive £1,000 but until that event none of them would be one whit the richer.

Jane told Charles in a letter that she was ashamed to think these dispositions should be such a disappointment to her that she had actually suffered a relapse in health, and had therefore felt obliged to entreat Cassandra to return home directly after the funeral.

> I live upstairs for the present and am coddled. I am the only one of the legatees who has been so silly, but a weak body must excuse weak nerves.

She must have felt, too, that the exertion of writing was becoming too strenuous a task for her, and that soon she would be unable to earn any more " Pewter " to assist the little *ménage* at Chawton.

Caroline Austen, who saw her shortly afterwards, found her incredibly changed. She was very pale, her voice weak, and she could only talk to her for a few minutes. It was to prove the young girl's last recollection of " Aunt Jane."

That same month she took up her pen once more and began her unfinished novel *Sanditon*. But the last date was March 17, and even then some of the later pages were written in pencil and her fine, delicate script was no longer so beautifully formed.

April passed, but even the spring days failed to revive her. In May it was settled to move her to Winchester, where she would have the benefit of Mr. Lyford's advice. She left Chawton for the last time on the 24th of that month, driving in James Austen's carriage with Cassandra.

> Now that's the sort of thing which Mrs. J. Austen does in the kindest manner ! But still she is in the main *not* a liberal-minded woman, and as to this reversionary Property's amending that part of her Character, expect it not—too late, too late in the day ;—and besides the Property may not be theirs these ten years. . . .

Henry Austen and William Knight rode beside the carriage, despite the heavy rain which was falling. Mrs. Heathcote had taken rooms for them in College Street, Winchester, and visited them every day. Her sister Alethea Bigg was, however, not with her, having been " frisked off like half England into Switzerland."

Jane spent her time for the most part on the sofa. Sometimes she went out in a sedan chair and hoped to be promoted to a wheel-chair when the finer weather came.

Then, in a letter to an unidentified correspondent, she wrote that beautiful tribute to Cassandra :

> On this subject I will only say further that my dearest sister, my tender, watchful indefatigable nurse, has not been made ill by her exertions. As to what I owe her and to the anxious affection of all my beloved family on this occasion I can only cry over it and pray to God to bless them more and more.

She rallied somewhat, and encouraging reports were sent to her mother at Chawton. Jane was able to sit up a little, and as Cassandra did not like the nurse, she invited Mrs. James Austen to come and help her. She arrived early in June and remained there until the end. From that time there seems to have been absolutely no hope and Mr. Lyford warned them that her case was desperate. The exact nature of her malady has never been discovered, although it is usually described as consumption. This could hardly have been the case since James Austen in writing to his son, then at Oxford, told him that his aunt was not suffering any severe pain " which is rather an extraordinary circumstance in her complaint," a remark that seems to suggest a far more grave disease. Still, he found her composed and cheerful, though perfectly aware of her condition.

She lay there surrounded by loving friends. Cassandra, Mrs. James Austen and Mrs. Heathcote, rarely left her. It is said that she " retained her faculties, her memory, her fancy, her temper and her affections—warm, clear and unimpaired to the last."

The end came on July 18, 1817, when Jane was little more than forty-one years old. For the last forty-eight hours she had lain there more asleep than awake. About half an hour before she finally became unconscious she knew herself to be dying and even said that she wanted nothing but death. " God grant me patience, pray for me, oh, pray for me," were among her last words.

She was buried on the following Thursday in Winchester Cathedral, where a black marble slab, object of so many literary pilgrimages, marks her grave. Cassandra watched the little cortège from her window, bearing her grief with an heroic resignation. She survived her sister twenty-eight years, of which ten were devoted to the care of her aged mother. She lies buried with her mother at Chawton.

§

There were many to mourn the premature death of Jane Austen outside her own family by whom she was always especially beloved.

Sir Walter Scott, after reading *Pride and Prejudice* for the third time, wrote with singular frankness :

The big bow-wow strain I can do myself like anyone now going, but the exquisite touch which renders ordinary commonplace things interesting from the truth of the description and the sentiment, is denied to me. What a pity such a gifted creature died so young ! . . .

And Tennyson visiting Lyme—the scene of Monmouth's rebellion —many years later, is said to have exclaimed : " Don't talk to me of the Duke of Monmouth. Show me the spot where Louisa Musgrove fell ! "

Lord Morpeth—afterwards the seventh Earl of Carlisle—wrote some delightful lines in the *Keepsake* of 1825, of which I may quote the following :

> Oh ! Mrs. Bennet ! Mrs. Norris too !
> While memory survives we'll dream of you.
> And Mr. Woodhouse whose abstemious lip
> Must thin, but not too thin, his gruel sip !

Year by year the number and fervour of her admirers increase. Her bit of ivory two inches wide has a value for us that can hardly now be estimated, but can only be compared to the delicate miniature portraits of her own day. It is true that she wrote only of the leisured classes, and that she rarely described the houses where her inimitable comedies were enacted. Only in *Persuasion* did the beauties of Lyme evoke any delineation of scenery from her and there it is simply confined to a few exquisite phrases. But her characters are alive ; her men fully as much so as her women, indeed, with so many brothers and nephews how could it be otherwise ? Wit she possessed as few women writers have ever possessed it, yet she wrote with a kindly forbearance of the very foibles she portrayed. Very rarely does she stoop to condemn. To amuse was her aim, and she will surely continue to amuse succeeding generations of readers as long as English literature lasts.

No one reading her delightful and sparkling letters to Cassandra and others could attach any importance to the unflattering description of Jane supplied to Miss Mitford and quoted in the life of that lady.

A friend of mine who visits her now says that she has stiffened into the most perpendicular, precise, taciturn piece of " single blessedness " that ever existed, and that till *Pride and Prejudice* showed what a precious gem was hidden in that unbending case, she was no more regarded in society than a poker or a fire-screen, or any thin upright piece of wood or iron that fills the corner in peace and quietness. The case is very different now ; she is still a poker, but a poker of whom everyone is afraid. . . .

The hint of malice is fully accounted for, since it has been discovered that the writer of this portrait was a friend of the Mr. Baverstock who laid claim to the estates of Edward Knight, thereby involving him in an expensive lawsuit.

Miss Mitford, although professing to discover a lack of taste in *Pride and Prejudice*, considered *Emma* " the best of all her charming works." Later she so far relented as to refer to her as " our dear Miss Austen," but that was after her death.

The first memoir of Jane Austen was the brief one supplied by her brother Henry for the original edition of *Persuasion* and *Northanger*

Abbey published in four volumes by John Murray in 1818. Then ensued a long silence of over half a century until James Edward Austen-Leigh was induced as an old man to write a memoir of his famous aunt. It was necessarily imperfect, for he had few authorities to consult, but in the following year—1871—he published a second and enlarged edition which contained the suppressed chapter of *Persuasion* and the promising but unfinished stories *Lady Susan* (which may have been the *Susan* sold to Crosbie and recovered at Southampton), and *The Watsons*. That Jane had little intention of returning to either of them, is evinced by her attempt to begin an entirely new novel, *Sanditon*, a few months before her death. I should like, however, to put forward the theory that *Lady Susan* was actually completed, since the entire plot of the story was revealed by Jane to her immediate relations, and that dissatisfied with it, as with the famous chapter in *Persuasion*, she destroyed the final portions of it. She may have hesitated to give to the world the picture of such a depraved and brutal person as Lady Susan, whose hatred of her own daughter was at such variance with anything the author had hitherto written. She had depicted bad daughters, but never a bad mother, and from *Mansfield Park* we know that she actually shrank from dwelling upon immorality or vice.

Few authors have been so fortunate in their families and environment as Jane Austen. She was one of a large family, all imbued with a strong clan feeling, devoted to each other and especially to her. Her sister was her most intimate and cherished friend. Fanny Knight, involved in ceaseless love-affairs in which her aunt's counsel was always sought, was to Jane like another sister. Her sympathy with the rising generation was unbounded ; she had a warm place in her heart for her innumerable nephews and nieces. To them too "Aunt Jane" was the dearest friend and confidante. They realized her genius and were proud of her success and fame, which came so late yet came in such abundant measure, placing her for ever among the Immortals of English literature.

George Eliot

GEORGE ELIOT

§

MARY ANNA (or Marian) EVANS, was born at Arbury Farm on November 22, 1819, her father being Robert Evans, formerly of Ellaston, Staffordshire, and her mother, who was his second wife, Christiana Pearson.

The family was of Welsh origin from Flint. Robert Evans, who was born in 1771, was the son of George, a builder and carpenter. As a boy he learned something of his father's trade, but forsook this for farming at Kirk Hallam in Derbyshire, where he acted also as agent to Mr. Francis Newdigate. When the latter inherited the Arbury estate in Warwickshire in 1806, Robert Evans accompanied him thither and the rest of his working life was passed in that neighbourhood. His first wife, Harriet Poynton, whom he married in 1801, died in 1809 leaving a son and daughter. He married secondly in 1813, and of this marriage were born Christiana (afterwards Mrs. Clarke), Isaac, born in 1816, and Mary Ann, the youngest of his five children. Of her stepbrother she knew little, for shortly after her birth he went to live at Kirk Hallam accompanied by his sister Frances, afterwards Mrs. Houghton, who was then only fourteen or fifteen years old.

A few months after Marian's birth the family removed to Griff, a charming red-brick house surrounded by beautiful trees on the Arbury estate, where the child's babyhood and girlhood were for the most part passed, and where she acquired that deep insight into country lore and ways which was to prove so invaluable to her when she wrote her two masterpieces, *Adam Bede* and the *Mill on the Floss*.

Her father was forty-six when she was born, thus she could never remember him as other than elderly and grey-haired. But she must always have been aware of his forcible and dominating personality. He was a shrewd successful man, with a knowledge of many things which were of use to him in his profession. He was well versed in forestry, mining and building, and was capable of administering large estates. In addition to acting as agent for the Newdigates, he was also employed in this capacity by Lord Aylesford, Lord Lifford and Mr. Bromley-Davenport. He was powerfully built, and of great physical strength. When it came to a combat of wills with his adolescent daughter he invariably remained victor.

When she was five Marian, possibly more for companionship than for any other reason, joined her eleven-years-old sister Chrissy at Miss Lathom's school at Attleborough. The children returned to Griff on Sundays to spend that day with their parents. Four years later they were sent to a more ambitious establishment at Nuneaton where it is said Marian made no friends among the girls, but became devotedly attached to one of the teachers, Miss Lewis, a strong Evangelical who inculcated this small disciple with her religious views, an influence that was never quite to leave her. Her last school to which she went when she was thirteen, for the first time unaccompanied by her sister who was now grown up, was at Coventry. It will be seen that Robert Evans, like Mr. Tulliver, believed in bestowing upon his children an excellent education. And during those years Marian gave evidence of talent in two directions. She was passionately fond both of writing and of music. At Coventry she was envied by the other girls on account of her weekly baskets of eggs, vegetables and fruit from Arbury.

At the age of sixteen she left school, and her mother, who was then mortally ill, died the following year. Shortly afterwards, in 1837, Chrissy married Edward Clarke, a surgeon of Meriden, Warwickshire. Although George Eliot affirmed that she never, after the *Scenes of Clerical Life*, drew a deliberate portrait, she confessed that when she described Celia in *Middlemarch* she had her sister continually in mind.

This marriage made a great change in Marian's life. She was now the only daughter at home and all the housekeeping duties devolved upon her. It was her duty to look after her father and that beloved brother Isaac, whom Tom Tulliver is said to have resembled. But these tasks did not interfere with her intellectual progress. She read voraciously and studied German, Italian and music under various masters. Although she never spoke any foreign language with ease she could read at least four, adding Spanish at a later date.

Miss Lewis was at that time her chief correspondent, and her letters to her reflect that lady's deep Evangelical piety. There is not much to tell of those girlhood's years. Like Emily Brontë she could cook, and made red currant jelly in the kitchen at Griff. Her first visit to London was made with Isaac when she was nineteen. Otherwise her life seems to have been completely uneventful until she was twenty-two when a great change supervened that was destined to colour her whole future existence.

§

Robert Evans was now sixty-eight years of age and felt that the time had come for him to retire. He therefore moved to a house in Foleshill Road on the outskirts of Coventry, while Isaac, who had recently married, continued to live at Griff and took over the management of affairs from his father.

Marian does not seem to have regretted Arbury. She soon made friends with some neighbours, the Brays, who encouraged her love of study. She had plenty to do, for her father, who was rapidly ageing, needed her care. She was too busy that summer to accept an invitation to stay with Miss Lewis at Margate, " though I think indeed that both my heart and limbs would leap to behold the great and wide sea, that old ocean on which man can leave no trace." The country-bred girl had never seen the sea, but she was perhaps unconsciously paraphrasing Byron's : *Time writes no wrinkle on thine azure brow.* In any case she was quite safe—the pious Miss Lewis could assuredly never have read the poems of such a monster of iniquity.

The Brays were free-thinkers, and undid the careful work of that lady, confirming in Marian a tendency to intellectual unbelief. Mr. Bray, a wealthy ribbon-manufacturer, employed his leisure hours in writing books. *The Education of the Feelings* was the first of these, and in 1841 he produced a second and more daring one, *The Philosophy of Necessity.* He had a delightful house called Rosehill on the outskirts of Coventry where Miss Evans was a welcome visitor and speedily made friends with other members of the family.

Mrs. Bray had a sister, Sara Hennell, and a brother Charles. Marian Evans awoke to the fact that there were other men in the world besides her father and the beloved Isaac. Men who were less interested in timber and crops than in books and philosophic thought. Cara Bray and Sara Hennell became her lifelong friends, although naturally the deep intimacy diminished later on when she followed new and strange paths which were ultimately to change her into George Eliot. But with Charles Hennell she was on a different footing.

These people were of a slightly superior class to her own ; they were older too and more cultivated. It is quite possible that Charles Hennell regarded Marian Evans as not quite good enough despite her learning, her intellectual ability, and it must be added her intimacy with his sisters. He became engaged very shortly afterwards to a Miss Brabant, the daughter of a doctor.

Marian was passing through that period of transition and revolt inevitable in the lives of young keen clever women who suddenly find themselves at odds with their own surroundings. To her father she had always been his little Polly, and perhaps he had not envisaged the fact that Polly was engaged in making a life of her own. Here in Coventry. . . . One day she announced that she could no longer accompany him to church. She had lost her faith ; it would be dishonest to go. Robert Evans was a man of notoriously powerful physique ; he had had his way with men, women, horses and cattle too long to sit down under such a speech as that. Little Polly was twenty-two years of age, but she was his daughter ; she must be made to mind. Otherwise she could no longer remain where she was. He would go and live with his other daughter, Chrissy Clarke, who could be relied upon never to display such abnormal tendencies.

Marian decided to live in lodgings at Leamington and earn her living by giving lessons. But first she went on a visit to her brother at Griff. Isaac, who had " High Church " leanings, less common then than now, inculcated by a tutor at Birmingham, could never have been much in sympathy with his sister's Evangelical piety, and probably did not regard this present phase as permanent. He was very kind to her and so was his wife. Perhaps he indicated the risk of setting up for herself, the lack of shelter if she left her father's roof. And then it would mean leaving Coventry and these dear friends who made her so welcome. . . . Perhaps the thought of the Brays was the most powerful influence of all. Marian returned home to resume her post as Robert Evans's housekeeper, and to attend the proper number of church services in his company. They must have looked a curious couple, the ageing but still powerful man, rugged, weather-beaten, absolutely true to type, and this pale sallow girl with the dull skin, expressive grey eyes, and strongly moulded features, and a hint of suppressed passion about the mouth and " broad commanding brows."

When Miss Brabant married she renounced the project of translating Strauss's *Life of Jesus*, which was considered the last word in German destructive criticism. She handed the monumental task over to Miss Evans and it helped to liberate her from what she termed the " wretched giant's bed of dogma." Christianity was never to mean anything to her again, although she could confess to a certain emotion in Catholic churches, possibly inspired by the music. However, out of respect for her father, who had undergone no such process of liberation, she continued to accompany him to church on Sundays.

The work occupied her for two years, and when it was completed a difficulty arose about obtaining the money for its publication, Charles Hennell and a friend between them raised the necessary sum of £300.

Her life was no easy one, for combined with the intellectual effort involved, her father's health was failing and she acted both as companion and nurse. " Poor thing," Mrs. Bray wrote to her sister, " I do pity her sometimes with her pale sickly face and dreadful headaches and anxiety about her father."

The book appeared in 1846, and two years later she accompanied her then dying father to Hastings. Although he could still walk and his appetite was good he refused to amuse himself. She must always be at hand to read to him and write his letters. She found relief, however, in writing copious letters to the Brays.

She read *Jane Eyre*, then recently published, and took the opportunity of inveighing against the Christian view of marriage.

All self-sacrifice is good, but one would like it to be in a somewhat nobler cause than that of a diabolical law which chains a man body and soul to a putrefying carcase. . . . However, the book is intensely interesting only I wish the characters would talk a little less like the heroes and heroines of police courts.

She was assisted in the task of nursing her father by Miss Bury (afterwards Mrs. Congreve) daughter of the doctor who attended him. Robert Evans died on May 31, 1849, at the age of seventy-six, and Marian was left to face life alone with a small income of £120 a year.

§

The Brays came to the rescue and invited her to accompany them on a trip to the Continent. They visited Paris, Lyons, Avignon, Marseilles, Genoa, Milan and Como, finally arriving at Geneva, where Marian resolved for the present to pitch her tent. She lodged in a pension at Plongeon and mingled with its little coterie of cosmopolitan guests. Among them were a Marquis de St. Germain and his family, who attended the Catholic church " all nicely drest " on Sundays, and a Mme Cornelius, wife of a wealthy Frankfort banker, " who had more reading than the marquise, being German and Protestant." But the Frenchwoman took a kindly interest in this solemn, solitary, ill-dressed, provincial woman, and abolishing the ringlets taught her how to do her hair more fashionably. Two things, she said, now stuck out on each side of her head like those on the head of the Sphinx, making her look if possible uglier than before. The Marquise took her to task also about her soul, telling her she was in " *une mauvaise voie sous le rapport de la religion.*"

Plongeon proved too expensive and moreover it was cold in winter. Marian found rooms in Geneva with a M. D'Albert-Durade and his wife. They were artists and shared her passion for music. There she paid 150 francs a month to include light, so that she was living well within her income. The town life proved to her taste and she attended Professor de la Rive's lectures on Experimental Physics.

At times she was desperately homesick. The cold foggy climate tried her strength. " I hate myself for caring about carpets, easy-chairs and coal fires," she wrote to the Brays. She missed the substantial comfort of Griff and Coventry. Otherwise she was happy. The Durades were kind, introducing her to their circle of friends. M. Durade painted a pleasing portrait of her, and she called his wife " Maman."

When she returned to England in March, 1850, M. Durade accompanied her. They crossed the Jura in sledges, joining the railway at Tonnerre. She stayed first at Griff and it affected her spirits. " Oh, the dismal weather and the dismal country and the dismal people ! " she wailed. Isaac must have been thankful to see his discontented sister depart for Rosehill, where presently M. Durade also came to stay.

For more than a year she made her home with the Brays and it was there she met Mr. Chapman, editor of the *Westminster Review*. In September of the following year, though she had no previous experience, he invited her to become his assistant editor. Forthwith she went to London and boarded with the Chapmans in the Strand.

Still wider horizons. . . . She had shaken the dust of Arbury and Coventry from her feet. Even the Brays were less wholly satisfying since that sojourn at Geneva.

One of her fellow-boarders was Frederica Bremen, the Swedish novelist, a woman eighteen years older than herself, whose books were translated into English by Mary Howitt. She had been in America, where she had known Emerson, Longfellow and Lowell, thus she had far more actual experience of life than Miss Evans. " She is equally unprepossessing to eye and ear," Marian wrote of her, although later she " repented of her repugnance." But she was always inclined to censorious criticism of her fellow-creatures.

She was now thirty-two years of age and had never been sought in marriage. Nevertheless, she aroused jealousy in the heart of Mrs. Chapman, who was not on the best of terms with her

GEORGE ELIOT

(From a drawing by M. D'Albert-Durade.)

Courtesy of the Directors, Bibliothèque publique et universitaire, Geneva. (*Copyright.*)

husband. But she did not at once go away. Many interesting people came to the house and among them was Herbert Spencer, her junior by one year. He had been an engineer on the Birmingham and Gloucester Railway, but he was now editing the *Economist*. Already he had published his *Social Statics*. Marian Evans wrote of the " deliciously calm new friendship " he gave her. " We see each other every day and have a delightful camaraderie in everything. But for him my life would be desolate enough."

Charles Hennell was dead. Mr. Chapman was a married man. Here was a man much of her own age, free, intellectual, gifted.

And he was genuinely attracted by her, saying that she had a remarkable intellect and was moreover gifted with a feminine grace and a charm of manner that kept him close to her side through entire evenings.

They went together to concerts and to the opera and theatre. Spencer told her she was a born novelist, but she did not believe him. People began to gossip and he took alarm. Once he stayed at Rosehill at the same time as herself by her special request. But nothing came of it. He took his father—a Quaker—to see her in London, and the elder Spencer was delighted with her. Still, no mention of marriage. He denied in his old age that he had ever been in love with her or thought of marrying her. And it was he who, oddly enough, introduced her to George Henry Lewes.

She was unhappy enough when she realized that Spencer, despite the deliciously calm friendship and delightful camaraderie, had no serious intentions. She left London for a time and paid visits. She stayed with the Combes at Edinburgh, her first experience of a large and wealthy house where she found herself as she expressed it in clover. On her way south she stayed at Ambleside with Harriet Martineau, with whom she had had a slight tiff on the subject of George Henry Lewes. The great Harriet had jeered at him for introducing psychology as a science in his articles on Comte. Marian retorted that Comte held psychology to be a necessary link in the chain of science. " Lewes had only suggested a change in its relations."

It was barely two years since Charlotte Brontë, then at the height of her fame, had been a guest at Ambleside. She was too delicate and nervous to endure the destructive, sledge-hammer criticism meted out to her by Harriet, and not long afterwards the unlikely friendship came to an abrupt end.

On her way south Marian Evans, restless and a trifle peevish, stayed at Rosehill. On the day of her return to 142, Strand, Herbert Spencer came and spent the evening with her. . . .

§

George Henry Lewes was a contributor to the *Westminster* so that Marian was brought a good deal into contact with him after their first introduction. He was about two years older than herself and had been something of a rolling stone. First he had tried the stage but his small figure and weak voice destroyed any hope of success in that direction. Then he " walked " the hospitals, but again could not endure the sight of so much suffering. He had now settled down to a literary life for which his exuberant versatility admirably qualified him.

Of his actual parentage nothing is known, but his grandfather was quite a well-known actor of the eighteenth century. This stage tradition clung to Lewes all his life. He never ceased to be an actor, perhaps even something of a clown.

Already he had produced a couple of novels, *Ranthorpe*, and *Rose, Blanche and Violet*, now practically forgotten and only occasionally exhumed by the student in the hope of learning a little more of this small queer enigmatic figure who possessed such an enduring influence over George Eliot.

He was like a dog, perhaps a spaniel, for with his long hair, whiskers and moustache, he had an extremely hirsute appearance. Small, agile, eager, his plain little face was deeply pitted with small-pox. He was said to be the ugliest man in London, and the pencil drawing which is so often reproduced as his portrait is really that of Leigh Hunt, whose hand rests upon a book bearing the author's name, an infallible guide to identity.

Marian's first impressions were unfavourable. He reminded her of a miniature Mirabeau whose face had also been pitted with small-pox and who had a strong growth of heavy hair. But gradually as she got to know him better she again " repented of her repugnance."

She was reading *Villette*, as indeed everyone was that year. There was to her something preternatural in its power. " Villette, Villette, have you read it ? " she wrote to the Brays. But Lewes was less enthusiastic. He told her that he had met the author, the famous Currer Bell, daughter of a Yorkshire parson, and described her as a " little plain, provincial sickly-looking old maid." Nor could he have discerned that preternatural power in her book since his famous advice to her to read Jane Austen is known to all. In fact, he didn't wish her to work on her own lines, but advised her to attempt something that would have been quite impossible to her. Probably not a single author has ever quite escaped this unhappy fate.

And then Charlotte had taken him furiously to task for his criticism of *Shirley* in the *Edinburgh Review*, the first two pages of which were headed " Mental Equality of the Sexes " and " Female Literature." He had aroused her indignation by criticizing her as a woman rather than as a writer.

After I had said earnestly—she wrote—that I wished critics would judge me as an author not as a woman, you so roughly—I even thought so cruelly—handled the question of sex. I daresay you meant no harm and perhaps you will not now be able to understand why I was so grieved at what you will probably deem such a trifle, but grieved I was and indignant too. There was a passage or two which you did quite wrong to write. However I will not bear malice against you for it ; I know what your nature is ; it is not a bad or unkind one though you would often jar terribly on some feelings with whose recoil and quiver you could not possibly sympathize.

Not a pleasant letter for a man to receive, but Lewes—who admitted that its tone was cavalier—thoroughly deserved every word of it for his ungentlemanly personal attack not upon the author but upon the woman. However, in our own day the attitude is by no means unknown, and a famous authoress has confessed that when she publishes her novels under a man's name, she receives far better reviews than for those that appear under her own.

Marian Evans offered a less sensitive and probably less temperamental subject for the slightly burlesque humour of George Lewes. There is no evidence that he could jar terribly upon her. On the contrary she saw in him a " man of heart wearing a mask of flippancy." At a performance of the *Merry Wives* he helped to carry off the dolorousness of the play. He was always " genial and amusing." She began to like him in spite of herself. . . .

But Lewes was not free. He was a married man with three sons and his wife had left him for Thornton Hunt, the dark handsome eldest son of Leigh Hunt. The two men with their families had set up a co-operative *ménage* in a big house in Queen's Road, Bayswater. The inevitable happened. Lewes had married very young, a woman slightly above himself in station who was extremely pretty. Her name was Agnes Jervis, and she was generally known as Rosebud. Hunt fell in love with her and they went away together for several days. She came back and Lewes forgave her. Then she left him a second time, informing him that her decision was final. Hunt had no more scruple about leaving his own young wife than she had about deserting her husband and her three boys. Lewes was thus at a loose end when he encountered Marian Evans.

It was her increasing intimacy with him, which could not escape the notice of her friends, the Chapmans, that induced Marian to

K

leave their house in the Strand and set up on her own in Cambridge Street, where she could receive him without comment. She had been for more than a year in London ; she was now thirty-four years of age and looked probably a good deal older with her heavy features and sallow skin. Never more than passably good-looking even when she possessed the freshness of youth, there was undoubtedly something attractive and arresting about the massive head, the prominent brows, the deep grey eyes, the thick auburn hair, now parted and smoothed down over her ears.

The winter of 1853 passed and in the Spring of the following year Lewes was ill. He was of slight, rather frail physique, but full of spirit and courage. To the last he bore his constant ill-health with a marked cheerfulness, indeed, it seemed impossible for him to doff his gay motley. When he was convalescent he went to stay with his friend Arthur Helps in the country. "No opera and no fun for me for the next month," Miss Evans lamented.

She could, however, help him by correcting his proofs when he was too ill to do this himself. And by May she was already hinting to her friends at the possibility of going abroad. June came and she asked Mrs. Bray to forward her books. July—and she packed some books for Sara Hennell. "I shall soon send you a good-bye for I am preparing to go abroad," she wrote. The good-bye was written ten days later, when she told them briefly her address for the next six weeks would be Poste Restante, Weimar. The letter was signed : "Ever your loving and grateful Marian." Not a word of Lewes nor of the momentous and irretrievable step she was about to take. And that very day she left London for Antwerp with George Henry Lewes. . . .

§

There was nothing in the least romantic about this sedate and even solemn elopement, and George Eliot's unhappy passion for Lewes has never figured among the classic love-affairs that from time to time have entranced the world. There was in it nothing of the young eager love that lent a certain glamour to the lamentable *scappatura* of Shelley and Mary Godwin, both now in their graves ; nor of that chivalry that prompted Robert Browning to lift a woman six years older than himself, and whom he believed to be perishing from some spinal complaint, from her "mattress-grave" and bear her away to a region of sunshine, fresh air and liberty, where she was to live and thrive for fifteen radiant years. Nothing either of the tragic passion that held Nelson in its chains. . . .

Nor did their exterior appearance imbue the adventure with any quality of romance. Miss Evans, with her roughly modelled horse-

GEORGE HENRY LEWES
Courtesy of Messrs. Benn.

like peasant face, her tallish angular figure with its unsheddable touch of prim provincialism, so little in accord with the advanced views she was now putting into practice, was not of the stuff of which heroines are made, and Lewes equally un-hero-like ran beside her like an active, intelligent, devoted little dog with a dog's faithful and rather anxious brown eyes.

Of the dawn as they passed up the Scheldt after a perfect passage, Marian wrote thus in her Journal :

The crescent moon, the stars, the first faint blush of the dawn reflected in the glassy river, the dark mass of clouds on the horizon which sent forth flashes of lightning, and the graceful forms of the boats and fishing vessels painted in jet black on the reddish gold of the sky and water, made up an unforgettable picture.

Their chief object in going to Weimar was to obtain further material for Lewes's *Life of Goethe*, which was already begun. And Weimar had the merit of being extremely cheap. They paid for board and lodging, only £2 6s. per week, which sum included wine and washing. But economy was necessary. Marian's income was small and Lewes had little beyond what he earned, besides having to support his mother and the three boys.

In August, Arthur Helps joined them, and it is said that by his advice they called themselves man and wife. He accompanied them on an expedition to Ettesburg and Marian was enchanted with the sight of the mountain-ash-trees in full berry. " I felt a child's love for the bunches of coral standing out against a blue sky."

Whether people were aware of their irregular relationship is extremely doubtful since they called themselves Mr. and Mrs. Lewes, and as such were received by the Princess Wittgenstein, beloved friend of Goethe. And, of course, there must be a visit to Goethe's house where, by special favour, they were shown the bedroom and study.

They went to the Opera. At a performance of *Ernani*, conducted by Liszt, Marian was struck with his appearance. " He looked splendid, the grand outline of his face and flowing hair were seen to advantage as they were thrown into relief by the stage lamps." Then he came to see them and played to Marian. She was enchanted. " For the first time in my life I beheld real inspiration—for the first time I heard the true notes of the piano."

But *Lohengrin* drove them from the house before two acts were over, though they enjoyed the *Flying Dutchman* and *Tannhäuser*.

After a short stay in Berlin they turned homewards. Marian had written to several of her friends informing them of the step she had taken and very few had replied. Even the Brays were shocked into silence. She thought of the inevitable return to England with something of anxiety and alarm.

On her arrival at Dover she wrote to Sara Hennell :

I am well and calmly happy—feeling much stronger and clearer in mind for the last eight months of new experience.

Perhaps the most painful thing of all was the attitude of Isaac Evans, leading his honest laborious life at Griff. For him his sister was thenceforth dead ; she had ceased to exist. And better dead, perhaps, he thought, rather than this shame. They had always held their heads so high. . . . Chrissy Clarke pursued the same line of conduct. To her simple provincial relations Marian was simply a woman who had " gone wrong."

Still she derived comfort from the sympathy of a few friends, such as Sara Hennell, Barbara Smith (afterwards Mme Bodichon), Bessie Parkes (afterwards Mme Belloc) and Mrs. Peter Taylor.

Now came their first and inevitable parting. Lewes must take his boys somewhere for the summer holidays, and in the circumstances she could not accompany them. Yes, there were still phases of his life into which she could not enter. Charles, the eldest, was twelve, and how could his father explain her to him ? He took them to Ramsgate, leaving her in lodgings at East Sheen. From there she wrote a long explanatory letter to Mrs. Bray which shows that she had now learned bitterly the place she must henceforth occupy in the eyes of the world. It wasn't only Isaac and Chrissy who had so relentlessly, so unforgivingly, turned down their thumbs. . . .

Light and easily broken ties are what I neither desire theoretically nor could live for practically. Women who are satisfied with such ties do *not* act as I have done. That any unworldly, superstitious person who is sufficiently acquainted with the realities of life can pronounce my relation to Mr. Lewes immoral I can only understand by remembering how subtle and complex are the influences that mould opinion. But I *do* remember this, and I indulge in no arrogant or uncharitable thoughts about those who condemn us, even though we might have expected a somewhat different verdict. From the majority of persons, of course, we never looked for anything but condemnation. We are leading no life of self-indulgence, except indeed, that being very happy in each other, we find everything easy. . . . I should never like to write about myself again ; it is not healthy to dwell on one's own feelings and conduct but only to try and live more faithfully and lovingly every fresh day. . . . I can find no strength or comfort except in " pressing forward towards the things that are before," and trying to make the present better than the past.

As an example of sophistry and self-deception, complete and deliberate, this letter, written apparently in all sincerity, can surely have few equals. We have a woman living with a man who was not and could not be her husband, not only attempting to vindicate her position, but also assuming a highly moral tone to extenuate her action. But the allusion to "unworldly superstitious persons" shows how completely any form of Christian religion had been flung overboard. Nor did she ever renounce her wish to appear before the world as a teacher of all that was good, and on the moral plane, great.

During Lewes's absence she wrote several articles for the *Leader*, and also for the belles-lettres section of the October issue of the *Westminster*. When he returned they spent a short time at Worthing, afterwards moving to Richmond, where they remained living very quietly for three years.

That autumn saw the publication of the *Life of Goethe*, the work by which Lewes will be best remembered. It is long, laborious and full of information, but whatever his charm as a brilliant conversationalist and raconteur may have been, nothing of this escaped into his writings. He had a naturally turgid style, which did little justice to the immense amount of valuable material he so patiently accumulated.

Marian sent a copy to Charles Bray.

I think you will find much to interest you in the book. I can't tell you how I value it as the product of a mind which I have every day more reason to admire and love.

Very clearly were they given to understand that she must be taken seriously or not at all.

She too was occupied with biographical articles and wrote one on that famous, tragic figure, Margaret Fuller, Marchesa Ossoli, who was drowned during an ill-fated voyage back to America together with her husband and child who had suffered from small-pox *en route*. This gifted woman had translated the *Conversations of Goethe and Eckermann*, written *Papers on Art and Literature*, and edited the *Dial*. Marian wrote another article on Mary Wollstonecraft, that brilliant and enigmatic pioneer of the rights of women, whose wild and passionate life had influenced the women of a whole generation, possibly even indirectly affecting Marian Evans herself, when she took the step which produced such consternation among her friends.

By the middle of January, 1856, she was able to tell Sara Hennell that one thousand copies of the *Life of Goethe* had been sold, the price being 30s.

It was she who held the purse, doling out sovereigns with "all the pangs of a miser." Indeed, during the first eighteen months of

their association it must often have been difficult to make two ends
meet, considering the heavy claims upon them. But they lived a
solitary and laborious life, sharing a small sitting-room where they
lived and wrote, and where she, nervous and unstrung, for hers was
no tranquil nature, suffered agonies from the busy scratching of
Lewes's pen.

There were elements of risk and uncertainty in her present life
that must at times have weighed heavily upon her. All her happiness and security were dependent upon the fidelity of this man
with whom she had thrown in her lot. Being what she was she
must have felt sometimes that her feet were uncomfortably close to
the edge of the crater. . . .

§

Owing to failure in the business of ribbon-manufacture the Brays
had to leave Rosehill. Marian invited them to spend a night at
Richmond. There was talk too of the Lewes boys being sent to
school to their friend, Mr. John Sibree, but he declined to receive
them for a reason that is not specified. It is more than probable
that their father's domestic life militated against their finding
acceptance at an English school, and he finally resolved to send them
to Hofwyl, near Berne. He had been educated abroad himself, so
was aware of all the advantages and disadvantages of such a proceeding.

In April they spent a couple of days at Sydenham with Herbert
Spencer, and as the financial situation was somewhat eased, they
went in May to Ilfracombe to enable Lewes to pursue those studies
in natural history which now became his chief work. Marian took
a proper, even excited interest in the " molluscs and medusæ " of
that fruitful seashore. The tide pools that held these marine marvels
were a joy to them both. They rambled about the Devonshire
lanes, where the " primroses sprinkled the sides of the hills with
their pale stars." Country-bred, she was always happier and in
better health when away from London.

Their serious reading was never neglected, but it was a shade
less heavy. Gosse's *Rambles on the Devonshire Coast* was of assistance
to Lewes, the *Life of Chatterton* by Masson, stimulated Marian's
biographical studies. They even made friends with the curate, Mr.
Tugwell, who was possibly unaware that Mrs. Lewes had no right
to the name by which she now elected to be known.

These semi-scientific studies under the ægis of Lewes stood her
in good stead. She was conscious of a tendency " that is now growing constantly in me, to escape from all vagueness and inaccuracy,

into the daylight of distinct vivid ideas. The mere fact of naming
an object tends to give definiteness to our conception of it." It was
the natural impulse of the creative artist to harness imagination to
hard facts. . . .

It was a happy time for her " despite the work, zoology and bodily
ailments." And from Ilfracombe she wrote a highly significant letter
to Mrs. Peter Taylor, in which she said : " *It will always be a pleasant
thought to me that you have remembered me kindly and interpreted me
nobly.*"

Her attitude was somewhat reminiscent of Macbeth's :

> What thou wouldst highly
> That wouldst thou holily ; wouldst not play false
> And yet wouldst wrongly win. . . .

§

From Ilfracombe they went to Tenby, a place which, familiar to
her, was new ground to Lewes. They enjoyed the sands and bathing
and the expeditions to St. Catherine's Rock with its caverns, to which
they went armed with " baskets, hammers, chisels and jars and
phials," returning laden with spoils in the shape of fossils. But all
the same she must have felt she was losing valuable time running
about after Lewes in this way. Very soon the positions were to be
entirely reversed.

Barbara Smith came down to spend a few days with them. And
hardly a week after her departure, as if the matter had been discussed between them, Marian wrote a significant entry in her
journal : " I am anxious to begin my fiction writing."

The idea had been in her mind ever since she had shown Lewes
the tentative beginnings of a novel while in Berlin. He was impressed with it " as a bit of concrete description " and it suggested
the possibility of her being able to produce a novel, though he feared
she did not possess any dramatic talent. He had, it will be seen,
still a good deal to learn about her.

Now at Tenby, in the intervals of all that terrible hammering
and chiselling, the subject was revived ; he even urged her to begin.
And of course it was all very solemnly and seriously discussed.
She hesitated before work that was not an absolute duty. She had
a sure market for her articles and reviews of books, which brought
her a small but definite income, and there was risk attached to the
writing of a novel. It would take a long time, and even then she
might not be able to dispose of it. Perhaps in her heart of hearts
she feared failure and the effect of that failure upon Lewes. . . .

But the impulse was too strong for her. One day in a " certain dreamy doze " he conceived a story entitled the *Sad Fortunes of the Reverend Amos Barton*. " A capital title," Lewes said enthusiastically. And indeed, it is no rare thing for a story to spring complete from a suddenly imagined title.

But he wasn't always encouraging. " It may be a failure, it may be you're unable to write fiction. You may write a *chef d'œuvre* at once—there's no telling." Not very helpful, one would say. Perhaps he too feared the risk, being himself the author of two utterly undistinguished novels. He lacked the imaginative insight so essential to the writer of fiction. Still, there were marvellous examples of recent successes scored by women in that very field. There was Charlotte Brontë, dead a few months back at Haworth, who had not hesitated to tell him there were aspects of his mentality which jarred terribly upon her sensitiveness. More straightforward and honest, though far more passionate than Marian Evans, she could never have deliberately occupied an equivocal position and then invited her friends to " interpret her nobly." Long ago— though this was unknown to him—she had left the man she loved, the country where he lived, in a moment of tragic despair because honour and duty and every code of morality forced the sacrifice upon her. There was Mrs. Gaskell, with her delicately humorous *Cranford*, her famous *Sylvia's Lovers*, a woman of rare imagination and sympathy ; Mrs. Oliphant, still in her twenties, but already of established reputation, working desperately for her sick husband and little children ; Charlotte Yonge, with her deep Anglican piety, who had won immediate fame with her *Heir of Redclyffe*. And in the past there had been Jane Austen for whose books Lewes had an admiration that would have satisfied any modern " Janeite." Would Marian ever take her place amid that brilliant and distinguished throng ? She was above all things a student, and the student is not always or even often of the stuff of which the successful novelist is made. There is all the vital difference between them of the taker and the giver. . . .

They again referred to her novel while walking in Kew Gardens in August, after their return to Richmond. A few days later Lewes left England to escort his two elder boys, Charles and Thornton, to Hofwyl, near Berne, where they remained for some years.

§

The novel was actually begun on September 22, 1856. During its progress she and Lewes discussed it with characteristic seriousness, even solemnity. Could she write dialogue ? *Amos Barton* assured him that she could. But pathos ? That must be proved by the manner in which she handled Milly's death. She wrote that chapter during his temporary absence in London, reading it to him on his return. " We both cried over it," she relates, " and then he came up to me and kissed me, saying : ' I think your pathos is better than your fun.' "

In these days such emotive reactions seem to us almost incredible, and I do not think many could now be found to shed a tear over Milly Barton. However, we must remember that we are dealing with a period when a group of brilliant young men, including Dante Gabriel Rossetti and William Morris, wept over the premature death of Guy Morville, the Heir of Redclyffe, and the grief of his young widow.

The story was finished on November 5, so it had taken her less than six weeks to write. And in *Amos Barton* George Eliot gave evidence of that power of epigrammatic, ironical phrasing which lends humour to nearly all her books. " An anthem in which the key-bugles always ran away at a great pace while the bassoon every now and then boomed a flying shot after them." Mrs. Patten, who " had got rich chiefly by the negative process of spending nothing." Mr. Pilgrim, the doctor who gave " late dinners with enigmatic side-dishes and poisonous port." Just a sharp phrase and these people were made to live. A hint of roughness too, but that was all in the picture.

Those were the days when the Reader was solemnly addressed. " Reader, I married him," wrote Charlotte Brontë, unforgettably. George Eliot adopted the same idiom. " Reader, *did* you ever taste such a cup of tea as Miss Gibbs is this moment handing to Mr. Pilgrim ? " Such rhetorical questions were of common use in her generation.

At the said tea-party the unfortunate Amos Barton was bitterly criticized. Mr. Pilgrim disliked him, not only because he had called in a rival doctor, but also because with some smattering of medical knowledge he had cured one of Pilgrim's own patients. Mrs. Patten had a very different grievance. Mr. Barton would talk to her of her sins and her need of " marcy." And she had never been a sinner ! . . .

Charlotte Brontë in *Shirley* had set a fashion in curates and this may have suggested certain passages in *Amos Barton*. Indeed, the story was intended to form part of a series entitled *Scenes of Clerical Life*, and as such Lewes offered it to Blackwood, aware that being only roughly about thirty-five thousand words in length it was not of sufficient size for an ordinary novel.

Lewes's accompanying letter was really almost sufficient to put off any self-respecting publisher.

According to my judgment such humour, pathos, vivid presentation and nice observation have not been exhibited (in this style) since the *Vicar of Wakefield*.

Blackwood, perceiving its merits, answered that " his friend's reminiscences of clerical life will do." *Amos Barton* made " very pleasant reading." The death of Milly was powerful and had affected him very much. " If the author is a new writer I beg to congratulate him on being worthy of the honours of print and pay." Still, he could make no definite offer for its publication in *Maga* till he had seen more of the series. He indicated the weak points of *Amos Barton*. There was the error of trying to explain the characters by description instead of allowing them to evolve. . . . He added : " The round-up is perhaps the lamest part of the story."

Lewes replied that he had communicated the letter to his " clerical friend " who was somewhat discouraged by it, but acting on his advice would submit the second story when ready.

Blackwood explained he did not wish to convey anything like disappointment, but he always " thought twice before putting that decisive mark ' In type for the magazine ' on any MS. from a stranger." However, as the rest of the series was still unwritten he had formed a sufficiently high opinion of *Amos Barton* to waive his objection and publish it without seeing the others, although he could not bind himself to accept its successors if he did not approve of them. " I agree with you there is great freshness of style," he wrote, adding that he proposed to begin the publication in January. " I am glad to hear that your friend is, as I supposed, a clergyman "

Lewes was too honest not to reveal the truth on this point. " My clerical friend merely meant the writer of the ' clerical' stories. I am not at liberty to remove the veil of anonymity even as regards social position." Nor did he wish his own name to be mentioned in regard to the stories lest speculation should happen upon the truth. Most people in London, though possibly not in Edinburgh, were aware by this time of his liaison with Marian Evans.

George Eliot, as we must now call her, began *Mr. Gilfil's Love Story*, which as a story is perhaps the most compact of the three, on Christmas Day. At the end of December, 1856, she received the January number of *Maga* containing the first instalment of *Amos Barton* and a letter from Blackwood enclosing a cheque for fifty guineas. He added that should the series continue as he anticipated, he hoped to publish the *Scenes* later in book form either on the half-profits system or in return for a definite sum for the rights.

I am very sensitive to the merits of cheques for fifty guineas—she wrote to Mr. John Blackwood.

Thus the year 1857 opened propitiously for them. Albert Smith wrote in praise of the story, saying he had never read anything that affected him so much as Milly's death, so that her astonishing loquacity in the circumstances must have escaped him. " The men at the club seem to have mingled their tears and their tumblers together," Blackwood wrote. " It would be curious if you should be a member and be hearing your own praises."

In writing to Blackwood she signed herself for the first time George Eliot, and told him that whatever measure of success her stories might achieve, she was resolved upon retaining her anonymity. She had observed that a " *nom-de-plume* secured all the advantages without the disagreeables of reputation." And later she said, with a touch of that ironical humour which salted all she wrote, that " if George Eliot turned out a dull dog or an ineffective writer—a mere flash in the pan—she for one was determined to cut him on the first intimation of that disagreeable fact."

Mr. Gilfil's Love Story was finished in March, and it is astonishing to find that Mr. Blackwood was faintly disappointed with it, although he published it probably on account of the unusually favourable reception accorded to *Amos Barton*. That same month they took a holiday, visiting Penzance and the Scilly Isles where they read Mrs. Gaskell's *Life of Charlotte Brontë* with great enjoyment. " As poetic as one of her own novels," was George Eliot's comment. " Janet's Repentance "—the weakest of the three stories that formed the *Scenes of Clerical Life*—was then in progress.

Herbert Spencer, who seems to have been " in the know," said that he had heard the *Scenes* being discussed with warm praise. Thackeray had expressed his hearty approval. People were already evincing curiosity as to the author and by some the series had been attributed oddly enough to Bulwer.

Letters from strangers—now irreverently termed " fan-mail "— began to pour in, a sure sign of an author's growing popularity.

Sir—wrote one of these unknown admirers—will you consider it impertinent in a brother author and old reviewer to address a few lines of earnest sympathy and admiration excited by the purity of your style, originality of your thoughts, and absence of all vulgar seeking for effect in those " Scenes of Clerical Life " now appearing in Blackwood ?

No doubt now as to the success of the venture nor of her power of writing fiction. More, she could hold her readers. Not many authors have risen to fame through a series of short stories,

—Kipling, the creator of Sherlock Holmes, and Katherine Mansfield being notable exceptions in more modern times. The cheques that flowed in gave George Eliot practical and stimulating proof of success. In addition to the payment for the contributions to *Maga* she received £120 for the first edition of the *Scenes* in volume form. But she stipulated to be allowed to write as she would " without cramping influence." *Maga* was intended for general, or what is termed family reading ; there must be nothing equivocal in its content. And the powerful brain at work on its tragic masterpiece, *Adam Bede,* could submit to no such restrictions.

They read *Aurora Leigh* for the third time that summer, no mean feat for two busy people. " I know no book that gives me a deeper sense of communion with a large as well as beautiful mind," George Eliot wrote.

§

On October 22, 1857, George Eliot made the following entry in her journal, perhaps little dreaming of the fame those two words were to bring, not only to herself, but to English literature.

Began my new novel, *Adam Bede.*

Two weeks later she told Blackwood that the book was making slow progress. Indeed, rapid work would have been impossible to her at any time. She was a slow conscientious worker, bringing a curious solemnity of purpose to her task.

A little sunshine of success would stimulate its growth I dare say— she wrote. Unhappily I am as impressionable as I am obstinate and as much in need of sympathy from my readers as I am incapable of bending myself to their tastes.

At the end of each year she was wont to give a brief summary of its happenings in her journal. Thus, 1857 had brought her " a deepening of happiness ; the blessedness of a perfect love and union grows daily."

Nor was the " little sunshine of success " lacking. Copies of the *Scenes* had been sent at her request to various celebrities, among them Charles Dickens, who said in reply that had he been left to his own devices he should have addressed the writer as a woman. " No man ever before had the art of making himself so like a woman since the world began," he affirmed. Froude wrote appreciatively and so did Mrs. Carlyle, who was at a loss to imagine why the book should have been sent to her. She knew of no one called George Eliot. But perhaps it was a delicate way of giving it to her husband ? She conceived the writer to be " a man of middle age with a wife from whom he has got those beautiful feminine touches in his book, a good many children, and a dog that he has as much fondness for as I have for my little Nero."

They had already received a visit from Major Blackwood during the preceding autumn, but her secret had not then been disclosed. Now in February Mr. John Blackwood appeared in person. " Well, am I to see George Eliot this time ? " he asked smiling. They left the room together and after a brief consultation decided to admit him to the secret since her private life could hardly at this juncture affect the sale of her books. Thackeray, he told her, spoke highly of the *Scenes*. Both he and Mrs. Oliphant were convinced they were the work of a man.

She showed Mr. Blackwood the first chapters of *Adam Bede*. After reading one page he said : " This will do." He discerned the surer touch. In the *Scenes* she had been feeling her way in a medium that was strange to her. And there had been that teazing doubt in Lewes's mind as to her competence for the task to which she must inevitably have reacted.

In April she refused to give her publishers any outline of the story. There was some fear perhaps in her mind, of the " cramping influence " of *Maga*. She and Lewes were then on the point of leaving for Munich. Both had earned a holiday. Her *Scenes* were selling adequately, and Lewes had scored a moderate success with his *Seaside Studies*. But even when abroad they kept their " workers' hours." By May she had finished the twenty-second chapter of *Adam Bede*. They went out a good deal in Munich, chiefly to quiet musical parties.

In June Lewes left her to visit his sons, and although he was only away a week, George Eliot was unable to endure the solitude and sought the society of her friend, Frau von Siebold.

When they left Munich they visited Salzburg, Ischl, Vienna, Prague, and finally Dresden, where they remained for a couple of months, renting a charming apartment of six rooms, for which they paid only eighteen shillings a week. She had a private study and worked there behind closed doors, and it was here she finished the second volume of *Adam Bede*, rising at six in order to ensure a long morning. They left Dresden towards the end of August, arriving in England on September 2, 1858. Soon afterwards she despatched the second volume of *Adam Bede* to Blackwood and only two months later the third was in his hands. He approved of the book and offered £800 for the copyright for four years.

It is fortunate for us that George Eliot left so complete an account of the planning and writing of *Adam Bede*. Her own early life at

Arbury provided her with the background she used picturesquely if
a trifle sombrely.   But the " germ " of the story lay in an episode
related long ago by her Methodist aunt, Mrs. Samuel Evans, wife of
her father's younger brother.   This aunt had visited a young girl
who was in prison condemned, according to the savage laws of those
days, for the murder of her illegitimate child, a crime to which she
refused to confess.   Mrs. Evans remained praying throughout the
night with her in the condemned cell and at last the girl (not astonishingly) broke down and confessed.   Mrs. Evans accompanied her to
the scene of execution in the morning.   It will be remembered
that George Eliot very wisely commuted the sentence to trans-
portation for life in her novel.   The incident which she had heard
related as a child had remained in her memory, and one night she
told it to Lewes.   He remarked that the prison scene would make
" a fine element in a story."   This made her decide to use it in
Adam Bede.

Her father served as a working model for *Adam Bede*, although
it was by no means an actual portrait, whereas the character of
Dinah was quite naturally evolved from that of her aunt, the earnest
Methodist, Mrs. Samuel Evans.   It was thought that Mrs. Poyser's
sayings resembled those of George Eliot's mother, but there could
have only been a family resemblance as she declared they were all
" fresh from her own mint."   She affirmed too, that there was not a
single portrait in *Adam Bede*.

The scene in the wood between Adam and Arthur Donnithorne
came to her in Munich during a performance of *William Tell*.   Up
till then she had not been able to visualize the inevitable collision
between the two men.

Throughout the book she altered little except that at Lewes's
suggestion she " spaced out " two of the scenes.   She wrote the last
volume in six weeks, despite headaches and a curious emotional state
that was probably the consequence of overwork and anxiety as to
the reception it would obtain.   " I love it very much," she wrote,
" and am deeply thankful to have written it."

The book appeared on February 1, 1859, and the first instalment
of the money—a cheque for £400—was punctually sent.   The prospect
of such unheard-of prosperity induced them to take a house at
Wandsworth and engage a servant.   Hitherto they had lived in
lodgings, so this was quite a new and adventurous departure.   Holly
Lodge, Wandsworth, was the address of their new abode and it
possessed " far more vulgar indulgences than I ever expected to have
again."

It was a tall building, the rooms were large and airy, and there was a view of the Crystal Palace which she did not appreciate. But this suburban home set up within her a longing for the real country with its orchards, meadows, hedgerows and streams. It was, however, apparently essential for their work that they should be near London. George Eliot's sister, Chrissy Clarke, died in March. She had written a few weeks before to effect a reconciliation with the sister from whom she had been so long estranged.

§

From the first there was never any doubt as to the immense success of *Adam Bede*. By April its sales had surpassed all expectation. Blackwood was able to tell her she was not only a popular author but a great author. Herbert Spencer brought her the news that Mr. Charles Buxton had quoted her in the House of Commons. "As the farmer's wife says in *Adam Bede*, ' it wants to be hatched again and hatched different.' " And Charles Reade declared it was the " finest thing since Shakespeare." She could bask now in a veritable sunshine of success.

And there were other tributes nearer to her heart. Miss Barbara Smith, now Mme Bodichon and settled in Algiers with her French husband, read *Adam Bede* and with a rare discernment recognized the author. There might have been some familiar word, some particular phrase to guide her, for she had known her long and intimately, and her subsequent letter of appreciation gave George Eliot more joy than all the reviews and tangible proofs of success, " since the evenings when I read my manuscript to my dear, dear husband, and he laughed and cried alternately and then rushed to me to kiss me."

This provides a curious and significant sidelight upon their emotional relationship, but then we, of a colder and more controlled generation, find it difficult to understand those ready tears which were wont to afflict both Lewes and George Eliot.

The tangible proofs of success were by no means wanting. By May she knew that at the end of the year she was to receive a further sum of £400 for *Adam Bede*, making £1,200 in all. She was never again to feel the pinch of poverty or the necessity of doling out sovereigns with a miser's reluctance. Her success consolidated too the hazardous adventure of her union with Lewes.

She still preserved her anonymity to a great extent, although this became more difficult when one Liggins, the son of a baker, announced that he was the author of *Adam Bede*. And even as Mrs. Carlyle was by some supposed to be Currer Bell, so *Adam Bede* was attributed in some quarters to Mrs. Gaskell.

When dining one night, after a performance of the *Messiah*, at the Crystal Palace with the Brays and Sara Hennell, Marian revealed herself to them as George Eliot. Their astonishment displeased her. " They seemed overwhelmed with surprise." The experience, she said, enlightened her a good deal as to " the ignorance in which we all live of each other." Their reactions were, however, perfectly natural since they were suddenly called upon to view their old friend—who had always been slightly below them in social status—as one of the outstanding celebrities of the day.

Perhaps, too, in her new and wider experience of life, she had outgrown these old friends of Coventry days. For the last five years she had seen little of them ; she must have lost a good deal of that provincialism they remembered. Now, however much they might disapprove of her mode of life, she was a person who counted quite definitely in the world of letters. They were impoverished, while she was, according to their standards, a rich woman. The evening must have been a complete failure. . . .

In July, George Eliot and Lewes went to Paris and Lucerne, where they stayed at the Schweizerhof. They could afford a good hotel now after years of putting up at cheap lodgings. From Lucerne Lewes went to visit his sons. George Eliot wrote to Charles, the eldest one who was now seventeen, and sent him a watch. They were only absent a couple of weeks and returned to Holly Lodge to learn that the fourth edition of *Adam Bede*, consisting of five thousand copies, had been sold in a fortnight.

She was in the fortunate position now of being able to refuse work. An offer came from an American periodical inviting her to contribute a serial to consist of twelve weekly numbers. She named her price—£1,000—to which the editor agreed. A few days later she definitely refused the offer although it had been raised to £1,200. She was engrossed in the *Mill on the Floss* and could not envisage such an interruption. Still few authors would have cared to forgo such a large emolument.

A further sum of £200 from Blackwood for a second edition of the *Scenes*, now enjoying a renewed prosperity on account of the immense success of *Adam Bede*, reached her in August. She was in no humour to write pot-boilers, even if there had been any necessity for her to do so. She and Lewes continued to live thriftily ; their indifferent health and anomalous position combined to prevent them from going into society, and their own entertaining was on a most moderate scale. It was therefore quite unnecessary for the authoress of *Visiting my Relations* to warn her in a letter against being beguiled

by love of money. They needed money in order to live and to
educate the boys, but it must be earned by diligent work. And
indeed, from the outset George Eliot took her career seriously, even
solemnly. The success of *Adam Bede* only made it a matter of
deeper anxiety. " I suppose there is a little sense of responsibility
mixed up with a great deal of pride," she wrote.

And she did well to be careful. An astounding success is rarely
followed by another of equal *éclat*, especially when it occurs early
in an author's career. Would the *Mill on the Floss*—at that time
entitled provisionally " Sister Maggie "—prove a worthy successor to
Adam Bede, the sales of which were still so remarkable ? A seventh
edition consisting of two thousand copies was in the press by October,
1859. The final cheque of £400 by the terms of the contract was
paid, but owing to the unprecedented sales, Blackwood proposed to
pay her a further £800 in the following January. She had thus
made £2,000 by the book in rather less than a year ; a large sum
for those days. When we remember that Charlotte Brontë never
received more than £500 apiece for *Jane Eyre*, *Shirley* and *Villette*,
while Jane Austen had to be contented with £110 for *Pride and
Prejudice*, we cannot help feeling a slight and perhaps rather dismayed astonishment.

People were now beginning to seek them out at Wandsworth.
Charles Dickens dined with them and invited George Eliot to contribute a serial to *All the Year Round* to commence four months after
Easter, but she declined on the grounds of insufficient time. As she
had stepped into fame with what was practically her first essay in
fiction, and, unlike many authors, had not had the anxiety of more
or less lengthy periods of diligent rejection, she had no bygones to
be exhumed from a literary sepulchre to satisfy the demand for her
work. Everything was "fresh from her mint," as she would have said.

Herbert Spencer dined with them, as did Wilkie Collins. There
were more offers for serials, one from Lucas for *Once a Week*, but
" Sister Maggie " stood in the way.

Sir Edward Lytton called. He considered the two defects of
Adam Bede were the dialect and the marriage of Adam and Dinah.
" But, of course, I would rather have my teeth drawn than give
up either," she noted. And whatever its defects, was it not still
selling beyond her wildest dreams ?

§

After a great deal of discussion, it was decided that the new
book should be called the *Mill on the Floss*, a title suggested by Blackwood. George Eliot had thought of " Sister Maggie," " St. Ogg's

L

on the Floss," and " The Tullivers or Life on the Floss." Blackwood, however, very wisely preferred the *Mill on the Floss*, and he won the day. Publishers are usually in the right as regards the title of a book, their business sense is more keen and they can measure its attractiveness in their advertisements. Still the Mill wasn't on the Floss—it was on a small tributary called the Ripple. This insignificant detail didn't, however, seem to matter, and perhaps no book has ever appeared before the world with a more beautiful title.

By January, 1860, she had finished the second volume. Lewes was at that time contributing a series of papers called *Studies in Animal Life* to *Cornhill*.

Offers came in for the *Mill on the Floss*. Harper's of New York offered £300 for the American rights, and Tauchnitz £100 for the German reprint. She finished the book on March 21, and a few days later they left for Italy.

Lewes always took her abroad directly a book was done. She suffered continually from exhaustion and that peculiar form of headache so common with the creative artist, known as hemicrania. He was himself a nervous, delicate man, who suffered, as she did, from constant headaches. The sojourns abroad were thus beneficial to both.

They arrived in Rome during a crowded Holy Week, and could not obtain rooms at the then fashionable Hôtel d'Angleterre, where the young Prince of Wales and his suite had been housed during the preceding year. They had to make the best of an uncomfortable perch in the Hôtel d'Amérique in the Via Babuino, but moved on the following day to rooms in the corso.

Neither of them had ever been in Rome before and they were bitterly disappointed. Indeed, some days passed before the sense of disillusionment gave place to one of rapture. The first word of praise was elicited by a visit to the Villa Doria-Pamphili " which has the beauties of an English park with views such as no English park can show." The Villa Albani, the Campagna, Frascati, Tivoli and the other towns of the Castelli followed in due course. In Rome itself they visited picture-galleries, churches, museums, the Catacombs, and the Protestant cemetery where they stood, as so many thousands of their fellow-countrymen have done across more than a century, beside the graves of Keats and Shelley.

The Holy Week ceremonies, with their stately ritual, did not appeal to George Eliot. They were, as she recorded in her journal, " a melancholy, hollow business, and we regret bitterly that Holy Week has taken up our time from better things." She even repeated that devastating cliché, to excuse herself for kneeling for the Pope's blessing, that " no one could be the worse for the blessing of an old man." But on the morrow she had a cold and headache and in other ways was " not conscious of improvement from the Pope's blessing." One wonders that she could have hoped it should operate favourably upon herself and Lewes, but as usual she wanted things " both ways."

From Rome they went to Naples, where they visited the usual sights, the beautiful Greek temples at Paestum earning her especial praise. From Naples they went by sea to Leghorn and thence travelled to Florence. After much sight-seeing they continued their journey to Bologna, travelling by night in the diligence. Then Padua, Venice, Verona, Milan, Como, Chiavenna and across the Splügen to Zurich and Berne, where they were joined by Charles Lewes, who had now left Hofwyl and was to proceed to England to try for an appointment in the Civil Service.

July found them back at Wandsworth, and to her delight she heard that the *Mill on the Floss*, published on April 4, while they were in Rome, had sold six thousand copies in the first three months of its existence, while five hundred more were in the press. She had received very favourable terms for it, as she was to have £2,000 for four thousand copies and pro rata for the 31s. 6d. edition ; £150 per thousand for those sold at 12s. and £60 per thousand for those at 6s. The *Mill* promised to be a bigger success than even *Adam Bede*. It was said that much of the author's own childhood was reproduced in Maggie Tulliver, that dark wilful passionate heroine, eternally at war with her little world. The uncles and aunts were skilfully and ironically portrayed. The Dodsons were especially popular and are said to have resembled her mother's family, the Pearsons. And who can ever forget Uncle Pullet, who " had a large natural faculty for ignorance " ?

Meanwhile in that active powerful brain *Romola*, fruit of the too brief Florence days, was being slowly and with difficulty conceived.

§

" Our big boy is a great delight to us and makes our home doubly cheery," George Eliot wrote after their return. Charles called her Mother, or rather Mutter ; he seems to have been on the best of terms with her. Never could he have known such a comfortable home, nor felt the ease of wealth. Still, he was eighteen and he must have been aware of the equivocal position she occupied in that house. Indeed, the arrangement was a highly indelicate one, and few people would have regarded it as a possible solution of the problem as to where he should live.

He passed into the Post Office at the head of the list and for his sake they determined to take a house in London. This was rendered the more easy by the finding of a tenant for Holly Lodge, and in September they rented a furnished house in Harewood Square. The yellow drawing-room displeased George Eliot, and she resolved to have a " paradise of greenness " when they were finally settled in a place of their own. For the moment they had, however, given up the plan of buying a house which she thought might ultimately entail " a more expensive mode of living." She therefore declined Blackwood's offer of an anticipatory cheque.

Arthur Helps brought her the news that Queen Victoria had spoken to him with great admiration of her books, especially of the *Mill on the Floss.* " It is interesting to know," she added loftily, " that royalty can be touched by that sort of writing. "

Before writing *Romola,* she completed a much shorter book, *Silas Marner.* But despite the large sums she was now earning she continued to practise a rigid economy. When she and Lewes went to the Monday " Pops " at St. James's Hall they sat in the shilling seats. It was their easiest and cheapest pleasure. " I go in my bonnet," she wrote.

In December, 1860, they moved to their new house at 16 Blandford Square, which they had taken for three years, hoping by the end of that time that the future of the three boys would be settled, enabling them to live where they liked. But she was never well in London. Her chief pleasure was to go to the Zoological Gardens, of which Lewes had become a member. Like Walt Whitman she found the birds and beasts congenial to her spirit.

There is a notable letter about this time to Mme Bodichon, which suggests that lady was thinking of becoming a Catholic.

The bright point of your letter is that you are in a happy state of mind yourself. . . . As for the forms and ceremonies I feel no regret that any should turn to them for comfort if they can find comfort in them : sympathetically I enjoy them myself. But I have faith in the working out of higher possibilities than the Catholic or any other Church has presented, and those who have strength to wait and endure are bound to accept no formula which their whole souls—their intellect as well as their emotions —do not embrace with entire reverence. The "highest calling and election" is to *do without opium,* and live through all our pain with conscious clear-eyed endurance. . . .

This passage shows her intense desire to be regarded as a great moral teacher, speaking from the heights of an almost inaccessible purity, even when she was perfectly aware that the world was justifiably ready to affix a label to her which she would have resented

most passionately and which must have taxed her capacity for
" conscious clear-eyed endurance " to the utmost.

And there were undoubtedly difficult moments. Although she
could say definitely that it was no trial to her to be cut off from
the world, that her happiness lay in her life with Lewes, in the work
which she pursued with such unremitting diligence and which was
productive of such rich rewards, she must have realized that had it
not been for the irregular connection many doors would have been
flung open to welcome the famous George Eliot. The social side of
her fame she could not savour, although many, many years afterwards her position was in some sort accepted and people forgot it
in their eagerness to know one of the most celebrated of women
writers.

And then, when all was said and done, who would accept her
teaching ? Her private life was wholly at variance with those
excellent moral apothegms she was such an adept at enunciating,
and she must have lived perpetually beneath the shadow of a shame
that darkened her days.

The friends she still retained were permitted that privilege on her
own terms. The one passport to her friendship was that she
must be called Mrs. Lewes, and to suggest that she was still Marian
Evans was an insult. This was forcibly impressed upon Mrs. Taylor,
who tactlessly addressed her by that name, in 1861. For six years,
she told her, she had ceased to be Miss Evans, " having held myself
under all the responsibilities of a married woman," adding with
hauteur, " I wish this to be distinctly understood."

When I tell you that we have a great boy of eighteen at home who
calls me mother, as well as two other boys almost as tall who write to
me under the same name, you will understand that the point is not one of
mere egoism or personal dignity, when I request that anyone who has a
regard for me will cease to speak of me by my maiden name.

Only—and therein lay the sting—she was still Miss Evans in the
eyes of the whole world. There could be no question of a marriage
between herself and George Lewes until his wife died, a desirable
event that never occurred in his own life-time. Nothing could
straighten out the tangle.

She encased herself in a protective armour, making it an iron
rule never to pay visits. She was compelled, she said, to renounce
" the few that would be really attractive and fruitful " for the many
which would be neither. She would receive, but she would not be
received. She laid down her own terms clearly and succinctly for
those who desired her friendship. In fact, she must be sought—she
would not seek.

She still attended concerts with Lewes sitting in the cheapest seats where they mingled with the crowd. The long pale rather horse-like face became a familiar sight to concert-goers in the London of that day. But the gas and bad air diminished her delight in the music.

§

In April, 1861, *Silas Marner* having made a most successful appearance, they went to Florence, travelling through France. They were both so overcome with their usual headaches when they arrived at Nice, that they were thankful for the luxuries to be found in a big hotel. At Florence they stayed at the Albergo della Vittoria on the Lung' Arno. But the climate did not suit them. Lewes suffered much from cough and sore throat. Still, despite her forty-two years and indifferent health, George Eliot was able to climb to the top of Giotto's Tower. She was soaking herself in local colour, not realizing that the whole subject upon which *Romola* was founded was utterly alien to her own thought and education.

During this visit they went to Camaldoli and La Verna, accompanied by Mr. Thomas Trollope. Thirty-four days of busy sightseeing and collecting of material followed, and then they returned home to accomplish the work which she said she began as a young woman and finished as an old one.

On their return they dined with Blackwood at Greenwich and saw a game of golf being played in the Park, a rare sight in those days or she would not thus have mentioned it.

It was an idle summer, with two boys demanding amusement and attention. Thornton, who was now at school in Edinburgh, came back for his holidays in July, and these changes and unaccustomed duties must inevitably have caused a temporary lull of intellectual energy. Also she was no longer enjoying that *solitude à deux* which was so dear to her. And looking at the matter squarely, there must have been some very awkward moments. It was inconceivable that careful parents—and the parents of those days were meticulously careful—should permit their sons and daughters to go to Blandford Square, however much the young Leweses should desire the companionship of their own kind.

It was not till October, when the holidays were over, that George Eliot began the first chapter of *Romola*. She was so depressed about it that a month later, while walking with Lewes in the Park, she almost renounced the idea of writing her " Italian novel."

Wilkie Collins, Herbert Spencer, Bulwer and Smyth-Piggott were faithful friends and constant visitors. Two or three women rallied round her, but there was little contact even with the Brays, Mrs.

Congreve or Mrs. Peter Taylor. Mme Bodichon was living in Algiers, so that their intercourse was necessarily limited.

And then she was at grips with Florentine history. For the first time she resorted to the British Museum Reading Room, studying the topography of Florence, the mediæval costumes. All her reading —and it was very extensive—during the latter part of 1861 dealt with the period of which she intended to write. And on January 1, 1862, with something of the character of a New Year resolution, she set down the following sentence in her journal : *"I began again my novel of Romola."*

That same month Mr. George Smith, the publisher, approached Lewes, enquiring whether he thought Mr. George Eliot would be open to a magnificent offer. " This made me think about money," she wrote, " but it is better for me not to be rich."

She could hardly expect Lewes to be so disinterested, he had too much on his hands. Only one of his sons was so far earning any- thing, and his own mode of life was by slow but sure degrees changing with their altered income. He was then just about to bring out a book called *Animal Studies*, and it was when Mr. Smith actually brought the proofs of it in person that he began his tentative over- tures. His offer proved indeed magnificent, for he was prepared to give £10,000 for her new novel, to include all the rights both at home and abroad as well as its serialization in *Cornhill*. This far surpassed the munificence of Mr. Blackwood, and such a sum properly invested meant a certain income to the couple who had had to start with little beyond their brains to support them.

Two days later George Eliot declined the offer in so far as *Cornhill* was concerned. Mr. Smith wished to begin the instalments in May, and she refused to give up any part of it until the end of the book was in sight. She had known from the beginning that it was not going to be an easy task ; more than once she had repented of undertaking it.

Had she been driven by the same financial stress as Mrs. Oliphant, whose children were dependent upon her earnings for the very bread they ate, she would without doubt have sat down and applied herself to the task without scruple or delay, so as to bring that end within sight. She had three months before her and she could be a fairly rapid worker when she chose. But she was ever uncertain about *Romola*, and her headaches became more violent and continuous from the amount of sheer hard reading it involved. She spent a few weeks at Dorking and it was not till May that they returned to London. The negotiations were then resumed, and it was arranged that she should receive £7,000 for the publication of

Romola in twelve monthly parts in *Cornhill*, receiving the money in like instalments.

There was regret, of course, at leaving Blackwood, but he seems to have accepted it in a friendly spirit. Perhaps he foresaw that a third masterpiece was little likely at present to emanate from that powerful brain. Books that should rival *Adam Bede* and the *Mill on the Floss* were after all highly improbable contingencies.

Romola progressed slowly ; it was not actually finished till June, 1863, when she had been at work on it for nearly two years. Indeed, more than two years had elapsed since the journey to Florence to collect material and copy.

The year 1863 opened with a certain anxiety since Thornton, the second son, was to go up for an examination for admission into the Indian Civil Service. He failed to pass and left a few months later to take up farming in Natal, where he received the spinal injury from which he never recovered.

George Eliot was alone for a fortnight that Spring, for Lewes went to Hofwyl to see his youngest son, Herbert. In May she wrote in her journal that " she had killed Tito in great excitement." After that she worked rapidly and the book was ready on June 9. A few days later Lewes carried her off to the Isle of Wight, where they stayed for the most part at Niton.

§

Did George Smith repent of his bargain ? The sales of *Cornhill* diminished beneath the untoward weight of *Romola*. The fresh ground George Eliot broke in this novel was little acceptable to readers who asked of her those incomparable middle-class and provincial scenes which had delighted them in *Adam Bede*, the *Mill* and *Silas*.

All her learning, her indefatigable digging in the libraries of Florence, could not enable her to reconstruct a period of whose essential struggles she knew nothing. Savonarola is never in the least like a Catholic, far less a priest. Romola after her conversion is more like a Methodist than a Catholic. And then the speeches that sometimes continued for a whole page, the Latin tags that embellished those enormous discourses ! . . . In almost every chapter we detect the heavy hand of Lewes. We know that George Eliot was often " hung up " while writing the book and that more than once she threatened to lay it aside ; so what more natural than that he should come to her aid ? He added his dullness to hers. No one, it can be safely said, could adequately reconstruct that fiery period of Florentine history without an inward, personal knowledge of Catholicism which George Eliot could not in the nature of things possess. If it be true that easy writing makes hard reading, it is equally true that difficult writing makes even harder.

The historical novel always has its devotees, but they do not comprise the greater part of the reading public. Travel in Italy during the 'sixties was then the privilege of the wealthy or the refuge of the impoverished; it was not the commonplace it has since become when everyone with £20 at their disposal may enjoy a comprehensive, if rather swift, survey of the peninsula. And English people were not then particularly interested in Savonarola. The Italian and Latin interpolations must have fretted the ignorance of many of those who had enjoyed *Adam Bede* and the *Mill*.

Still praise flowed in although not in the same measure as heretofore. George Eliot answered one of her critics, Mr. R. H. Hutton, whose article on *Romola* had especially disconcerted her. Across her pedantic attempt at self-justification, it is possible to detect a bitter disappointment, a hint of wounded pride, a yearning for the appreciation that had been denied from such a quarter.

I am sorry she has attracted you so little, for the great problem of her life, which essentially coincides with a chief problem in Savonarola's, is one that readers need helping to understand. But with regard to that and to my whole book my predominant feeling is—not that I have achieved anything but—that great, great facts have struggled to find a voice through me and have only been able to speak brokenly. . . .

She must have learned through Mr. George Smith that the book as a serial in *Cornhill* had proved a failure. And this is hardly astonishing, since it does not possess a single quality that editors will tell you is necessary for a story which is to be published in instalments. While he looked ruefully at his bargain—for £7,000 is never a negligible sum—Mr. Blackwood, on the other hand, must have rejoiced that he had not made a more munificent offer in order to obtain *Romola* for *Maga*.

§

Herbert soon followed Thornton to South Africa, to that openair farming life which is supposed to be so healthy for young Englishmen. That they neither of them survived it for many years is nothing to the purpose, but George Eliot, who provided the outfits, money for the journey, in fact all that was essential to expedite the departure of two unwanted youths, has sometimes been blamed for her decision to exile them. It is true that she didn't want them at home; they interrupted her work; they had not the wit and address of the " dear boy " Charles. And Lewes did not believe

they were his sons. Thornton Hunt had stood godfather to
" Thornie," who was named after him ; and both children were born
after their father had grave reason to doubt the " Rosebud's "
fidelity.

Charles was different. He behaved in a most filial manner to
George Eliot, addressing her as Mutter or Mater. She called him
" Grub " and wrote earnestly affectionate letters to him, in which
the possessive tone is emphasized. When he was about to leave
Hofwyl with something of regret, she wrote as follows :

I fear you will miss a great many things in exchanging Hofwyl with its
snowy mountains and glorious spaces for a very moderate home in the
neighbourhood of London. You will have a less varied and more arduous
life : but the time of *Entbehrung* or *Entsagung* must begin, you know, for
every mortal of us—and let us hope that we shall all—father and mother
and sons—help one another with love.

But Charles was a young man ; he knew perfectly well that his
own mother was alive and living apart from his father, and that the
" Mrs. Lewes " he called Mutter, had right to neither title. Still he
was a sensible and wary youth and recognized the source from which
flowed the wealth that had lifted them all from hazardous poverty
to a condition of unexpected opulence. And he took his cue from
this letter. He must work ; he must earn his own bread, shape his
own career. His education had been an unusually expensive one,
and now he was called upon to repay in some measure all that had
been done for him.

Thornton and Herbert were given less opportunity to offer this
mutual help in the way of love. They were packed off to make their
own way in the world while still in their 'teens, but this was no
unusual procedure in the last century when boys were flung out of
the nest as quickly as possible to fend for themselves.

With the " boys " off their hands Lewes and George Eliot were
able to look about for a house, and after a great deal of discussion
and many quite unnecessary fears, they finally decided upon a
somewhat ambitious abode at 21 North Bank, Regent's Park,
called the Priory. It was a charming Regency house of character,
faced with stucco and standing in its own grounds, where roses and
other flowers flourished. One of its long bay windows opened upon
the garden where there were shady trees. It was quiet, away from
the noise of traffic, in short, it was a desirable spot for a busy nervous
woman. Of course it was a larger and far more important abode
than anything they had hitherto inhabited, but then it was a far
cry from the small lodgings at Richmond where the scratching of
Lewes's pen had nearly driven her mad to their present opulence.

Still, there is a suggestion that she would have preferred something simpler when she writes : " I think after all I like a clean kitchen better than any other room. . . ." It was little Polly Evans speaking from Griff. . . .

They could not at once move in as there was much painting and papering to be done. There is no evidence in George Eliot's books that she had any " feeling " for furniture or even decoration. She lacked taste judging from her clothes, which had been a source of mortification to her friends ever since those far-off Genevan days, when the Marquise de St. Germain had taught her how to do her hair. Thus we find that she gladly relinquished the task of decorating the new home to Mr. Owen Jones. He too reproached her for her " neglect of personal adornment " and at the subsequent—and disastrous—house-warming she appeared attired in grey *moiré* antique trimmed with real lace.

It was a terrible evening. A greater " frost " could not have been imagined. Invitations were sent out to a hundred and fifty people deemed worthy of such a unique privilege, for Lewes wished to celebrate at once their new home and the inauguration of the *Fortnightly Review* of which he was to be editor. It was all planned on a large attractive scale. Music, to be supplied by professional performers. A marvellous supper . . . the rooms gaily lit with countless candles. George Eliot handsomely attired in grey *moiré* antique. Lewes in unaccustomed evening dress which he had donned with the air of a martyr. Nothing to do now but to await the arrival of the hundred and fifty invited guests. . . .

Presently a couple drifted in. The chairs, the musicians, the lights and flowers provided the melancholy evidence that a large company was expected. But as yet no sound of that rapid succession of carriages approaching the Priory could be heard. Another couple was followed by a single man. Twelve persons with difficulty were mustered to that entertainment. The music began. Lewes did his best with his chatter, his invincible histrionic quality, to make the entertainment pass off as if nothing untoward had happened. But for George Eliot it was an evening of unmitigated humiliation. When the few faithful ones had departed she was in tears. Not all her fame as a writer, not all the wealth she had won, could induce people to come to her house. It was a tacit refusal to acknowledge Mrs. Lewes. . . .

Of course, the weather was bad. . . . Some of the guests had pleaded illness, others could not venture out on such a wet night. George Eliot tried to talk but her tongue felt like lead, as she afterwards expressed it. The next day she was ill in bed. How happy were those who died young ! . . . The year 1865 had had its distinctly bad moments for her. " I am going to work doggedly at my novel, seeing what determination can do in the face of despair."

The cold reception accorded to *Romola*, the humiliation of her almost unattended party, had robbed her of something of her spring. It was in this mood that in March she began *Felix Holt, the Radical.*

Perhaps the one happy event was the marriage of Charles Lewes to Miss Gertrude Hill, sister of the famous Octavia Hill, and granddaughter of Lewes's old friend, Dr. Southwood Smith. She was very handsome, had a beautiful contralto voice, and the young people adored each other. Indeed, he had fallen in love with her as a mere boy and was in his twenty-second year when he married her.

Once more George Eliot enjoyed that *solitude à deux* which she preferred to any other life. There was space and to spare at the Priory ; it offered her all she could wish for the calm uninterrupted exercise of her talent. But there was no urgent need for her to write, as there had been twelve years earlier ; she was already in possession of an income that amply sufficed for their needs, and it seemed that no part of it need be diverted upon the entertainment of others. Thus, there was not that imperative need to produce, since the *Fortnightly*, under the ægis of Lewes, promised success. She had everything . . . and yet something was wanting.

§

George Smith, discouraged perhaps by the financial returns of *Romola*, declined to give the £5,000 for *Felix Holt* which Lewes demanded. Blackwood was more complaisant and published the book. It was finished at the end of May, 1866, " after days and nights of throbbing and palpitation, chiefly, I suppose, from a kind of nervous excitement which I was not strong enough to support well."

Lewes was also feeling the strain, as well he might. A week later they left for Holland, where at Rotterdam she visited the synagogue, where an attempt had been made to assassinate Spinoza. She also attended an evening service at which no women were present, and was moved to tears by the spectacle of this feeble survival of what had once been a sublime religion ! . . . They spent about a fortnight there and then, more on account of Lewes's health than her own, proceeded to Schwalbach to take the waters. At the hotel they dined in their own room. She couldn't face a *table d'hôte* composed chiefly of her own countrymen and presided over by an English parson. " I am miserably *gênée*," she wrote, " by the glances of strange eyes." Her marvellous reputation, as well as her irregular relations with Lewes, made her undoubtedly an object of the keenest, though not always the pleasantest, curiosity.   And perhaps she realized that those of her compatriots who would be most eager to seek her acquaintance would be the very ones she would least wish to know.

They took refuge in the solitude they preferred.   Something that was ultimately sensitive and desirous of praise and approval in her made George Eliot shrink from the strange eyes, full of curiosity, perhaps even full of condemnation.

On their return she resumed work on the *Spanish Gypsy*, a drama in verse.   They planned to remain in England that year, but when winter came Lewes's health made it absolutely essential that they should go to the South.   On their way to Biarritz they stayed in Paris and made the acquaintance of that historic character, Mme Mohl, at whose house they met Renan.   From Biarritz they travelled through Spain to get the atmosphere for the new drama.   In March they returned to a cold and snowy England.

There was a cheque from Blackwood for £2,166, which included the first instalment for *Felix Holt* and £500 towards the £1,000 he had offered for ten years' copyright of her cheap editions.   In July the final instalments reached her.   She had thus made £13,000 in two years.

They were able now to indulge their love of travelling.   Germany, Switzerland and Italy were all in turn revisited.   But in the year 1869 she set herself a definite task.   There had been no novel since *Felix Holt*, and the publication of the *Spanish Gypsy* had not been a conspicuous success.   There is little lyrical quality in her poetry ; she was always much more of a philosopher than a poet.   But now she must write a novel, and that novel was *Middlemarch*.   There was also to be a poem on *Timoleon*. . . .

§

Browning was perhaps the influence that had stirred within her an ambition to write poetry.   He was now a frequent visitor at the Priory, was admitted to that charmed circle where the Sibyl sat attired in solemn clothes, her abundant greying hair draped in black lace.   He quoted freely and talked "admirably of versification," he was, indeed, an enthusiast on the subject.

And then she and Lewes had visited Oxford, had been introduced to that intriguing *ménage*, the Mark Pattisons' at Lincoln College. The elderly don, Rector of Lincoln, and his brilliant wife, nearly thirty years younger than himself, did undoubtedly give George Eliot the nucleus of her new novel, although Pattison did not resemble Casaubon any more than his wife resembled Dorothea. Still, there was the situation, ready to hand, and Mrs. Mark Pattison

gave the excellent people of Oxford much food for speculative
gossip. She was beautifully dressed at an epoch when the wives
of other dons wore more sober and conventionally provincial gar-
ments ; she was clever, being an excellent French scholar ; she was
something too of an artist. Rhoda Broughton, in her brilliant novel
Belinda, used the plot—if plot it can be called—in a lighter and yet
more deeply tragic manner.

The work was laid aside for the moment and George Eliot and
Lewes went to Italy, seeing Ravenna and Assisi, which were both
new to them, and revisiting Rome and Florence. This was a highly
important journey for her, since she met her future husband, Mr.
John Walter Cross, for the first time. The encounter took place in
Rome, where George Eliot and Lewes were staying at the Hotel
Minerva, and was the outcome of a chance meeting with Cross's
sister, Mrs. Bullock—then on her honeymoon—in the beautiful picture
gallery of the Palazzo Doria. Mr. Cross arrived in Rome a few days
later with his mother and an unmarried sister, and was invited to
the hotel. He always retained a very vivid impression of George
Eliot sitting beside his mother on a sofa, and was especially struck
by her fine brows, thick auburn hair, the long head broadening at
the back, the penetrating grey-blue eyes, and the " finely-formed
thin transparent hands." He was particularly eager to meet her for
he was an ardent admirer of her novels. Cross was then a young
man, under thirty years of age, and there was undoubtedly something
of hero-worship in his reverent attitude. This was a novel experience for George Eliot, who had never been lionized and had
lived more or less the life of a recluse since her association with
Lewes. Many of the sweets of success were denied to her, and
although a few old friends remained faithful, she had never mingled
freely with her congeners. Proud and sensitive, there was always a
little teazing doubt in her mind as to her reception, a fear lest
people should fail to interpret her " nobly." Cross, however,
accepted her without hesitation, and what is more his quite con-
ventionally-minded relations were enchanted to have the privilege
of meeting so famous a person. Their interpretation was perfectly
adequate and they parted with mutual regret and a determination
not to lose sight of each other.

George Eliot left for Florence on the following day. Cross must
often have felt how near he had been to missing her altogether.

Trouble awaited them on their return to the Priory. George
Eliot thought she had placed the " boys " to great advantage when
she gave them outfits and guns and packed them off to South Africa.
And now here was Thornton back on their hands, after six years.

He had left them a splendid young fellow of nineteen, over six feet in height ; he came back to them a hopeless invalid to whom it was impossible not to offer sanctuary. He was suffering from a long-standing spinal injury, and was " sadly wasted." For the next few months he claimed the whole of their care and attention.

At first he reacted to these ministrations, but as time slipped by he grew steadily worse and could not be moved even into the garden of the Priory. Mme Bodichon, who was then in England, went twice a week to sit with him. Fiction was laid aside during this gloomy interlude and George Eliot occupied herself with writing those eleven sonnets, which though never great poetry have a certain delicate charm, as when she says :

> But were another childhood world my share
> I would be born a little sister there.

While sitting with the dying man she read Shakespeare and her beloved Dante. But Byron never held any message for her and she dismissed him with a certain acerbity. " He was the most vulgar-minded genius that ever produced a great effect in literature." This of the poet who wrote that matchless lyric *The Isles of Greece*, and was capable of such a phrase as " *She walks in beauty like the night.*"

In August—the month when *Middlemarch* was begun—there was a visit to Weybridge and the exciting friendship with the Cross family was duly resumed. The Bullocks were present, and Mrs. Bullock, who was something of a musician, sang some songs of her own setting from the *Spanish Gypsy*. One of these, *On through the woods, the pillared pines*, affected George Eliot so deeply, that she rose and embraced the young composer with tears in her eyes. This spontaneous emotion reveals a quality of sensitiveness that is not often revealed in her books. But the circumstances were slightly exceptional, for both families were passing through a time of great anxiety. There is no doubt that Lewes and George Eliot were most deeply concerned about the sufferings of Thornton, while grave fears were being entertained by the Cross family for the safety of Mrs. Bullock, who was then nearing her first confinement. Nor were these premonitions of disaster without fulfilment, for within a month she had died in childbirth, and a few weeks later Thornton was released from his long sufferings. These bereavements crystallized the links between George Eliot and her new admiring friends.

Thornton Lewes had an attack of paraplegia in August and from that time grew visibly weaker. He died in October. George Eliot described him as a " sweet-natured boy, frank, impulsive, and still a

boy despite his twenty-five years." She could at least assure herself
that she had done all that was humanly possible for him during
the last months of his life.

Opinions differ in the matter, for some of her biographers have
declared she was always like a mother to Lewes's sons, and there is
no doubt Charles was dear to her. But the other two ? . . . We
can form no opinion as to whether she really held they had any
claim upon Lewes. It is certain, however, that when Thornton lay
dying she sent for his mother to come and see him, and remained
in the background herself during that poignant meeting. It was then
nineteen years since " Rosebud " had left the six-year-old child. . . .

§

In May, 1870, George Eliot and Lewes stayed at Oxford with the
Mark Pattisons. There they met a quiet grave girl of eighteen,
first on the croquet ground and again one night at supper. She was
Miss Mary Arnold, daughter of Thomas Arnold, and after supper she
remembered that George Eliot took her aside and held her enthralled
with a description of her Spanish journey. She could hardly have
discerned in this young attentive listener one who not a couple of
decades later was to achieve, as Mrs. Humphry Ward, a fame not less
than her own and whose financial rewards were even more remarkable.

Miss Arnold could recall the spontaneous dislike she felt for
Lewes, and many years later described the scene on the croquet
ground.

The chestnuts were all out, one splendour from top to toe, the
laburnums, the lilacs, the hawthorns red and white, the new-mown grass
spreading its silky carpet round the college walls, a May sky overhead,
and through the trees glimpses of towers and spires, silver-grey, in the
sparkling summer air : the picture was one of those that Oxford throws
before the spectator at every turn. George Eliot stood on the grass in the
bright sun, looking at the flower-laden chestnuts, at the distant glimpses
on all sides of the surrounding city, saying little—that she left to Mr.
Lewes !—but drinking it in, storing it in that rich absorbent mind of hers.

Later that summer they went to Cromer and Whitby. They were
at Limpsfield when the Franco-Prussian War broke out, and George
Eliot was whole-heartedly on the side of Germany, which is hardly
surprising, for she was always far more in sympathy with the Teutonic
than with the Latin culture, despite her vaunted passion for Dante.

As it was impossible to go abroad then they rented Mrs. Gilchrist's
cottage at Petersfield for a few months. George Eliot was still
struggling with an attempt to write poetry, but it did not come
easily to her.

In December, Lewes's aged mother died. It does not seem that she and George Eliot ever met, so we can only suppose that she failed to interpret her nobly. But Lewes contributed to her support till the end.

By the end of 1870 only one hundred pages of *Middlemarch* had been written. The book progressed slowly and the first part was not published until a year later. It was issued in eight parts, appearing in volume form in 1873. By the readers of that day it was preferred to her other books, the supposition that it was something of a *roman à clef*, lending a certain zest to the interest it aroused. Be that as it may it surpassed in rich pecuniary rewards all its predecessors. Its sales were enormous, for upwards of twenty thousand copies were sold in a year, and she found herself the richer by £12,000. George Eliot was aware now that her power of holding the public was by no means exhausted. *Romola* had proved an acid test ; with *Middlemarch* she was reinstated in popular favour.

There were visits to Oxford and Cambridge in 1873. College life was unfamiliar and she gave dark blue caps and shirts to the Cambridge crew. At Oxford they stayed with Jowett. They took the waters at Homburg that summer, making a stay in France afterwards. But now those peaceful watering-places of France seemed to her more attractive than the more fashionable ones of Germany.

All this time the intimacy with the Cross family deepened. And there were other friendships. Mrs. Burne-Jones, for instance, who had the temerity to express affection for her. " I like not only to be loved but also to be told that I am loved," she wrote in reply. There was something of Maggie Tulliver in that wistful phrase.

Sometimes she would look into the new novels of the day to see what the younger generation were doing. Nearly a couple of decades had passed since she published her first venture in fiction ; she had been producing practically ever since, and perhaps she felt a decrease of power within herself. Her work was more laboured ; it was an effort, it lacked the delightful spontaneity of *Adam Bede* and the *Mill*. It tended to be prosy and didactic. And then had not Tennyson told her that everyone nowadays wrote so well ? What would he have said sixty years later when the young—sometimes even the very young—reveal an assured technique, even a penetrating insight into what at least constitutes their own world ?

But the effect of these literary excursions upon George Eliot was " paralysing." She knew she could not emulate the picturesque prose of Ouida (alas, so unread and forgotten now !) whose intimate knowledge of Italy sprang from a long residence in that country. That vigorous pen had been at work for more than ten years, pouring

M

forth romance after romance in beautiful and even haunting prose, despite the superficial absurdity of many of the scenes and characters. There was Rhoda Broughton, then at the height of her fame, never obtruding her profound literary knowledge in her books, but betraying it by many a sign, and possessing the power of endowing a situation with humour as well as with deep underlying tragedy. No, these were all "paralysing," and although George Eliot read Anne Thackeray's stories with enjoyment and Trollope's out of affection they did not help her. She could not learn that more modern idiom. . . .

§

George Eliot and Lewes had not so far embarked upon a country house of their own, and usually rented a furnished one for the summer unless they went abroad. Thus in 1875 we find them settled at Rickmansworth in a " good old red-brick Georgian house with a nice bit of garden and meadow and river at the back." The summer of that year was, however, a wet one, and she found the place damp and misty.

Letters to Mr. Cross display a warm affection. He was so very much younger—more than twenty years—so that she could write to him in this wise without being misinterpreted.

Let us have news of you all soon. Let us comfort each other while it is day, for the night cometh.

Like all the women of her day, George Eliot had alluded to herself as old from the time she was forty, so at fifty-six it was only natural that she should watch for the approach of night.

At the end of July they received the news of the death of Lewes's youngest son, Herbert, in South Africa.

On the 15th of June we went to a house we had taken at Rickmansworth. Here in the end of July we received the news that our dear Bertie had died on June 29th.

That was the brief entry in her journal. Otherwise the event passed without comment. " Our dear Bertie. . . ." The climate had proved as fatal to him as it had done to " Thornie." He was twenty-seven years of age and left a wife and child. Nothing is known of his last illness nor did his passing bequeath any kind of melancholy or interruption of their usual life.

Daniel Deronda was then in progress. The first scene was suggested during their visit to Homburg where George Eliot saw a girl of five-and-twenty gambling at the tables. Some uprush from her early education made her shrink appalled from the sight, " of one so young completely in the grasp of this mean money-making demon."

Stimulated by the success of *Middlemarch*—and if she affected to despise money, it is quite certain that Lewes, who had for many years been a very poor man, did not do so—George Eliot worked steadily at this new venture. Whilst writing it she would not " risk reading any other English fiction." When they went for a brief visit to Wales their manuscripts were prudently deposited in the bank as became such precious assets. They returned from Wales in October and the two first volumes were in print by December 1. She herself professed to think poorly of the book, but Mr. Lewes and Blackwood " were full of satisfaction."

Indeed, it must be said that throughout her career George Lewes gave her that encouraging and stimulating praise which her spirit needed. Most authors have probably learned from experience that while they may please an unknown public whose appreciation is often conveyed to them by spontaneous letters, they nearly always have to endure a lack of encouragement on the part of relations and personal friends. Did not " Margaret Ogilvy " sigh over her son's books, regretting that James Barrie was, alas, not a Stevenson ? Yet surely R.L.S. never tasted such success nor received such pecuniary rewards as did her son later in his career. . . . It is said that Mrs. Benson conscientiously read all the many books written by her three sons, and rarely found anything to like in them. . . . Lewes wished Charlotte Brontë to model herself upon Jane Austen, while Mr. Clarke, the Royal Librarian, urged the immortal Jane to write a historical romance upon the House of Cobourg. Authors, therefore, should take heart of grace. . . .

Still, whatever may be the verdict of future generations *Daniel Deronda*, with its Jewish hero, does make the dullest reading in the world. It is dreary and even gloomy and one marvels at the satisfaction of Lewes and Blackwood. But at the time it was not without its admirers, even among persons who counted, and it evoked considerable discussion when it was first published in 1876. Bernal Osborne was heard to affirm that the very best parts were the scenes between Grandcourt and Lush. This pleased George Eliot, who comforted herself with the reflection that he had probably seen more of the Grandcourt and Lush kind of life than most of her critics.

They were both suffering more than usual that year from indifferent health—it is wonderful to observe what an important part these headaches, colds and minor ailments played in their lives—and in June they went abroad with the intention of going South. But

George Eliot was taken ill at Aix and feared the prospect of even greater heat, so after a visit to Les Charmettes they went to Berne and Ragatz. The latter place completely restored her health ; she was able to walk for four or five hours a day. Still, she was beginning to dread those long journeys which were Lewes's delight. After spending three months abroad, they returned home. During their absence they had heard of the deaths of those two remarkable women—George Sand and Harriet Martineau.

Daniel Deronda in four volumes greeted her on arrival at the Priory. In this form the sale at two guineas exceeded that of *Middlemarch*, so that she had no cause to complain of any falling off in public interest or estimation. It was her last novel, though not her last book.

In October they paid a visit to Mr. Bullock at Six Mile Bottom with all its memories of Byron and Augusta Leigh. Their host had now changed his name to that of Hall. Here they met Turguéniev, deeply distressed at the death of George Sand. " What a heart of gold was hers, what an absence of all false and unworthy sentiment, what a brave man she was and what a good woman ! " The clouds that darkened his last years had not then begun to gather, and he was busy with a translation of Flaubert's *La Légende de Saint Julien l'Hospitallier*.

His encounter with George Eliot was an immense success. " They had innumerable bonds of sympathy " comments Mr. Cross.

§

In December, 1876, George Eliot resolved to buy a country house and decided upon the Heights, Witley, near Godalming, with eight or nine acres of land. Despite the beauty of the surrounding landscape, she feared it might prove insufficiently bracing for health. But one of its great attractions was that it was within fairly easy reach of Weybridge and the delightful Cross family.

They spent Christmas with them that year, only " the greater part of the time I was not well enough to enjoy greatly the pleasures their affection prepared for us." One can imagine that George Eliot was a trifle heavy in hand on a festive occasion.

The New Year opened stormily " with threat of war in the East." But " as to our private life all is happiness, perfect love, and undiminished intellectual interest."

Now she corrected *Romola* for a cheap edition, reading it for the first time for ten years and apparently with pleasure. She could still feel that it was written with her " best blood," and sobbed with " painful joy " as she read those long-forgotten sentences. She used to say that after a year she no longer felt that complete identification with her books " which gives such zest to the sense of authorship," but this is an experience which is probably common to all prolific writers.

I generally like them best at that distance, but then I feel they might just as well have been written by somebody else.

The summer was spent at Witley, and George Eliot enjoyed many games of tennis, despite her fifty-seven years. They found themselves in a sociable neighbourhood where they were kindly and hospitably received. Perhaps—who knows ?—Mr. Cross had prepared the way. There were the Harrisons at Sutton Place. Not far off was Tennyson, whose acquaintance they made. The Edmund Gurneys—then recently married—lunched with them ; the Du Mauriers came to dinner. Mr. Cross, then greatly preoccupied with his mother's illness, sought consolation at the Heights. It was greatly in his favour that he got on so well with Lewes. . . .

" Oh, that we were all of one mind, and that mind good ! " George Eliot wrote to Mrs. (afterwards Lady) Ponsonby, whose acquaintance she had recently made and to whom some of her loftiest and most moralizing letters were now addressed.

She refused to contribute a volume on Shakespeare to the " English Men of Letters " series. And although it was true she was moving cautiously in society, no one must for a moment imagine that this could lead to any more public display, and she declined an invitation from Mrs. Peter Taylor to speak at a meeting with considerable *hauteur*.

I thought you understood that I have grave reasons for not speaking on certain public topics. No request from the best friend in the world— even from my own husband—ought to induce me to speak when I judge it my duty to be silent.

§

Il y a dans les liaisons qui se prolongent quelque chose de si profond ! Was literary London veering round to this opinion expressed by Benjamin Constant in his *Adolphe* ? More than ten years had passed since that disastrous house-warming when the musicians performed to empty chairs, and now instead of formal parties the Sunday receptions at the Priory had taken a definite place in the London spectacle. Many intelligent observers of the sedate " seventies " have recorded their impressions of these solemn gatherings.

Not many women. . . . To obtain that rare privilege they must ask for it even as one might with humility request an audience of

Royalty. And the British matrons of that day were certainly not going to plead for favours from " Mrs. Lewes," although some of the younger and more adventurous women did not hesitate to do so. But there were men in plenty, the list of names including many celebrities, among whom were Tennyson, Browning, Sir Leslie Stephen, Locker Lampson, Herbert Spencer and Huxley. Still it was an ordeal. George Eliot sat on the left of the fireplace, remote, aloof, sibylline, a chair placed near her for the favoured interlocutor. George Lewes made tea—it would be too much for " Her." And the rules were strict. The one unpardonable offence was to mention her books, and as six o'clock struck the company must disperse. No one stayed longer ; that would have been unthinkable. None of that last lingering, that unwillingness to tear oneself away which so flatters the successful hostess. It was all solemn and orderly and punctual. No free-and-easy mingling, though Lewes chattered bravely to keep things going. George Eliot did not move among the crowd, saying a word here and there, giving a friendly smile and gesture to the shy newcomer as the hostess who is also a woman of the world will do. She sat there speaking only upon serious themes, while Lewes roamed eagerly, anxiously, among the guests, his absurd little boyish form oddly at variance with his wrinkled face and grey hair and whiskers. A clown but a brave one. . . .

Ill-advised persons brought propitiatory gifts to lay at that shrine. But George Eliot had all Charlotte Brontë's dislike of such offerings —an echo perhaps of that atavistic primitive fear which is expressed in the Greek adage : Distrust the hand that brings a gift. . . . Locker Lampson brought a cherished Rembrandt etching—surely enough to melt the heart of any woman—but had it been an oleograph reproduction or a steel engraving of some modern picture, it could not have been more coldly received. But she had little feeling for art, except where music was concerned, and the only picture that was ever known to move her was Raphael's *Madonna di San Sisto*. And a worse fate awaited Henry James, who gave her one of his own books and found it hastily thrust into his hand in the hall as he was leaving by a nervous apologetic Lewes. " She " had so little time. . . . James bore no malice ; he liked to be permitted—as he was then a young man—to sit at her feet even if his proffered gifts were rejected. " The great George Eliot is both sweet and superior," he wrote, " and has a delightful expression in her large, liny, pale, and equine face. I had my turn sitting beside her and being conversed with in a low but most harmonious tone, and bating a tendency to *aborder* only the highest themes I have no fault to find with her." The long duration of the adventure—now a couple of decades old

—combined with the harmonious and distinctly highbrow atmosphere that prevailed at the Priory, the personality of the two elderly
protagonists who lived a life of such apparently prosaic respectability
seemed to challenge Mrs. Grundy to remember the negligible fact
that the real Mrs. George Lewes was still alive. George Eliot had
won through, and at Witley the same story was repeated and people
were attracted to the Heights by the fame of its châtelaine.

For once she did not see eye to eye with Lewes when in his
exuberant hospitality he invited the Burne-Joneses with their
children, to spend Christmas with them. Was he craving for young
fresh faces around him ? Charles spent the feast with his wife's
relations ; there were three babies now to call George Eliot grand-
mamma. She could not face such an infraction of that cherished
solitude-à-deux, and she wrote to cancel the invitation.

We are two dull old people and they ought to have a group of young
persons to be joyful with. . . .

At the end of the year she bade a solemn farewell to her journal
which she had kept so meticulously for upwards of a quarter of a
century and which gives us such invaluable insight into the manner
in which her work was accomplished. Perhaps, however, when she
wrote the words she had some premonition of the tragic change that
awaited her in 1878. . . .

§

In June, George Eliot and Lewes dined with Mr., afterwards Lord,
Goschen, to " meet " the Crown Prince and Princess of Germany.
Queen Victoria's daughter ? . . . No one could surely venture to call
her ugly names after that. There were present also, Lord and Lady
Ripon, Dean Stanley, the Queen's favourite prelate, whose views
on hell were so comfortingly heterodox, and the Bishop of Peter-
borough. Literature was represented by Froude and Kinglake.
Royalty . . . the Church of England . . . the news was communicated speedily to the Brays. And surely this would be a lesson
for Griff. . . . But Griff remained aloof in an obstinate, impenetrable
silence.

Again the summer was spent at Witley. More neighbours enlivened
the Heights, Sir Henry and Lady Holland, Mrs. Thellusson, Mrs.
Greville, and the Allinghams as well as the Harrisons, Du Mauriers
and above all Tennyson. George Eliot, weary perhaps of fiction,
was writing a dull book, *Theophrastus Such*. But careful and thrifty
as she was, they were no longer dependent upon her earnings and
she might well have laid her pen aside.

However, a cloud had gathered despite the brilliant social success that was now so tardily hers. Lewes was ill. His little gnome-like form was less thin than emaciated. He suffered at times from spasms of unbearable pain. He was then sixty-one and looked like a wizened monkey. When the pain passed his gay spirits returned ; he would even sing the tenor part of the *Barber of Seville* with great *brio* in a high weak voice. His audience in the drawing-room at Witley consisted of George Eliot and Mr. Cross. It never occurred to him to be jealous of Cross. He was so young and " She " was close on sixty. . . .

They were back at the Priory when Lewes's illness definitely declared itself. One November afternoon they went for a drive and on their return he complained of fatigue—he, who so rarely complained in his constant preoccupation for " Her " health. Fever and severe pains in the head were accompanied by symptoms of a more serious character.

Sir James Paget came and assured her that the trouble would soon be allayed ; he gave grounds for hope. George Eliot did no work—she never did any more—for just before he was taken ill the faithful Lewes had despatched *Theophrastus* to Blackwood. It was indeed finished in a " state of exhilarated activity," the very day of that fatal drive. And Lewes's work was also finished ; he would never tie up any more parcels nor see that she was not sitting in a draught. He died ten days later, on November 28, 1878, falling, as she said, " gently asleep." It was then little short of a quarter of a century since they had flung that challenge in the face of an astonished public and eloped to Antwerp and Weimar.

" Here I and sorrow sit," she quoted on January 1, 1879, and a little later she wrote tragically to Mrs. Burne-Jones : " The world's winter is going, I hope, but my everlasting winter has set in."

It had been bad enough to know she was never Lewes's wife, but it was far, far harder to face the fact that she was not his widow.

Charles Lewes assisted her in the task—to her a sacred one—of arranging his father's manuscripts. For the rest she shut herself up after the manner of Victorian widows following an august example. She hugged her grief. She would have no one know that any other activities absorbed her ; even the fact that she was correcting the proofs of *Theophrastus* was rigorously concealed. Her grief must be dramatized. . . .

Her love for Lewes had undergone no change during those twenty-four years of practically unbroken companionship ; it was the one passion of her life. For him she had sacrificed her good name, her reputation, the place in the world that her great fame must have secured for her. Nor had his life been without sacrifice ; he had renounced all thought of a career of his own in the world of letters, so that he might devote himself wholly to shielding her and her talent.

Still, despite all he could do for her, and he did a very great deal, he was powerless in the one direction. The life she had chosen could never have been easy, and its difficulties were increased a thousand-fold when she became so suddenly celebrated. As Mr. and Mrs. Lewes, obscure and comparatively unknown except to their own immediate circle, they could have passed unobserved, but fame flung its relentless searchlight upon George Eliot and all the world knew she was living with a man who was not her husband. There were moments when the pricks must have become almost unbearable to one of so sensitive and reserved a disposition. Her shrinking from strange eyes at a table d'hôte dinner, her flat refusal to speak in public, her clinging to that precious solitude with Lewes, all tell their own tale of a permanently defensive attitude. People called her Mrs. Lewes as the sure and only passport to her friendship, but she had no right to the title. She wished to be known as a great moral teacher, but who would accept such lessons seriously from a woman in her lamentable position ? . . .

Had she loved Lewes less she must have left him when fame and fortune were laid so abundantly at her feet. But there was never any question of that nor, indeed, any sign of wavering on either side. All her manuscripts were dedicated in that exquisite script of hers to her beloved husband, for as such she had taught herself to think of him. She did everything that was possible to place his three sons adequately in the world. Charles's children were her " grand-children " ; his wife was her daughter-in-law. Only the supreme sacrifice which Christian morality would have imposed upon her had been wanting. Not for any reason in the world would she have renounced her love for George Lewes. She preferred in her own words to " do without opium and live through all her pain with conscious clear-eyed endurance."

But to face the world alone, never a wife and now not a widow, was a task that proved beyond her strength. . . .

§

Some two months after Lewes's death she wrote to John Walter Cross, who had been assiduous in letters and enquiries, but had so far been rigorously excluded from the shrine.

Some time, if I live, I shall be able to see you—perhaps sooner than anyone else—but not yet. Life seems to get harder instead of easier. . . .

Still, she wished to live a little longer to accomplish certain things for Lewes's sake. His manuscripts to be arranged for the press, a studentship to be founded at Cambridge in his memory.

Even as late as February 7, when the bulbs had begun to push up in the Priory gardens and the birds were singing in the trees, she had not been able to venture beyond the gates. Mme Bodichon offered herself as companion for a trip abroad, thinking this might distract her, but it was firmly declined. " Each day seems a new beginning—a new acquaintance with grief."

But on the twenty-third of that month Cross was admitted for the first time. He invited her to stay with him and his sisters at Weybridge. His mother had lately died so that he was himself in great grief. She refused the invitation, pleading that the work she had in hand necessitated constant reference to her books. But the ice was broken. Her solitude had been invaded.

Other people came. In March Gertrude Lewes brought her children to tea. Mr. Henry Sidgwick was admitted in order to discuss the plans for the studentship. On March 22 she saw Mrs. Burne-Jones and Mrs. Congreve. Only they must never, never tell anyone they had been to the Priory. No one must know she received visitors, still less that she was correcting the proofs of *Theophrastus*, or that she drove daily to Kilburn and walked " in perfect solitude " among the fields and budding hedgerows. The world must still believe her to be plunged in irremediable and unmitigated woe. There was no effort to accept grief simply and take up her daily life of writing, walking and seeing a few intimate friends without this seal of secrecy. But she could evince indignation at this " unjustifiable war " in South Africa. . . .

As the Spring advanced she began to feel a " dreadful need " of Mr. Cross's counsel, which he was only too eager and anxious to give. They saw each other constantly—of course no one must know !—they read Dante together and she stimulated his admiration for her favourite cantos. " It was renovation of life," wrote this humble worshipper, for had he not always offered her that adulation which a young man will often bestow spontaneously upon an elderly and famous woman ? In May he persuaded her to play to him ; it was the first time she had touched the piano since Lewes's death. And then—most momentous step of all—she left London and went to Witley and they met regularly twice a week, even oftener.

She was still very thin, and Mme Bodichon records that in her " long loose black dress she looked like the black shadow of herself." Nevertheless the world began once more to interest her ; she emerged, she mingled with her friends. And then towards the beginning of June she fell ill.

It wasn't a question this time of severe headache, of lassitude; there was a definite malady. Sir James Paget and Sir Andrew Clark came down to consult with the Godalming doctor. Oh, she had all she wanted—she wrote to assure Mrs. Burne-Jones. . . . She had her servants, her excellent doctor; she had constant care. And besides that there was a devoted friend who came daily to make certain that she needed nothing.

In July she was better—marvellously better—and invited Gertrude and Herbert's widow with their children—five in all—to come down and eat the strawberries. By September she was stronger and had put on flesh. She selected among several candidates a young Edinburgh man, Doctor Charles Roy, to be the first recipient of the " George Lewes Studentship."

During the winter and the early spring of 1880 she was back at the Priory, where Mr. Cross was her constant companion. He was especially welcome because he had admired Lewes so much, and was always ready to speak of him in reverent terms. She was no longer afraid of meeting people; the Kilburn lanes never saw her. She and Cross visited the National Gallery, the British and South Kensington Museums. And Cross went very warily during those months of probation. Still, more than a year had passed since Lewes's death. . . .

Towards the end of March George Eliot went to Weybridge to stay with Cross and his sisters. The ladies received her with due affection and sympathy during the two days of her visit. They knew and approved of their brother's wish to marry her.

On April 9, after due hesitation, George Eliot became engaged to him. It was true that she was sixty-one and he not yet forty, but as he seemed to desire it so very much. . . . " A friend much valued and trusted by Mr. Lewes and who now that I am alone sees his happiness in the dedication of his life to me." It was undoubtedly an egoistic attitude towards the man who was after all giving her a very great deal, but she was firm in her conviction that she was bestowing rather than accepting an honour.

And then, during all this gloomy period of mourning, he had been unfailingly attentive. She could write to his sisters of " your brother's great gift of love for me." She went back to Weybridge later that month, this time as his affianced wife, but the secret must still be kept. It was not until May 5 that she revealed it to Mme Bodichon and a few very intimate friends.

It would not, she explained, make any difference to what she intended to do for her "grandchildren," since Mr. Cross had his own fortune. He seems, indeed, to have been completely disinterested, and his reward is that he will be everlastingly remembered as "George Eliot's husband."

They planned to give up the Priory, home of so many years, of such dear associations, and Cross took a house at No. 4 Cheyne Walk, Chelsea. The summers would be spent as usual at the Heights. They were to go abroad for the honeymoon.

Afterwards many people blamed her both for marrying Cross and for not telling them beforehand of her intention. But she explained that she had not really made up her mind until a fortnight before the marriage, and throughout that time was in a state of doubt and struggle.

There was a touch of triumph in that entry she made in her journal on May 6, 1880.

> Married this day at 10.15, to John Walter Cross at St. George's, Hanover Square. Present, Charles, who gave me away, Mr. and Mrs. Druce, Mr. Hall, William, May, Eleanor and Florence Cross. We went back to the Priory where we signed our wills. Then we started for Dover and arrived there a little after five o'clock.

A marriage in church. . . . Griff must surely now emerge from its long obstinate silence. And to do it justice Griff did.

§

Some memory of that flight to Antwerp twenty-six years before must have been present in her mind, only that now she need no longer fear the gaze of strange eyes. Marian Evans—that ambiguous figure known as Mrs. Lewes—had no longer any existence. The past had swallowed her up. As Mrs. Cross she could look the whole world in the face.

Now she travelled in luxury as the bride of a rich man. They had a "millennial cabin" on the Channel steamer. The first halt was at Amiens where they visited the Cathedral and in the evening re-read "our dear cantos" of the Inferno. Then on to Paris where they had an apartment *au premier*. No need now to dole out sovereigns with miser hand ; they were both rich. To Grenoble and a visit to the Grande Chartreuse, her only regret, expressed rather oddly in a letter to Charles, being that "Pater" had not seen it. And to Mme Bodichon :

> All this, a wonderful blessing, falling to me after I thought my life was ended. . . . Deep down below there is a hidden river of sadness, but this must be always with those who have lived long—and I am able to enjoy my newly reopened life. . . .

Her friends were astonished, even dismayed, although to us now her marriage must seem the most natural step she could have taken, since it removed her from that equivocal position she had endured too long. Such an abrupt severance with the past ! . . . But was there no one with sufficient imagination to realize that despite the brave face she had shown to the world, the mere fact that she was not Lewes's wife had all the time been gnawing at the very core of her happiness ? Cross had offered her something which it had not been in Lewes's power to give, divorce at that time being by no means the simple thing it has since become.

She wrote to Charles Lewes :

Marriage has seemed to restore me to my old self. I was getting hard, and if I had decided differently I think I should have become very selfish. To feel daily the loveliness of a nature close to me and to feel grateful for it is the fountain of tenderness and strength to endure.

But really on the face of it she had very little to endure, for Cross seems to have been a most model husband, identifying himself completely with her interests, even to reading the *Inferno* on his honeymoon. . . .

Like Maggie Tulliver, she had that passionate need, not only to love, but to be loved, which lies at the root of many women's characters. With her it was accompanied by an equally urgent desire for approbation. She feared alike censure and criticism, and Lewes had done his best to shield her from both. With that example before his eyes, John Cross knew exactly where his duty lay and performed it most admirably.

Her new position, assured and secure, must have bestowed upon her an immeasurable tranquillity, a peace of mind to which she had long been a stranger.

During that honeymoon journey her health improved, and she " felt uninterruptedly well and strong." Her brother Isaac, who had taken no notice of her for twenty-six years, wrote a letter of congratulation to his errant sister, thus breaking that long silence. She was delighted with it, and in her reply told him that her only regret lay in the disparity of years, Mr. Cross being so much younger than herself.

Milan, Padua, Venice, the old ground she had so often traversed with Lewes. " I shall be a better, more loving creature than I could have been in solitude," she wrote from Verona. Only no one must for a moment imagine she had forgotten the past. From Venice she wrote :

Instead of my former affection being displaced in my mind I seem to have recovered the loving sympathy I was in danger of losing. . . . The spring seems to have risen again.

But they tarried too long in Venice, making light of the heat after the fashion of unaccustomed Northerners. Cross fell ill from the effects of the climate. When he was well enough to be moved, they went to Innsbruck and thence to Munich. During their absence she lent her house at Witley to Charles and his family, since they did not intend to return to England till August.

Cross had known her for eleven years and during that time she had been almost constantly ailing. Now she was amazingly well and apparently tireless, walking for miles, visiting museums and picture galleries, and showing no sign of fatigue. She no longer alluded to herself as an old woman—that would have been a mistake to a husband twenty years her junior.

Now they were back in England, and of course visits must be paid to Cross's sisters and to his former brother-in-law, Mr. Hall at Six-Mile-Bottom. Then Witley, as the house in Cheyne Walk was not yet ready for them. But in September Mrs. Cross's old symptoms reappeared, and for a few days she was alarmingly ill. Towards the end of the month when she was convalescent, he took her to Brighton for a change.

There was an improvement at first, but later in October Sir Andrew Clark went down to Witley to consult with Mr. Parsons, the Godalming doctor. In November she was able to resume her daily walks and drives. During her illness she wrote and told Mrs. Congreve that she had " been cared for with something better than angelic tenderness."

Her health improved ; they resumed their readings. Dante, the Bible, Milton, Wordsworth, and a few French novels, probably at Cross's suggestion. There was no sign of weariness on his part.

Her commanding brows and deep penetrating eyes were seconded by the sweet restrained impressive speech which claimed something like an awed attention from strangers.

An awed attention such as he had himself offered long years ago when first admitted to the Presence in the somewhat banal *décor* of the Hotel Minerva at Rome. . . .

§

As the house in London was still unfinished they lingered on at Witley, and a fine November rendered the country pleasant enough. They did not go to Cheyne Walk till December 3. On the following day they attended a concert at St. James's Hall with Neruda,

Piatti and Zimmerman among the performers. No need now to hide
themselves amid the crowd occupying the shilling seats. . . .
Life went on in much the usual manner. Reading and music in
the evenings. Walks and drives, visits from friends during the day.
Mrs. Congreve and Mme Belloc were admitted to this new *ménage*.
They saw the books—several thousands of them—arranged precisely
as they had been at the Priory. But this time the decoration and
colour schemes were not entrusted to " our good friend, Mr. Owen
Jones "—Cross had seen to it all himself.

And the visitors wondered a little, why when she seemed so well,
walking with ease and energy, and playing the piano, she remained
so woefully thin. It was, however, a common feature of her malady.

Two weeks after their arrival in London they attended a performance of *Agamemnon* in Greek, given by Oxford undergraduates.
A Saturday " Pop " followed, but the day was cold, the hall at once
overheated and draughty. Her cloak slipped from her shoulders
and she refused to put it on again. That evening she played to her
husband as usual, but on the following morning at breakfast she
conplained of sore throat. However, she received Herbert Spencer
when he called and began a letter to Mrs. St. Loe Strachey which
was left unfinished on her desk.

The next day—a Monday—she was critically ill, and on Wednesday, December 22, Sir Andrew Clark pronounced the pericardium
to be seriously affected. " Tell them I have a great pain in my left
side," she murmured just before becoming unconscious. She died
that same day, little more than two years after Lewes, and was
buried in a grave beside his at Highgate. She had been married just
over seven months, and was then little short of sixty-two years of age.

§

Mr. Cross gave George Eliot's journal and portions of her letters to
the world, and since then, from time to time, the veil has been partially
lifted from that enigmatic personage. But her journals reveal to us, as
nothing else can, the manner in which her books were imagined and
written, the careful way in which Lewes sheltered and nurtured
that talent at once so late in developing and putting forth its fruit
which forms part of the permanent treasure of English literature.

The novel writer is, as a rule, a novel reader, but it was not so
with George Eliot. From time to time she made an effort, as we
have seen, to read contemporary fiction, but, to use her own words,
it paralysed her. She was not really in sympathy with it, because
her career had begun as a student ; she had " turned novelist "
somewhat late in life, and had something of contempt for her craft

as practised by others who sought only to entertain and had no serious message to give to the world. That is why, perhaps, her own books owed so little to the idiom of her day ; they sprang, as it were, ripe from a brain that had been for years occupied in translating Strauss's monumental *Life of Jesus*, and Spinoza, and had perhaps never contemplated the possibility of producing any original work, least of all in the realm of fiction.

The strong formative influence of her life was undoubtedly that of George Lewes. He was not a man whom women generally liked —witness the instinctive antipathy to which Miss Arnold, afterwards Mrs. Humphry Ward, confessed. He was plain, almost grotesque, and he could jar every nerve in Charlotte Brontë's body with his criticism, which, if it was not intended to hurt, could have had no significance at all. But he was shrewd, sagacious, clever, versatile and utterly unconventional, and such as he was, George Eliot loved him with an enduring passion that death could not destroy. Perhaps it would be unjust to say as many have done, that he worked her too hard, although we can read between the lines of her journal and see how near she was to breaking down after each of those enormous books. But on the other hand, he did up the parcels, poured out the tea, restored unwelcome gifts to the astonished donors, and dealt with publishers in a manner that was surely beyond praise. And all the time, how eagerly she deferred to his opinion, how tender was her feeling for him ! . . . He gave her what she most craved for—a love and approbation that little Polly Evans had never known, either at Griff or Coventry, and which had indeed been utterly lacking in the simple farm-life from which she had sprung.

All her life she had feared solitude as a child fears the dark, and indeed, this began in her case with an actual dread of the dark. She turned to Lewes when other men had failed her, to save her from that solitude, just as after his death she turned to Cross to relieve that isolation of body and spirit. It is not easy to associate that strong massive face with its hint of masculinity with such primitive complexes, but they were of overwhelming importance in her life and must be held responsible, at least in part, for those actions for which the world is perhaps most prone to blame her. She needed a physical presence to disarm those fears that formed so large a part of her nature. Her marriage to Cross is thus as easily explained as her association with Lewes ; indeed, her marriage was the one perfectly simple and inevitable action of her life.

Mrs. Oliphant

MRS. OLIPHANT

§

MARGARET WILSON was born in 1828 at Wallyford, near Musselburgh, the youngest of six children of whom three were dead. Her two surviving brothers, Frank and William, were at least a dozen years older than herself. Her mother, delighted at the advent of a bright, intelligent little girl, made her her constant companion and devoted herself to her, although rarely deviating from that severity which was deemed necesary in those days for the proper upbringing of young children. In later years, Mrs. Oliphant confessed she had never heard an endearing word from her.

Of her birthplace she could remember nothing, her earliest recollections being of their next home in the village of Lasswade on the road to Dalkeith and some six miles from Edinburgh. She could vividly recall the return of her elder brother Frank every Saturday night to spend Sunday with his people, as well as his early departure to Edinburgh in the dark of Monday morning, for it was always in winter that she visualized the little scene. The cheerful room, the bright fire lit by Mrs. Wilson's hands, and beside which she, a very small child, sat toasting a cake of dough, while her mother bustled about to ensure that her boy should be adequately fed before his long walk back to Edinburgh, were duly observed and remembered. There were candles on the table, and outside it was dark, " but with a subtle sense of morning."

This elder brother was then to Maggie a kind of god. He was a bright clever lad, fond of his little sister, though impatient with her at times after the manner of boys. He was the " good " boy, while Willie, the younger, a handsome, gay attractive youth, early fell into those habits of self-indulgence and intemperance which made him a constant source of anxiety and shame to them all.

Maggie was six years old when her parents removed to Glasgow where Mr. Wilson had some appointment at the Customs. To her mother's intense grief the two boys had to be left behind to pursue their studies in Edinburgh.

For Maggie, only her mother, of her two parents, really counted.

The father remains always a shadowy, morose, indefinite figure in the background of her life. He took no notice of her and very little of anyone else, and when he returned home in the evening, she must keep very quiet so as not to disturb him. Mrs. Wilson, on the contrary, was the chief figure in that little household, a clever, cultivated, competent woman who kept everything going on a very meagre income, contriving to imbue that modest home with a certain degree of comfort. A woman of quick temper and defiant speech she could " cut to the quick with a flying phrase." But she was generous and hospitable, while her husband detested guests and in later years actually withdrew when any were invited. It could never have been a very happy or united household, despite all the brave efforts of Mrs. Wilson to render it so.

She was never young as her daughter remembered her, and one day when she was about forty-five she suddenly discarded the brown " front " she wore, disclosing her own lovely white hair. To Maggie she gave her dark liquid brown eyes and smooth soft skin, as well as those more intellectual qualities—a love of reading and poetry. She had too the Scotswoman's pride of race, and taught her the importance of the " old, chivalrous, impoverished " Oliphant family. " She might have been a queen," added her daughter.

The next removal was to Liverpool, and it was in that city that Maggie passed her girlhood and adolescence. From being her mother's constant companion—there is nothing to show she received any schooling—she developed early, and at sixteen was already the object of admiration among the youth of the place. When little more than that age she became engaged to a young man on the eve of his departure for America. She described him as a " good, simple, pious, domestic, kind-hearted fellow, who was neither good-looking nor clever." Their correspondence, at first frequent and copious, gradually dwindled and quarrels ensued. Then his letters ceased altogether, and Maggie, realizing that the affair was at an end together with the girlish hopes and dreams bound up in it, believed that her heart was broken. But in reality, this early experience of love stood her in good stead. It strengthened her character, disillusioning her in a sense and robbing her of all sentimentality. Nor does it seem that her love-affairs ever meant very much to her. Her marriage, though prosaic and even hard, was a perfectly happy one, but I doubt if she ever " fell in love " with her husband or anyone else.

§

As a girl she had few amusements and pleasures. Like the Brontës she never went to a dance, and her sole recreation lay in reading.

MRS. OLIPHANT
(From a photograph.)
By kind permission of Miss Janet Oliphant.

After the breaking of her engagement her mother fell ill and she was her only nurse. This young keenly intelligent girl spent long hours in that sick-room, and detesting needlework in those days she began to write, more as a means of passing the time than from any thought of becoming an author. This first little book was warmly appreciated by her mother and Frank, but Maggie recognized its worthlessness while she realized too that she possessed the power to do something far better. She did not attempt this, however, until her mother had recovered and the family had moved to Birkenhead, while Willie, who seemed to be settling down after a wayward youth, was about to leave for London to study at the London University and prepare himself for the Presbyterian ministry. She was twenty when she finished *Margaret Maitland*, and Willie was entrusted with the manuscript. He took it to Colburn, who immediately accepted it on the half-profits system, and on the publication of the third edition she received what to her must have seemed the very substantial sum of £150. There was, she said, something of her own childhood in little Grace, something of her mother in Mrs. Maitland.

The Wilsons seemed to treat the whole affair as a most tremendous joke. Mrs. Wilson laughed and cried with pride and happiness at her little daughter's success. She thought Mr. Fullom, who conducted the correspondence, the most wonderful man and prophesied great things for Maggie from his acquaintance.

But the delight of the family was short-lived. Willie fell once more into deplorable habits of intemperance; and as a consequence was deeply in debt. Probably those debts swallowed up most of the earnings of his sister's novel. When he was sufficiently recovered to return to London, it was arranged that his sister should accompany him. She was then little more than twenty years old, and that this formidable task of looking after him should have been relegated to her at so early an age gives a convincing proof of the maturity and stability of the girl's character. It was for her a presage of the future, since throughout her life responsibility after responsibility was thrust upon her, and she shouldered each successive burden without a thought for the expense or drudgery it entailed. As a bread-winner she began and as a bread-winner she was to end. She accepted life with all its bitter hardships with an indomitable courage.

Perhaps it was fortunate for her that she did not belong to the class that considered it derogatory for a woman to earn her livelihood by her pen. From the first she was encouraged to write.

While in London, she lived in lodgings with her brother, and in the same house dwelt two cousins, nephews of her mother, Frank and Tom Oliphant.

To her was entrusted the slender purse just sufficient for their needs. Willie was quiet and amenable; he gave little trouble, except on one occasion when she discovered he had incurred a debt. Maggie dealt with the situation with an energy and initiative that did her infinite credit. The money must be paid without an appeal to their parents, partly to shelter Willie and partly to prevent the economic burden falling upon them. She settled that the midday meal must be forgone twice a week until the debt was paid. She shared the necessary sacrifice, and the brother and sister ate only a bun apiece to sustain themselves until tea-time.

Frank Oliphant, who was then studying painting, was not unmindful of this dark, clever attractive girl, who had already made something of a name for herself. He was indeed more aware of her presence than she of his. But he took her to the National Gallery and sometimes even to the play—an unheard-of dissipation in the Birkenhead days—although her reactions could hardly have encouraged him. Her taste was undeveloped and Leonardo's *Christ in the Temple* actually shocked her " with a sense of profanity."

Of a dreamy unpractical artistic nature, Frank Oliphant saw in his cousin the very woman who would prove a true helpmate to him in his career. She, however, took little heed of him, being too deeply absorbed in Willie and his delinquencies, and also with her work which already filled every moment of her spare time.

This experience must definitely have robbed her of all youth, a period which with her had never been very care-free. She was always, and perhaps inevitably, a disillusioned woman with no very great belief in love. The passionate love depicted in the Brontë novels was entirely incomprehensible to her ; she read of it with unsympathetic astonishment. She did not see life in those terms of dark and often hopeless passion ; she could hardly believe it could play such a vital part in a woman's history. With her love was always a side-issue, not an all-absorbing emotion. Where it most nearly touched her heart was in her own motherhood, destined to be so sorely wounded. . . .

She had begun *Caleb Field*, a story of the Great Plague, the very day *Margaret Maitland* was finished, and before she was even aware that her work would be favourably received. And on her return to Birkenhead, after three months of constant vigilance in London, she continued the book, sitting at the table in the little parlour round which all the family gathered. As in the case of Jane Austen there was no privacy or seclusion. Talk went on, and Maggie, like that earlier writer, joined in it. Oddly enough this did nothing to check the flow of her imagination ; indeed, it would be difficult to conceive of anything that could even momentarily arrest that eager, facile pen.

§

Willie was now a Presbyterian minister to the delight of his family, who confidently believed that his reformation was complete and permanent. He was appointed to a remote village in the North of England where a charming little cottage was assigned to him. The position was, of course, utterly without importance and the income very small, but he was started in life and that was the great thing. No one seems to have had any fear that the very loneliness of the place would affect him. Indeed, all went well for a time and then an anonymous letter reached the Wilson family, shattering at a blow all their hopes. Mr. Wilson as usual did nothing, but left it to his wife, then a delicate and prematurely aged woman of sixty, to cope with the situation. She left home that very night, travelling to Edinburgh and thence to Berwick. Of late, except for a certain falling off in the regularity of her son's letters, there had been no apparent cause for anxiety, but what she found on arrival confirmed her worst fears. After a few miserable days, during which she nursed her son back to health, she returned with him to Birkenhead. Maggie and Frank awaited them at the ferry ; they drove home in silence, none of them uttering a single word of reproach, but doing all they could by gentleness to show him that he was welcome.

It was the death-blow to all their hopes for him. The brief days of his ministry were at an end, and he settled down to a life of appalling inactivity and indolence, smoking, reading newspapers and novels and apparently perfectly contented with this melancholy existence, while they looked on in despair at the lamentable spectacle. He had not even sufficient perseverance to transcribe Maggie's work for her, although she tried by this means to give him occupation.

Two shadows darkened the girl's life, her father and Willie. The former's career was almost ended and the latter's was abruptly frustrated. She must have realized how necessary it was for her to earn money with which to carry on the home, and she permitted nothing to interfere with her ceaseless industry.

Not long afterwards Mrs. Wilson's nephew, Frank Oliphant, came to stay with them. He must have seen with dismay how heavy his cousin's burden had become. But when he suggested that together they "should build up the old Drumthwacket" he met with a definite refusal. Nothing daunted, he returned to the charge some months later and was accepted.

Before her marriage Maggie visited some of her Wilson relations in Edinburgh, and there began her lifelong association with the firm of Blackwood. *Caleb Field* was already published and she had just finished a new novel, *Katie Stewart*, of which the plot was based upon the life of her mother's great-aunt who had lived to a very advanced age and could remember and describe the entry of Prince Charles Edward into Edinburgh. These reminiscences, related to Mrs. Wilson, were in turn told to her daughter, who was able to use them to great advantage. In consequence of her introduction to the Blackwood family, she offered the book when ready to their firm and actually received the proofs of it on her wedding day, May 4, 1852.

She was then twenty-four years old. Her husband, a clever young artist, exhibited in the Royal Academy, also designing a stained-glass window for Ely Cathedral ; indeed, towards the latter part of their life in London he seems to have devoted himself to this craft rather than to painting. The young couple had little beyond what they earned, but Mrs. Oliphant's growing popularity as a novelist made the step seem less imprudent than it might otherwise have appeared. In the early days of her married life she was able to count upon about £400 for each novel, and as she wrote with the greatest ease and facility, they were thus assured of a sufficient income from this source alone.

They lived in London, first at Harrington Square and later in Ulster Place, near Harley Street. Unfortunately, Mrs. Oliphant's parents followed them to London and took up their abode there, and as Mrs. Wilson and Frank Oliphant were mutually antagonistic this proximity did not contribute to the young wife's peace of mind.

Frank Wilson, mortified at being thus abandoned by his parents and sister, whose marriage apparently aggrieved him, forthwith married his cousin Jeanie Wilson and set up a *ménage* of his own.

§

In the year following her marriage, Mrs. Oliphant gave birth to a little girl, Margaret. Exactly a year later she had a second daughter, and immediately after this event Mrs. Wilson's health began to fail. She died in September, 1854, and in the following February Mrs. Oliphant lost her younger child, Marjorie, who at eight months old was a beautiful infant with large dark eyes. The bereaved mother was aghast to discover that this grief afflicted her more profoundly than the loss of her own beloved mother. Later in the year she gave birth to a third daughter, who died almost immediately.

Mr. Wilson disappears from the story about this time, vanishing like the silent shadow he had always seemed to his daughter. The Oliphants now moved to Ulster Place. Materially things were going well with them ; he was selling his pictures and she her books. He was also obtaining orders for stained-glass windows and rented a house near-by, which he used as a studio and where he employed a certain number of workmen. Here in 1856 their elder son, Cyril, a child full of life, vigour and intelligence, was born.

They saw something of the literary and artistic life of London, although it does not seem that at that time Mrs. Oliphant knew any of the " giants " who then held the field of fiction, Dickens, Thackeray (whose daughter was afterwards to become her intimate friend) and Charlotte Brontë, who was still living when they first married. Nor does it seem that they came into contact with any of that brilliant group which included Millais, Rossetti, Burne-Jones and William Morris. But they saw a good deal of William and Mary Howitt, who figure so frequently in the literary annals of those days, skirting, as they did, the fringe of the Pre-Raphaelites, and dabbling somewhat excessively in spiritualism. Mary Howitt alarmed Mrs. Oliphant by telling her of the number of babies she had lost through some defective valvular action of the heart ascribed to too much mental activity on the part of the mother, a not very cheering communication to make to a busy novelist who had lost two cherished children.

Often they would spend the evening with Mr. and Mrs. Samuel Carter Hall, at whose house they met Rosa Bonheur, " a round-faced good-humoured woman with hair cut short and divided at one side like a man's." Mrs. Hall had made something of a reputation for herself with a couple of Irish novels.

Then there was Dinah Mulock, author of *John Halifax, Gentleman*, a best-seller of its day and a book that deserves to be remembered if only for its admirable description of the Severn " bore " and the bread riots of the Hungry Forties. She was, Mrs. Oliphant said, a tall young woman with a slim pliant figure " and eyes that had a way of fixing the eyes of her interlocutor in a manner which did not please my shy fastidiousness." She observed the same tendency in Mrs. Browning on the solitary occasion on which she met her.

The scene of this book was laid in Tewkesbury, and Dinah Mulock is commemorated in the Abbey by a medallion. But she spent much of her young girlhood in London, where she lived in Chatham Place, that unhealthy region near Blackfriars, where poor Lizzie Siddal, wife of Dante Gabriel Rossetti, passed so much of her life both before and after marriage. Chatham Place, long since destroyed, also housed an even more remarkable figure, Emma Lyon, afterwards Lady Hamilton, who was nursemaid in a doctor's family there. . . .

Mrs. Oliphant brought about an introduction between Mr. Blackett the publisher, and Miss Mulock, at the former's request. Perhaps he discerned in that tall slender woman with the disconcerting gaze qualities not apparent to the younger writer. *John Halifax* was published under his ægis in 1856, and met with an immediate success, incidentally popularizing, it is said, the name of Muriel. Mrs. Oliphant was a little dismayed, as well she might be.

She made a spring thus quite over my head with the helping hand of my particular friend, leaving me a little rueful. . . . Success as measured by money never came to my share. Miss Mulock in this way attained more with a few books and these of very thin quality than I with many. I don't know why. I don't pretend to think that it was because of their superior quality.

Things were going well for the little household in Ulster Place. Mrs. Oliphant had her two children, charming and healthy ; her work was prospering and she was extremely happy in her quiet domestic life. But the peace was of brief duration. In the summer of 1858 she went out one evening after their early dinner to buy some dessert knives on which she had set her heart. The shop was near ; a friend who had dined with them was sitting with her husband ; she left the house without any premonition of calamity. Yet when she returned, she found some slight commotion as if something untoward had occurred during her brief absence. They assured her there was no cause for alarm, but her husband in coughing had had a very slight hæmorrhage. . . .

So little did she think of it, so far was it from alarming her—for she had no experience of such things—that she actually fulfilled a plan she had made to stay with a friend, Mrs. Moir, at Musselburgh, that summer. Yet once away from him panic seized her, and she went to Edinburgh one Sunday morning and sent a telegram—a much rarer thing in those days—to ask how he was. She waited about all day and received no answer, and later came a letter scolding her for her folly.

Nevertheless, it was for Frank Oliphant the beginning of the end. He had trouble with the workmen he employed to execute the windows for which he had a certain number of orders ; they proved untrustworthy when he was no longer able to give them a close supervision, and this preyed on his mind. Presently it was decided that he must no longer remain in England, the house was to be given up ; they were to migrate to Italy. Before this was finally arranged he consulted a Dr. Walsh, then a famous lung specialist, and Mrs. Oliphant accompanied him to Harley Street, waiting outside for him. She tells us how she walked up and down the street during that dreadful interval, praying to keep herself from crying. He emerged with a smile, telling her there was very little amiss except overwork. He would be well when once he could get away.

Afterwards in Rome, Robert Macpherson—who had married Mrs. Jameson's niece—told her that Frank had learned his doom that day from Dr. Walsh, but had not had the courage to reveal the truth.

I was angry and wounded beyond measure, and would not believe that my Frank had deceived me or told another what he did not tell to me. Neither do I think he would have gone away, to expose me with my little children to so awful a trial in a foreign place, had this been the case.

She forgot, perhaps, that he was not without hope of recovery in a more genial climate. Others had benefited from a sojourn in Italy, why should not he?

§

They left for Italy in January, 1859, with the intention of going to Florence. After many tribulations—for they were all utterly unaccustomed to continental travelling, then by no means the simple thing it is now—they arrived at Genoa where they had rooms with a beautiful view over the Gulf. Tom Oliphant accompanied them as far as Paris, perhaps aware that he was little likely to see his brother again. Not one of the little party knew any French or indeed any other foreign language, and the brunt of the arrangements naturally fell upon poor Mrs. Oliphant, who had an invalid husband and two young children on her hands.

The landlady at Genoa was English and took pity upon the forlorn and chilled little group of travellers, offering them a fine suite of rooms—a great *sala* and two bedrooms—for eight francs a day. The frescoed walls, the blazing fire, the warm carpet, so different from anything they had hitherto encountered on their journey, seemed to put fresh life into them all. Mr. Oliphant would indeed have preferred to remain there.

With no experience of the Italian climate and believing it to be a warm one even in winter they took rooms in Florence, on the sunless side of Via Maggio, which must have been perishingly cold since central heating was unknown in those days and at the best a wood fire compares ill with a coal one. The weather was bitterly cold. Their resources were of the scantiest since apparently all they had to depend upon was the sum of £20 a month provided by Mr. Blackwood in advance for Mrs. Oliphant's stories and articles. Living was cheap enough in Florence then, but this sum was totally inadequate for themselves, the nurse and two little children, stranded thus in a foreign town. Those first months must have tried Mrs. Oliphant's courage to the utmost.

Her husband suffered from rheumatism in addition to his malady ; he was terribly depressed, sitting all day beside a little stove in gloomy silence, while she sat near the window trying to write those articles upon which their very bread depended.   A visit to the Uffizi plunged him into still deeper gloom, for it only showed him more clearly his own demerits as an artist.

One or two visitors came to see them, doing their best to cheer the sick man.   Mrs. Oliphant published *A Winter Journey, Felicità*, and *A Week in Florence* in Blackwood's magazine during the next few months.   But she was treading new and strange ground.   Hitherto her stories had been for the most part Scottish ones, and her knowledge of Italy was necessarily superficial and imperfect.   She was, however, amid all her anxiety, beginning to collect material for one of her more serious and permanent works, *The Makers of Florence*.

Things improved as the bright Spring weather set in.   Florence under blue sunny skies, aglow with flowers, was a very different place from the city she had first seen submerged in a dense fog. Even Mr. Oliphant recovered his spirits to a certain extent.

Then with the strange restlessness peculiar to his malady, he suddenly announced his intention of going to Rome.   Mrs. Oliphant was not unnaturally aghast at this decision, but it does not seem to have occurred to her to combat it even on the grounds of her own health, since she was by this time aware that within a few months she would give birth to another child.   Moreover, she feared the summer heats of Rome—for in those days malaria was still a common malady—for her two young children.   They had made a few friends in Florence, including the Scottish minister, Mr. Macdougall.   However, in Rome there was Robert Macpherson, artist and photographer, with his wife, and there was also that less attractive and reliable figure, Willie Wilson.

During her stay in Florence, Mrs. Oliphant's work had suffered from her deep anxiety, the sense of helplessness in a strange country ; still there was sufficient money in hand to enable them to make the move. They went by road to Leghorn and thence by sea to Cività Vecchia, from which port they drove to Rome.

Robert Macpherson was not sympathetic to Mrs. Oliphant.   He was too noisy and unconventional to please her quiet fastidious state, " a big, bearded, vehement man, a combination of Highlander and Lowlander, Scotsman and Italian, with the habits of Rome and Edinburgh all rubbed together. . . ." He was among the first to take up photography professionally.

His wife, Gerardine Bate, was of a very different quality, spoiled, untidy, disorderly, fond of gaiety but pretty, witty and vivacious. She helped him with his photography, and the marriage would have been fairly happy had not her mother lived with them and encouraged her in all her youthful follies and love of gaiety, and admiration, taking her part too in her quarrels with Robert.

The Oliphants did not remain long in Rome, for in May they accompanied the Macpherson family to Nettuno, then a mere fishing village and extremely primitive. Mrs. Oliphant used it in her article *The Seaside in the Papal States*, subsequently published by Blackwood. The sea air revived Frank Oliphant, and he even did a couple of sketches. From Nettuno they went to Frascati, but there he became very much worse. His digestion failed ; he was unable to eat, and by the time they returned to Rome on October 1, it was obvious to all that he was a dying man. They inhabited a furnished apartment in Via Babuino, where a consultation took place, Dr. Small calling in a celebrated French physician. The latter saw no use in disguising the truth and told Mrs. Oliphant that *franchement* her husband could not recover. That word *franchement* made a profound impression upon her ; she could never hear it uttered in after years without a shudder.

Even now her courage did not desert her. She nursed her husband night and day until the end came and he was buried in the Protestant cemetery, where little more than thirty years before Shelley's ashes had been laid. Then she waited on in Rome until the birth of her second son Francis, or Cecco, as he was always called in remembrance of those Italian days.

Everyone was very kind. The Macphersons helped her in the task of packing up for that melancholy return journey. Mr. Blackett offered to come out and escort her home. Mr. Blackwood told her to draw upon him for any money she might need. Before the end of 1859 they were all once more in London. . . .

§

Never could prospects have looked darker for a young widow of thirty-one with three little children—one of them a baby in arms— to support. " What did your husband leave you ? " a friend inquired. " Three children, my two hands and a thousand pounds worth of debts," was the answer made without bitterness. Indeed, her only available assets consisted of the small amount of furniture they had stored and an insurance policy of £200.

The task was a formidable one for a woman without any income and apparently with no one to whom she could turn. Her brother Frank had his own wife and family to support, still he offered her to share his house at Birkenhead. This she did for a short time, but the experiment was not a success and she took her children to Fife, renting a small house at Elie, the Blackwoods being quite near at Gibleston. The summer passed pleasantly enough ; she had her faithful nurse Jane, who had accompanied them to Rome to help her in looking after the children, and Maggie was now of an age to be a little companion to her.

For the winter she took the ground floor and basement of a house in Fettes Row, Edinburgh. It was bitterly cold and the outlook was dark. She had not been successful with her writing, which, considering her Italian experiences, was hardly to be wondered at, and even Mr. Blackwood, always a kind and generous friend, had been compelled to reject some of her stories. He had a very high standard for *Maga*, and it was not easy to pass those so carefully guarded portals. Despite this Mrs. Oliphant had the temerity to go to the firm with the suggestion that she should contribute a serial to those pages.

They offered no encouragement, indeed both Mr. Blackwood and his brother, Major Blackwood, shook their heads over the proposal. Her work had, perhaps not astonishingly, failed to fulfil the promise of those earlier books. She went out of the room hurriedly after this rebuff, afraid lest they should see the tears in her eyes. If her work were to be thus rejected how was she to support that little family who looked to her to supply all their needs ?

And then her indomitable courage came to her aid. She went home, helped to put the children to bed, and sitting up nearly all night, wrote the first draft of the *Carlingford Chronicles*, of which *Salem Chapel* and the *Perpetual Curate* were the best known and most successful. The story was accepted, and her name and fortune were made.

It may have been that George Eliot's *Scenes of Clerical Life* which had appeared serially in *Maga* had suggested the idea of the *Carlingford Chronicles* to her. From her girlhood spent at Liverpool and Birkenhead, she had plenty of experience of clerical scenes, and she proceeded to use these with that pleasant fluent spontaneity which always characterized her work. Nevertheless, it did sometimes occur to her to envy George Eliot and her sheltered life, her talent, so carefully nurtured by the vigilant Lewes, since she herself was utterly destitute of all assistance and influence in those early struggling days of her widowhood. Small wonder that she brought a very different attitude to her work from that of her famous if slightly ponderous contemporary. She had to make a home and provide for her three children, and she had not even the desolate security of a Haworth Parsonage, the luxurious prison of a No. 50 Wimpole Street, upon which to rely for shelter.

A year or two later she took a pleasant little house at Ealing in order to be near the Blacketts, and here she continued her *Carlingford Chronicles*, receiving adequate sums for the various volumes. Indeed, for *The Perpetual Curate* she was paid as much as £1,500. But there were inevitable moments of anxiety, and life was never quite free from intervals of discouragement, almost of despair. . . .

Still, she never lost hope. The day might be full of distractions, but when night fell upon the little household there was peace, and it was at night that she accomplished the greater part of her work. She was actually capable of working for eleven hours at a time. She had two outstanding gifts, a simple fluency of style, and the art of telling an interesting and wholesome story. Her imagination, her power of visualizing scenes, never failed her. But she professed astonishment when later she read of such technical matters as form, phrasing and style, the deliberate selection of words, the balance of sentences. That writers should deliberately practise their art as Stevenson did, was something of a revelation to her. She admitted, however, that she took pleasure in a " little bit of fine writing " which only happened when she was moved by her subject.

I have always had my sing-song guided by no sort of law, but by my ear which was in its way fastidious to the cadence and measure that pleased me ; but it is bewildering to me in my perfectly artless art, if I may use the word at all, to hear of the elaborate ways of forming and enhancing style, and all the studies for that end. . . .

While in Scotland she had made the acquaintance of Dr. John Carlyle, of whom Mrs. Carlyle used to say he was one of those people who must have been born with creaking shoes. At his suggestion on her return to London, she went to see his brother in Cheyne Row in connection with the life she proposed to write of Edward Irving. He received her quite graciously, but told her " the wife " could tell her more about Irving than he could.

I remember—she wrote—his tall thin stooping figure between the two rooms of the library on the ground floor in the pleasant shadow of the books, and subdued light and quiet in the place which seemed to supply a very appropriate atmosphere. I did not even know and certainly never should have learned from any look or tone of his that I had run the risk of being devoured alive by thus intruding on him.

She was at that time staying with her friend Mrs. Powell in Palace Gardens, and a few days later was told that a lady was waiting in her carriage outside and wished to see her. This was no other than " the wife " herself, Jane Welsh Carlyle, with her dark handsome tortured-looking face and black hair still untouched with grey. She invited Mrs. Oliphant to drive with her so that they might discuss her old friend Irving, who had taught her Latin when he was twenty and she only six years old.

A little later Mrs. Oliphant gives a very pleasant glimpse of Mrs. Carlyle who came to see her one afternoon just after little Cecco had had a kind of convulsion. She had given him a hot bath and was sitting near the fire, the child on her knees wrapped in blankets, when Mrs. Carlyle arrived. She sat by her " so kind and tender and full of encouragement . . . telling me all kinds of comforting things. . . ."

It was Mrs. Carlyle who told her on one occasion that George Eliot had mistaken her rôle, saying :

Nature intended her to be the properest of women, and that her present equivocal position is the most extraordinary blunder and contradiction possible. . . .

§

Mrs. Oliphant had spent a couple of years at Ealing when Gerardine Macpherson paid her an ill-fated visit. She was taken seriously ill and very nearly died. Mrs. Oliphant nursed her, and there is nothing to show that she grudged or resented the extra burden which this task must have thrust upon her, making heavy inroads on her time and strength.

However, Mrs. Macpherson recovered and suggested, somewhat imprudently, that they should all return to Rome together. Perhaps the prospect of the southern sunshine attracted Mrs. Oliphant, for she at once made plans for the journey, despite the bitter memories the city held for her. She was pretty well off too, thus no thought of the expense deterred her. Thrift was unknown to her, and she placed an almost reckless reliance upon her pen which for nearly half a century never failed her.

Her own party consisted of herself, three children and Jane, and it was further reinforced by Mrs. Macpherson and Mrs. Tulloch— wife of Principal Tulloch—and her two elder girls. After an uncomfortable journey to Marseilles they went to Genoa, Leghorn and Cività Vecchia by a French steamer. On their arrival towards the end of 1863 the Oliphants and Tullochs lodged together in a furnished apartment in Via Capo le Case, engaging a couple of Italian servants.

There was not—Mrs. Oliphant wrote—an omen of evil in any way. Our leaving of home, our journey, our life here, have all been among the brightest passages of my life ; and my Maggie looked the healthiest and happiest of all my children, and ailed nothing, and feared nothing— nor I for her. . . .

Maggie was then eleven years old, a lovely intelligent child, already a companion to her mother and acting too like a little mother to the " bundle of boys " as she termed them, with affectionate contempt. As her first-born and her only surviving daughter she was especially dear to Mrs. Oliphant's heart.

About January 23, 1864, the child was taken suddenly ill with gastric fever, and on the 27th she died after only four days' illness. She was buried beside her father in the Protestant cemetery, forming another sad and tragic link with Rome for the bereaved and broken-hearted mother.

I feared from the first moment her illness began, and yet I had a kind of underlying conviction that God would not take my ewe-lamb, my woman-child from me. . . .

She still had her two boys, bright, intelligent little fellows. Cyril —or Tids as he was usually called—was then eight years old, and Cecco little more than four. These were all that were left to her of her family of five.

Mrs. Macpherson took her out to their apartment at Frascati. The great, gaunt, half-empty rooms, situated at the top of a villa and inadequately heated by small stoves, were utterly comfortless. Mrs. Oliphant had loved the place in summer with its splendid views across the Campagna to the sea, but its winter desolation combined with the bitter cold, the lack of servants and all comforts, was insupportable. She hurried back to Rome, unable to bear the anxiety she felt for the children she had left there.

There was no talk even then of their returning to England. In March they stayed at Albano and Mrs. Oliphant fell in love with the enchanting little hill-city of Nemi perched high above the sunless waters of its deep volcanic lake, once the scene of such dark and sinister tragedies. For one wild moment she had visions of settling there and bringing up her boys abroad. Would things have been different then ?—she used to wonder. . . . In any case the scheme was quickly abandoned, and as the Spring advanced she took her little party to Naples and Capri. There she was able to write a sketch, *Life on an Island*, for *Maga*. Indeed, there was no sign of any idleness or shrinking from work during that sad time. *The Perpetual Curate* had been published before she left England and she was then writing one of her best-known novels, *Miss Marjoribanks*.

In May they finally left Rome and despite several subsequent journeys to Italy she could never bring herself to return there. They went north to the Lake of Como, staying at Bellagio, and then spent the remainder of the summer in Switzerland, Mrs. Tulloch's little girls being still with her.

o

The following winter was spent in Paris, where she met Montalembert, whose book she had translated during the early days of her widowhood and whose biography she was later to write. They had a pleasant apartment looking over the Champs Elysées, and the brilliant stream of life continually passing beneath her windows proved, as she said, a kind of salvation to her.

Cyril began his education under a tutor and both boys soon learned to speak French with a fluency they were never destined to lose. Cecco learned to read in a fortnight, and Mrs. Oliphant saw with pride that intellectually her sons were gifted above the average. And to use her own words she was " going on with a flowing sail," earning and spending with astonishing ease and thinking little of what the morrow might bring. The little grave in Rome was not forgotten, but grief itself must be set aside for the harsher and more urgent claims of life. . . .

§

When the question of Cyril's schooling arose, Mrs. Oliphant was at first undecided as to whether she should send him to Eton or Harrow. It never occurred to her that a less expensive school would have been more suited to her means. But she had travelled far since the early days of the little cottage at Lasswade, the obscure, rather penurious life at Glasgow and Liverpool, where thanks, however, to her mother's thrift and management, nothing of essentials had been lacking. She was ambitious now for her sons, and there was perhaps never a woman who took the question of money less seriously, a common failing with those gifted with the artistic temperament.

In 1866 she settled at Windsor, having ascertained that Cyril could go to Eton as a day boy, sleeping at home. She took a cheerful, charming little house at No. 6 Clarence Crescent, living there for six years and for the following twenty at a bigger one close by. It was about a mile from Eton, which was a drawback, the boys having to be there so early. Cyril, who was now ten, was to begin his studies at once, and Cecco as soon as he was old enough. " My boys," she wrote, " have brains enough to get on, I think, even amid the hurly-burly of a great school."

Miss Marjoribanks, finished while she was in Paris, appeared early that autumn, at about the same time as George Eliot's *Felix Holt*, a book which did not elicit Mrs. Oliphant's approval, and she had the courage to tell Blackwood so.

It leaves an impression on my mind as of *Hamlet* played by six sets of grave-diggers. Of course it will be a successful book, but I think chiefly

because *Adam Bede* and *Silas Marner* went before it. Now that I have read it I have given up the idea of reviewing it. . . .
I hope you don't think me so utterly stupid as to have any doubt about the perfection of George Eliot's writing ; I don't suppose she could express herself otherwise than exquisitely if she were to try, and there are a thousand tones of expression which nobody else could have hit upon and which give one a positive thrill of pleasure to read them . . . but I am mightily disappointed in the book all the same. One feels as if a great contempt had seized her for the public and her critics. . . .

Perhaps the fact that Blackwood had too sharply criticized *Miss Marjoribanks*—one of the very best of her books—lent a certain asperity to her letter.

Those first years at Windsor were perhaps the most care-free she was ever destined to know. Cyril was growing up a handsome, attractive boy with qualities and abilities that differed somewhat from those of the average schoolboy. At the age of twelve and without any special preparation, he won the Prince Consort's prize for French. The sons owed much to that cultivated literary atmosphere that characterized their home.

Mrs. Oliphant soon made a number of friends. She was both generous and hospitable, loving the stir of life about her. She had a great desire to give her boys as much amusement and recreation as possible, organizing picnics, parties and theatricals for them and their friends. They were neither of them at all difficult to manage ; they were gay, brilliant and industrious, giving bright promise for the future. And Mrs. Oliphant was earning a large income which, however, was often spent in anticipation. For this she is not to be blamed, for it must be remembered that she was crippled at the outset by the debt of one thousand pounds owed when she was left a widow.

All went well for two years, indeed, it seemed as if the happy united little household had fallen upon an interval of unexampled prosperity when in 1868, Mrs. Oliphant suddenly heard that her brother Frank, now the father of four children, was a ruined man. After a day of misery and suspense, expecting him to come to her, she went in search of him. She found only his wife, who was naturally in deep distress. For some years his health had been failing and he was afflicted with a kind of palsy which prevented him from writing, although he was still able to do his work.

Without a thought for the heavy expense involved, Mrs. Oliphant took charge of the two elder children, Frank and Nelly, while Mrs. Wilson with the two younger girls joined her husband in France.

I am not sure—Mrs. Oliphant wrote—that I had not a sort of secret satisfaction in getting Frank, my nephew, into my hands, thinking with that complacency with which we always look at our own doings that I could now train him for something better than they had thought of.

Nelly went shortly afterwards to live with her mother's sister, Mrs. Sime, but Frank formed a permanent part of the little household at Windsor and it was a delight to Mrs. Oliphant to note the pleasant generous manner in which her own sons accepted the new situation. He went to Eton with them, although to avoid expense he returned home for his meals. But he was a strong boy of fourteen and the fatigue entailed did not affect him. He worked hard and proved clever, steady and intelligent. He was old enough to realize all that was being done for him and to appreciate his aunt's generosity.

Mr. Wilson obtained work on a new railway that was being made in Hungary, and thither he went, accompanied by Jeanie his wife and the two little girls. The Oliphants resumed their old life with its simple gaieties, its parties and theatricals. The cloud had passed and was almost forgotten. . . .

Then one evening they were at supper after an expedition on the river, and Mrs. Oliphant could always remember the pretty look of the table, the salads and pink salmon, the ornamented sweets, the bright, happy faces gathered about her, the boys in flannels, the girls in their light summer frocks, when a fresh blow fell. In the midst of the talk and laughter a telegram was brought to her. She opened it without a qualm of anxiety and read the following words : *Jeanie is dead and I am in despair.*

Mrs. Wilson, who had been suffering from quite a mild attack of fever, had died very suddenly in her sleep. Looking at Frank's bright, happy face, Mrs. Oliphant resolved not to tell him of his loss until the evening festivities were over. She permitted nothing of her own emotion to escape her.

Frank Wilson returned to England with the two little white-faced girls, worn out with grief and fatigue, and too young perhaps to realize the extent of their loss. Mrs. Oliphant met them at Victoria and took them home with her. She found her brother's health completely shattered, although his sorrow was less than she had anticipated. For six years he lived in her house, too much broken-down to attempt any work. She had to recognize with increasing bitterness that all love between them was dead. The happy companionship of Lasswade and Birkenhead could never be recovered ; they were more like strangers than brother and sister. Their ways had lain too long apart for either of them to feel happy in these new conditions.

Mrs. Oliphant now had to provide for a household of seven persons,

three of whom **were** boys whose education was becoming increasingly
costly. Fortunately for all, her health remained unimpaired. She
continued to sit up far into the night to earn the money that was
necessary to keep the home together, and never could she have had
greater cause to remember and to derive courage from the old
motto of the Oliphants : *A tout pourvoir.* . . .

> If I had not had unbroken health and a spirit almost criminally elastic
> I could not have done it. I ought to have been worn out by work and
> crushed by care half a hundred times by all rules, but I never was so. . . .
> It was in its way an immoral or at least an unmoral mode of life, dashing
> forward in the face of all obstacles and taking up all burdens with a kind
> of levity, as if my strength and resource could never fail. . . .

Small wonder that with those extra burdens her output, necessarily increased, showed signs of haste, while the occasional careless-
ness of its quality was more pronounced. She wondered sometimes
whether she would have done better work if she had been less sharply
pressed, but less than ever could she run any risks. It was not until
part of her burden had been lifted that she wrote books such as
The Beleaguered City and the *Little Pilgrim in the Unseen,* " to please
herself," as she said.

Of course there were moments of acute financial anxiety, such as
when she found herself confronted with the refusal of a novel upon
which her income for the coming months depended.

> I always had a lightly flowing stream of magazine articles—she wrote—
> and refused no work that was offered to me, but the course of life could
> not be carried on on these, and a large sum was wanted at brief intervals
> to clear the way.

But at that moment it was as if every channel was closed—she
seemed to be at what she called a dead standstill.

> It was like nothing but what I have already said—a mountainous road
> making a sharp turn round a corner when it seems to disappear altogether
> as if it ended there in the closing in of the cliffs. I was miserably anxious
> not knowing where to turn or what to do. . . .

In despair she took her novel to George Smith, but although he
received her courteously, he was not prepared to make an offer for it.

She went back to Windsor almost in despair, and was, as she
admitted, dull and cross for the rest of the evening. There was,
however, a single ray of hope—a man had written asking if he might
come and see her on a matter of business, but as there was nothing
in the letter to make it seem of particular importance, she had
appointed the following day for the interview. That was one of the
darkest nights she had ever spent. . . .

And then in the morning her visitor came. He proved to be

from the publishers of the *Graphic*, for which he invited her to write a serial, the first instalment of which was to be ready in a week or two. The sum offered was £1,300. " The road did run round that corner after all," she added.

§

Dr. Arthur Benson, when a small boy at Eton, could remember Cyril Oliphant entering chapel at the end of the procession of Oppidans as a " small, lightly built curly-haired boy, handsome, attractive-looking, stepping rather jauntily and with an air of entirely unembarrassed amusement—indeed, a charming-looking creature with an expression which seemed at once sensitive, impressionable and whimsical."

He could recall, too, the little grey-haired lady in her widow's dress, who so often attended the services at Eton with her dark brilliant penetrating eyes and the face which would have been beautiful but for the somewhat prominent mouth. More than ever was his boyish interest awakened when he discovered that this was Mrs. Oliphant, the famous novelist, and the author of *The Makers of Florence*, which he had recently received as a Christmas present.

The years passed without any incident of note, until in 1875 Frank, who on leaving Eton had gone to the Royal Indian Engineering College at Cooper's Hill, passed out, taking a very high place which enabled him to choose in which part of India he would serve in the Public Works Department. Naturally he chose the Punjab—the most popular of all and towards which all his ambition had been directed. Cyril too had left Eton and was to go to Oxford, where it was hoped with his brilliant abilities he would win a Balliol scholarship. Mr. Wilson, whose health had now considerably deteriorated, expressed a wish to leave his sister's house and live on his own. Mrs. Oliphant would have preferred to place him in a doctor's care, but this prospect did not please him. She could not insist for the old sympathy between them was long since dead, and he was often slightly censorious of his sister, her ways and mode of life.

Frank Wilson, the son, was now a tall youth of twenty-one, with thick auburn hair and heavy moustache. He was big and strong and looked older than his years. Mrs. Oliphant was devoted to him ; he had been for nearly seven years like another son to her. She was determined, therefore, to give him a final treat before he left for India, and arranged to go to Switzerland with him and her own boys. They were to spend a couple of days in London first, so that they might attend the Eton and Harrow match. The three of them left for Lord's that morning in the highest spirits. " Frank tall and strong, my Cyril with his beautiful face, my Cecco only a boy and little, straining to keep up with them, all dressed in their best. . . . They were all my world."

The next day she was summoned home to Windsor by a telegram. Her brother had been taken suddenly ill, and after a few days he died, a prematurely worn-out man, scarcely more than sixty years old. Grieved as she was, his death could only have meant a relief to her. It was one burden the less. With Frank out in the world, earning his own living, she had only her sons and the two little Wilson girls to provide for, and perhaps Frank would now be able to give her some slight assistance with their education.

The scheme of going to Switzerland was postponed till a little later, when they went to Interlaken. Frank and Cyril escorted the two little girls, Madge and Denny, to their school at Arolsen, and then joined Mrs. Oliphant, who made friends that summer with Miss Anne Thackeray, afterwards Mrs. Richmond Ritchie. At Grindelwald they were joined by the Leslie Stephens—Thackeray's son-in-law and daughter. Leslie Stephen was then editor of *Cornhill*, and after a little pressure from his womenkind accepted a couple of Mrs. Oliphant's stories for that magazine which meant, she said, the bulk of a year's income.

That summer, which had promised so well, freeing her from a perpetual source of anxiety and care, was perhaps the last tranquil one Mrs. Oliphant was ever destined to know. Her subsequent anxieties, she said, were almost greater than she could bear. " God alone knows what was the anguish of those years." The thought of her brother Willie must have been too often before her mind. . . .

Cyril Oliphant went to Balliol that autumn despite the fact that he had failed to win the coveted scholarship. And now began for his mother what she called " the heat and burden of the day." She had known anxiety, grief, bereavement, had drunk very deeply of the cup of sorrow, but except for death her own little home circle had remained untouched by anything approaching shame. She was, however, destined, as she once said, to see her troubles repeated. As there was something of Willie in Cyril so she was fated to see Cecco early fall a victim to his father's malady.

Yet even in that pitiful *Autobiography*, in which she left so much to the imagination and which despite its *naïveté* must surely be one of the most pathetic of human documents, she could do no more than write elliptically and allusively of that time, only hinting at the nature of this fresh calamity.

My dearest, bright, delightful boy missed somehow his footing—how can I tell how ? I often think that I had to do with it, as well as what people call inherited tendencies, and alas, the perversity of youth which he never outgrew. He had done everything too easily in the beginning of his boyish career by natural impulse and that kind of genius which is often deceptive in youth. Notwithstanding all distractions he took a second-class at Oxford—a great disappointment yet not disgraceful after all. And I will not say that, except at the first keen moment of pain, I was in any way bitterly disappointed. . . . Perhaps he thought I took it lightly and that it did not much matter. Then it was one of my foolish ways to take my own work very lightly and not to let them know how hard pressed I was sometimes, so that he never, I am sure, was convinced how serious it was in that way and certainly never was convinced that he could not, when the moment came, right himself and recover the lost way. But only the moment—God bless him !—did not come until God took it in His own hands. . . .

She blamed herself bitterly afterwards for keeping them in ignorance of the struggles she had undergone to maintain and educate them, for her habit too of laughing at the " superior people," those who took themselves too seriously, the " boys of pretension and all the strong intellectualisms." By doing this she believed she had imbued her sons with a certain prejudice against the studious, hard-working reading men.

And she had brought them up, not exactly luxuriously, but always in a manner that must have made them feel she was a far richer woman than she was. There had never been any lack of money ; the house at Windsor was a centre of hospitality and pleasant gatherings, thus it is hardly surprising that her boys should have remained in ignorance of the fact that their present prosperity depended upon their mother's health and capacity for working, and their future upon their own exertions.

Nor did she at once realize Cyril's failure, or if she did she never alluded to it in her letters. On the contrary, she wrote proudly and optimistically about him while he was at Oxford, had plans for entering him at the Inner Temple believing he would succeed at the Bar.

When the time came for Cecco to go to Oxford, she took a house there in Crick Road so as to be near him during his first term, which shows a certain anxiety on her part. Indeed, she herself wrote of him :

My Cecco took the first steps in the same way, but thanks be to God, righted himself and overcame—not in time to save his career at Oxford, but so as to be all that I had hoped—always my very own, my dearest companion, choosing me before all others. . . . He had not much more than emerged from the desert of temptation and trial, bringing balm and healing to me, when he fell ill. . . .

She did not greatly enjoy Oxford, being at no time a very sociable woman except in her own house. With strangers she was shy and reserved, for which her early training was possibly accountable. Still, she met many of the notable people of the Oxford of that day. The Master of Balliol, Dr. Jowett, the Rector of Lincoln, Mark Pattison and his brilliant wife, the Max Müllers and many more.

A great many people called on me—she wrote—and I had a sprinkling of dinner-parties of the most superior description ; in short everybody was very kind, and I got a good deal of attention. I rather think I was set up as the proper novelist in opposition to Miss Broughton who has gone to live at Oxford and has much fluttered the dove-cotes, though I don't exactly know how.

Cecco was all the more comfortable in the beginning for having his home at hand, and has got thoroughly into the Oxford life, which is a great comfort to me, and I think Tids' work too was all the better for his mother's presence. The latter personage has his final examinations next term, which is a very anxious business. They all seem to expect him to do well.

It cost her at least five hundred a year to keep both sons at Oxford, and afterwards, as she then imagined, there would be all the expenses of starting Cyril at the Bar. Her work was therefore continued with indefatigable industry. In the year 1877 she published no less than three three-volume novels as well as books on Cervantes, Dante, and Molière, in conjunction with an Eton master, Mr. Tarver, for Blackwood's series of " Foreign Classics for Young Readers." In 1878 there was but one three-volume novel, but in 1879—Cecco's first year at Oxford—she published two, as well as a collection of her *Tales from Blackwood.* Her publishers included Smith and Elder, Blackwood, Macmillan, Hurst and Blackett, Longmans, and Chapman and Hall. No sign as yet of diminishing popularity, still less of flagging power. . . .

§

In the autumn of 1879, just after Cyril had left Oxford and when the horizon was still outwardly fairly bright, a fresh calamity fell upon Mrs. Oliphant. She received the news of the death of Frank Wilson in India from typhoid fever. He had then been absent about four years and was doing well in his profession of engineering in the Indian Public Works Department. He was the one about whom she had experienced the least anxiety. Physically strong, steady, diligent, though without the fatal brilliancy of her own sons, he possessed all the qualities which augur success.

I had trained him with pain and trouble, and sent him out to India with every hope and blessing four years ago, and here is the end, so far as this sad world is concerned. We were a week waiting an answer to a telegram which never came—in an anxiety I cannot describe, and which ended on the 29th in an official announcement of his death.

My boy Frank was the one I was most secure about and had least anxiety for. All seemed so well with him ; he was so robust and vigorous, nothing wrong about him either real or fanciful. . . . I have my three orphan nieces now deprived of the last prop that absolutely belonged to them, under my roof this Christmas. . . . You will give a pitying thought I am sure to these three poor girls.

Cyril went to London each day to work in the chambers of a barrister to prepare himself for his career. She was happy to have him with her and endeavoured, though without much success, to persuade him to work. In the summer she paid visits with her sons, staying first with Mr. Woodall, a Member of Parliament, at Burslem, where a boy of thirteen called Arnold Bennett was already watching the activities of the Five Towns with an observant eye. It was unusual for her to take such a long holiday, but she probably did so on account of her sons. They went on to Wales, staying at Barmouth for some weeks. But there is no doubt that Mrs. Oliphant was anxious to be relieved of her burden of incessant writing, which had now occupied her for thirty years. She wrote to Mr. Craik— who had married Dinah Mulock—in December, 1880 :

.I wonder if you who are in the world and hear of everything that is going on, think it at all possible that I could get something to do of a permanent character, which would relieve me a little from the necessity of perpetual writing. I don't mean to say that I am tired of writing or that it exhausts me, or that I don't like it better than any other occupation, for these assertions would not be true. But as I am growing old (she was then nearly fifty-three), I have more and more desire for a regular quarter-day, a regular occupation, and so much money certainly coming in.

. . . I think if I had enough of steady income to justify me in getting a small house in town I should be thankful—but at least for the steady income I should be thankful anyhow.

All the private income she had indeed to depend upon was the pension of £100 a year which Queen Victoria had allotted to her in 1868. Thus, if anything were to happen to herself these four children who were now dependent upon her would be left without visible means of support. And already she must have had fears for Cyril. . . .

In writing to Mr. William Blackwood on December 26, 1880, she added :

It seems to me while I write that probably you will be in London for George Eliot's funeral. How sad it is ! . . . There is something very solemn in the thought of a great spirit like hers entering the spiritual world which she did not believe in. If we are right in our faith what a blessed surprise to her ! . . .

In the following April Mrs. Oliphant went to Venice to collect material for her book *The Makers of Venice*. She took with her Cecco and Mrs. Coghill, a cousin who had become an intimate friend. At Venice she met Henry James, whose *Roderick Hudson, Daisy Miller* and *The Portrait of a Lady* had already earned him a well-merited fame. They visited Verona, Florence and Paris, returning home early in May. It was during that summer of 1881 that her anxiety about Cyril reached its culminating pitch. In September she took him to Scotland to stay with Mrs. Blackwood, a visit which they both enjoyed. But that she was very tired and anxious about that time is revealed in a letter written to Principal Tulloch who had then been very ill :

But think, please, if it had been me who had been ill, what would have become of me ?—no income going on whether one could work or not— no wife to take care of me. You are far better off than I am in these respects, and to tell the truth I am often tired to death of work and care— always work, work, whether one likes it or not. But I am wicked to complain. . . .

An attack of giddiness had, however, warned her that she was overworking. She had to rest for a whole day on the sofa—an almost unprecedented departure for her.

In the beginning of 1883 she was seriously anxious about Cyril's health. He had had several very alarming attacks of illness and Sir Andrew Clark, who was called in, considered his condition serious. However, by April he was better and there seemed a chance of his being able to help his mother. Sir Arthur Gordon—afterwards Lord Stanmore—was appointed Governor of Ceylon and invited him to be his private secretary. He was to receive a salary of from two to three hundred a year, which, strange to say, Mrs. Oliphant considered inadequate.

I suppose a private secretary lives with his chief or it would not lighten my purse much to make such an arrangement. However, I think the practical work for him is everything, and the entire change of scene an advantage too.

He was not to go out to Ceylon for some months and in the meantime Mrs. Oliphant took Cecco to Göttingen, where he was to study German in the hope of obtaining an appointment at the British Museum.

In January, 1884, she went to London and stayed for a few weeks in Hans Place at a house which had been lent her. Cyril started for Ceylon on January 29, and she and Cecco went to Bordighera and thence to Venice. She had good accounts of her elder son. He was at Kurunegala with the Governor for an elephant *kraal,* and at first things seemed to go well with him. But presently the news reached her that he was very ill indeed, had had repeated attacks of fever and was now on his way home. The doctor declared that the climate of Colombo would be fatal to him. Mrs. Oliphant hurried back from Italy and was just in time to meet him on his arrival in the *Cathay* at Gravesend. He was, however, looking better than she expected, the sea-voyage having restored him. But it was his one and only attempt to work except for the slight volume on de Musset he prepared for her series of Foreign Classics.

Once at home his health gave her fresh cause for anxiety, and she took him and Cecco to St. Andrew's for the summer. Again she found herself involved in all kinds of expenses which she was ill able to meet. Fortunately she was able to let her house at Windsor.

Cyril out all day and golfing—she wrote from St. Andrews—is much better and has got back all his old mahogany colour ; but he is still not very strong—much less strong than he looks. Cecco is very well and fatter than is expedient at his age. I have got through the most portentous amount of work in my long spell of quiet, but have still an intolerable quantity before me, after the delays and idleness of our long rambling. . . .

They returned to Windsor in the autumn and resumed their normal life, only with this difference, that Mrs. Oliphant clearly saw that Cyril—save for a little desultory writing—would never have the health to maintain himself. But there was still Cecco. He had given her so far but little anxiety and his complete devotion to her was one of the happiest experiences of her life.

§

In 1886, Principal Tulloch died and Mrs. Tulloch went to Windsor to stay with her daughter, Mrs. Tarver. Queen Victoria, who had had an immense admiration for Tulloch, visited his widow and re-mained with her for half an hour. Some days after her departure Mrs. Oliphant was summoned to the Castle. It was the second audience she had had with the Queen, and on this occasion she saw her quite alone and they had a long talk, chiefly about Mrs. Tulloch. She was, Mrs. Oliphant said :

. . . very sweet and friendly, hoping to see more of me and other amiabilities. . . The Queen was extremely kind and gracious to me, so kind that all one's little embarrassments about such an interview went completely away.

One to whom Mrs. Oliphant was very dear wrote thus of this episode :

Between these two, so far apart in station, there was a strong bond, for although Mrs. Oliphant might have said like Disraeli, " we authors," yet it was not that which drew them together, but the human sympathy of two lonely women left in the prime of life and to face and fight the world for all they held dearest, without their natural supporter and counsellor. Always this Greatest Lady had shown to her humbler neighbour—for to them both Windsor had become home—a gracious courtesy and generosity, for which all those who love Mrs. Oliphant will ever bear a deep and devoted gratitude.

A few days later the maid announced excitedly that " two soldiers from the Castle " had brought a parcel for Mrs. Oliphant. It contained a large illustrated edition of *Queen Victoria's Highland Journal* accompanied, as Mrs. Oliphant wrote :

. . . by a very pretty note from Sir Henry Ponsonby evidently dictated by the Queen, saying that she is well aware how humble her efforts are at authorship, but as a true Scotchwoman the Queen ventures to send them to you.
I thought it right, as I believe she likes to have one's thanks sent to herself, to write to her, thanking her for the books, and now I have a most gracious autograph letter.

Suffering much from rheumatism Mrs. Oliphant went to do the cure at Wiesbaden that summer, while Cecco returned to Göttingen to brush up his German. She was a little anxious then about his health. He wrote occasional stories and articles for *Blackwood* and reviewed books for the *Spectator*, and was still in hopes of obtaining some appointment, although he had been refused by the Society of Antiquaries for which his genealogical researches especially fitted him.

But such hopes were, alas, never to be fulfilled. In the early months of 1887, when he was little more than twenty-seven years old, his health began to give Mrs. Oliphant serious cause for alarm. Indeed, the first symptoms of tuberculosis were revealed during an attack of laryngitis. She took him to Pau, where he seemed to get much better, and by May they were back at Windsor. Indeed, it was supposed that he would be well enough to take up an appointment at the British Museum for which he had passed the test with exceptional brilliancy. To his mother's grief and to his own, he was rejected by the Commissioners on the score of health, Sir Andrew Clark declaring it would be fatal to him to live and work in London.

No wonder Mrs. Oliphant's heart failed her a little when she heard this decision, for she saw that neither of her sons would ever be able to take up any regular employment or give her substantial help. More than ever would they depend upon her exertions, and she was now sixty years old and as destitute of resources as when she began to write forty years earlier.

§

The *Life of Principal Tulloch* was finished in June and published
that same year—1888. Two three-volume novels and two short
stories as well as her monthly contribution to *Maga* under the title
of the "Old Saloon" appeared that year. There was no falling off either
in the quantity or quality of her work, indeed, the health of her two
sons made it more than ever imperatively necessary that she should
earn. Cecco went alone to the South of France and Spain, so that
she could write more uninterruptedly. But in the early weeks of
1889 she planned to go to Beaulieu with her two sons, leaving her
younger niece, who showed talent as an artist, to study in Paris.

While they were actually at the Gare de Lyon waiting to start for
the South, Cyril was taken so seriously ill that it became clear he
was unfit for the journey. Mrs. Oliphant left him in charge of a
doctor and joined Cecco at Beaulieu, whither Cyril came as soon as
he had recovered. By June they were back at Windsor.

It was about this time that Barrie's *Auld Licht Idylls* came into
her hands, and with unfailing flair she discerned their fresh and
original quality.

Mr. Barrie's *Auld Licht Idylls* I think exceedingly clever. Indeed there
seems to be genius in them though the Scotch is, as you say, much too
provincial. . . . Barrie I must applaud, for I think his faculty is great. . . .
He came here to see me one day. I have been rather nervous ever since
lest I should see myself in a newspaper, but he has been merciful. . . .

Sir James Barrie wrote a charming account of that meeting in his
Introductory Note to her posthumously published book of stories,
The Widow's Tale. He declared that she had "ordered" him to
Windsor and that he journeyed thither in as much trepidation and
pride as if the command had come from another Great Lady "resident
in the same place."

They say she was not tall—he wrote—but she seemed tremendous to
me that day. I find an old letter in which I dwelt on the height of her
and her grand manner. . . . In her presence I think those whose manner
is of to-day (he wrote in 1898) must always have felt suddenly boorish.
She belonged to a politer age; you never knew it more surely than when
she was putting you at your ease with a graciousness that had something
of command in it. Mrs. Oliphant was herself the fine Scots gentlewoman
she drew so incomparably in her books, most sympathetic when she
unbent and a ramrod if she chose—the *grande dame* at one moment, almost
a girl, it might be, the next . . . she always gave you the impression of
one who loved fine, beautiful things and always wore rare caps and fine
lace as if they were part of her.

He saw her for the last time shortly before her death :

The wit had all gone out of her eyes though not quite from her talk ; her face had grown very sweet and soft. She was less the novelist now than a pathetic figure in a novel. . . .

Indeed, when Mrs. Oliphant reviewed Barrie's book *Margaret Ogilvy*—that beautiful portrait of his mother—some remembrance of her own early days, the cherished figure of her own mother, must have risen to her mind. Fortunately she could not foresee the day when the author should forsake Thrums for Kensington Gardens, and attempt the apotheosis of the Boy who never grew up—than which, in real life, no sadder sight surely exists—in the sentimental illusion known as Peter Pan. . . .

§

Macmillan had invited Mrs. Oliphant to write a book about Jerusalem, and thither she went in the spring of 1890, meeting Cecco at Turin on the way. Both her sons and her niece Madge, afterwards Mrs. Vallentin, accompanied her. She was then terribly anxious about Cecco. He was woefully thin and, to use her own words, " it makes my heart sick every time I look at him."

It was a strenuous journey for all the little party, and on their return Cecco went to the Engadine which was then, as now, regarded as a desirable place for sufferers from his malady.

Mrs. Oliphant stayed for a few days with her cousin, Mrs. Coghill, but on her return to Windsor she found Cyril seriously unwell, while Cecco's letters were the reverse of reassuring. " I feel as if he were coming back less well instead of better," she wrote. " God grant I may be wrong, but my life seems sometimes almost too full of anxieties to be borne. . . . I hope that in a week or so Cecco will be back, but I almost fear the sight of his dear thin hands. I am cheerful enough, you know, outwardly, and don't talk of my troubles, but they are very heavy and sore. The mountains of work I have to toil through are the best help I could have."

Proud and undefeated, she never relinquished that task, now made more than ever necessary by the ill-health of both her sons.

Cecco returned in the autumn and was at Windsor when Cyril fell ill with what seemed to be a slight attack of bronchitis. It was only on the night of his death—November 9, 1890—that more serious symptoms supervened. He was then but thirty-four years old and his little book on De Musset, written for the series edited by his mother, was just going to press.

Mrs. Oliphant bore this blow with her usual fortitude. When the funeral was over she accompanied her younger son to Davos, where he was to spend the winter. But this bereavement had taken heavy toll of her ; the reaction came ; she suffered from rheumatism and lost something of her spring.

At Davos she had her first serious illness. She was then sixty-three and perhaps prematurely aged by the long battle of life. The doctors decided it would be imprudent for her to remain in that high altitude, and in the spring she took Cecco to San Remo, returning to Windsor in May. He was then well enough to do a little work in the Royal Library, and he also contributed an article on Davos to the *Spectator*.

After that Mrs. Oliphant was constantly abroad, seeking health for her son, hoping against hope that his malady might at least be arrested. She must often have had in mind those far-off days in the Via Babuino at Rome, when her husband lay dying in those comfortless rooms. At least she could give her son all possible alleviation, could leave no single stone unturned. . . .

In 1893, her elder niece Madge was married, and at the wedding the guests noticed how appallingly ill Cecco looked. He was terribly emaciated and coughed perpetually.

He died at Windsor in October, 1894, the last survivor of her five children. Thenceforth her younger niece, Denny—" my daughter now for so many years "—was her constant and loving companion. She had indeed long since adopted her as a daughter. . . .

For with Mrs. Oliphant those who knew her best loved her best. In her own family circle she was able to doff something of that inherited Scottish pride and delicate reserve which prevented her, one always thinks, from ever revealing herself fully to acquaintances and strangers. But to her own family and servants she was exceptionally dear, and she had to the end a host of loving and faithful friends.

§

Mrs. Oliphant's books enjoyed a great popularity for a very long time, but even before the end she was conscious, not of any failing in her own power and imagination, but of a sharp divergence between herself and the new generation of writers that sprang to fame in the 'nineties, a period of immense literary activity. If we are to believe —and, alas, how can we not ?—that her preface entitled " On the Ebb Tide," that formed an introduction to one of her last books, *The Ways of Life*, was autobiographical in that it revealed something of her waning hold over the public, there can be few sadder things in literature. For in it she spoke with a rare candour " of the wonderful and overwhelming revelation which comes to most people, that their career, whatever it may have been, has come to a stop, and that henceforth they must accustom themselves to going out with the tide."

The flood which in its rise seemed almost individual, pervaded by something like conscious life of force and pleasure, becomes like an abstract relentless fate when it pours back into the deep gulf of a sea of relentlessness. . . .

The moment when we first perceive that our individual tide has turned is one which few persons will find it possible to forget. We look on with a piteous surprise to see our little triumphs, our not-little hopes, the future we had still believed in, the past in which we thought our name and fame would still be to the good, whatever happened, all floating out to sea to be lost there, out of sight of men. In the morning all might seem to go on as sure as ever—that is for our time which means the same thing— as the sky over us or the earth beneath our feet ; but before evening there was a different story, and the tide was in full retreat, carrying with it both convictions of the past and hopes in the future, not only our little laurels tossed and withered, and our little projects, but also the very heart of exertion. . . .

No complaint or even bitterness. Everything in life had been taken from her, why not this little fame she had earned by the sweat of her brow ? It was the calm acceptance of a natural law by an exceptionally wise and clear-eyed woman.

She has her revenge in that preface—wrote Miss Mary Coleridge— the later Victorians may turn to it for consolation when the subjects of Edward VII weary of them. . . .

The art of writing had then become more highly technical. Writers were preoccupied with such matters as form, phrasing, balance. And to the newer generation of authors Mrs. Oliphant's books were found lacking in these subtleties. It was not enough to tell an interesting story—that she could always do as well as anyone—but her manner of doing it had nothing of the idiom of that new epoch. It was the natural fate of an author who had written too long and in the opinion of the critics too much. . . .

But critics in blaming a novelist for excessive output should glance back a hundred years and remember the bitter stress under which Sir Walter Scott worked after the failure of Constable & Co., in which he was unfortunately implicated ; the needs of a large family which compelled Charles Dickens to continue his perpetual lecturing, since that brought him more money than writing with less expenditure of time, long after the doctors had warned him against the fatigue involved. Writers do not as a rule spring from the ranks of the rich. Often they have families or dependent relations to support. No one censures a man or woman for incessant work in an office, and writing, like any other profession, must be pursued with unremitting diligence when the family budget depends upon it. Where

P

the claims upon authors are heavy it is practically impossible for them to put by any substantial sum for the future. A few in our own time have enjoyed such prodigious successes that they have been able to leave considerable fortunes at their death. But a glance at the heart-breaking Civil Pensions List will show that these are the happy exceptions and are probably those who began with an assured income. Almost every year the name of some author of a bygone " best seller " is published among those to whom the meagre pensions are allotted. These are they who have lived long enough to watch the tragic ebbing of the tide and to realize that they have no message for the new generation. Old age and sickness must have exhausted their economies while inability to work or perhaps to place that work completes the mournful little history. There are indeed few professions so hazardous as that of the author who has no adequate private means. That is why so many of our own poets have died in the most sordid poverty. . . . .

§

Mrs. Oliphant worked for the best part of half a century and completed during that time over one hundred books, many entailing a good deal of research, besides innumerable short stories, articles and reviews. Forty-nine years separated her first book from her last. She never laid down her pen—although it had worn a hole in her finger which made it agony for her to write—until nearing the end. She wrote a little poem about Queen Victoria's Diamond Jubilee within a week or two of her death. . . .

Her novels always began with a kind of spirited *élan* fated sometimes to flag a little. But they were invariably interesting and wholesome, and eminently readable from that spontaneous dexterity of manner with which they were presented, the shrewd but kindly worldly wisdom that characterized them. I think people will turn to them again as already they have returned to Trollope with whom she had something in common. They will be rewarded if in so doing they read *Kirsteen*, the *Chronicles of Carlingford*, the *Beleaguered City*—one of the most imaginative of all her stories—*Katie Stewart* and *Margaret Maitland*. They will find in many of these a picture of Victorian life that has perhaps rarely been equalled. And they will marvel, perhaps, that one brain and one pen could have achieved so much at once valuable and interesting.

In addition to the novels which emanated so ceaselessly from her pen to enable her to educate her own and her brother's children, as well as to help numberless lame dogs over innumerable stiles, she wrote full biographies of Edward Irving, Montalembert, Principal Tulloch and Laurence Oliphant. She was one of the first to write a life of St. Francis of Assisi in English. She wrote, too, that series of the " Makers " of Rome, Florence and Venice, which, appearing before the immense " spate " of books on Italy, are still of considerable value to the student and which must have involved a great deal of " spade-work." For forty-five years she contributed articles, stories, reviews of books, historical and biographical sketches to *Maga*. She was able to complete two volumes of that monumental work *Annals of a Publishing House : William Blackwood and his Sons*, for which her long association with that firm so eminently qualified her, before she died. Her article on Siena, to which place she journeyed a broken women a few months before her death, was published later in the year in *Blackwood's Magazine*. Two posthumous works were also published in the year following her death.

Thus she covered a very long period of the Victorian era—longer, I believe, than any other novelist. When she began to write many of the most popular authors of the day were at the height of their fame. When *Margaret Maitland* appeared *Jane Eyre* had only been for two years before the world, and *Shirley* and *Villette* were yet to come. The name of Brontë was still unknown, disguised beneath the pseudonym of Bell. *Vanity Fair*, with which Thackeray scored his first important success, was published in 1847, two years before *Margaret Maitland* appeared. *Adam Bede* was not published until ten years later, for although George Eliot was nine years older than Mrs. Oliphant she did not essay fiction until her thirty-seventh year. George Meredith, born the same year as Mrs. Oliphant, did not publish *Richard Feverel* till her first book was ten years old. Trollope, who was thirteen years her senior, began to publish only one year before herself. It was the same with Mrs. Gaskell, who was eighteen years her senior. Bulwer Lytton was then at the height of his fame, earning almost incredible sums for those novels, which— if we are to believe Joseph Conrad—remain still the joy of the fo'c'sle.

Newer authors, such as Ouida and Rhoda Broughton, first won fame in the 'sixties, when Mrs. Oliphant had been writing industriously for more than a dozen years. It was thus difficult for people to believe that she was not a great deal older than she was, and when her first Tauchnitz appeared, she had to correct an error on this point, and satisfy Mr. Blackwood that she had really been born on April 4, 1828.

For poets she had as contemporaries Tennyson, the Brownings, Swinburne, the two Rossettis. And not many years before her death she was to feel astonished and even a little envious at the almost fantastic financial success of Mrs. Humphry Ward. . . .

I do not believe there is another instance, except possibly that of Miss Braddon, of a woman writing so arduously and unremittingly over so long a period. Care and anxiety were her close companions through life, for even the happiness of her early married days was marred by the mutual antagonism of her husband and her mother, and the long painful illness of the latter. The only marvel is that she should have maintained her position in the world of letters against such fearful odds, and at a period too when so many giants of her trade so securely held the field. Perhaps her secret was that she could tell a story sympathetically and artlessly, and that she should have begun, too, with Scottish stories may afford some explanation of her early success. She was the pioneer, after Sir Walter Scott, of that Scottish school of fiction which was destined to find its most brilliant exponents in Stevenson and Sir James Barrie.

It is recorded by Dr. Arthur Benson that after her death W. E. Henley, a great admirer of her work, urged Henry James, to whom incidentally Mrs. Oliphant had offered considerable hospitality, to read *Kirsteen*.

That you should have any pretensions to interest in literature and should dare to say that you have not read *Kirsteen* !

Henry James—to use his own words or perhaps we should say Henley's—took his bludgeoning patiently and humbly and went home to read the book. His verdict was, as might have been expected, eminently unfavourable, for he was never a good judge of work that did not conform to his own intricate pattern, and his estimate of the writer was more than a little ungenerous since she had shown him both kindness and friendship. Still he had the grace to add : *Yes, no doubt she was a gallant woman* . . . .

A gallant woman ? . . . I do not think she could have wished for another or a better epitaph. For she *had* fought valiantly and against almost overwhelming odds from the time she was left a widow with three young children and debts amounting to £1,000, not only for herself but for that little household (and not always such a little one) that looked to her for all the necessities of life. There had been the three boys whom she had educated at no small cost and for whom she had had such high hopes, and was it through any fault of hers that the eldest and most successful should have succumbed to typhoid fever so early in his Indian career, or that the others through hereditary tendencies and physical disability should have fallen prematurely by the wayside ?

§

The last few weeks of Mrs. Oliphant's life were spent at Wimbledon. She amused herself with writing a dramatized version of *Esmond*, which she sent to Mrs. (afterwards Lady) Ritchie, telling her it had helped her through those twilight hours which she found the hardest of all. Nor was she surprised to hear later that there were already two other recent versions, since Laurence Oliphant had told her the same idea always occurred to three persons simultaneously.

In April, 1897, she went to Siena accompanied by her niece and Miss Tulloch, but she was even then very ill and suffering, and only remained there long enough to obtain such details as she deemed necessary for the writing of her projected book on the subject.

This is a very interesting place—she wrote—though there is an element of guide-book in what I am desired to do about it which does not please me much, and to which only my poverty and not my will consents. . . .

Only my poverty. . . . Yes, it had come to that after her half-century of strenuous, unremitting work.

After her return to Wimbledon she knew that the end was approaching. She was then in her seventieth year.

" I have no pain, I am only waiting, and I hope I shall not have to wait very long, lest I should grow impatient."

And in another, even more pitiful letter :

I am dying but not suffering much. Good-bye. . . .

From that bed of sickness she dictated the following little poem :—

> On the edge of the world I lie, I lie,
> Happy and dying and dazed and poor,
> Looking up from the vast great floor
> Of the infinite world that rises above
> To God and to Faith and to Love, Love, Love !
> What words have I to that world to speak,
> Old and weary and dazed and weak,
> From the very low to the very high ?
> Only this and this is all :
> From the fresh green soil to the wide blue sky,
> From Greatness to Weariness, Life to Death,
> One God have we on Whom to call :
> One great bond from which none can fall :
> Love below, which is Life and breath,
> And Love above which sustaineth all. . . .

She died on June 25, 1897, with the names of her two sons continually on her lips. She was buried with them at Eton.

A gallant woman. . . .

§

There were many to mourn her outside her own family. A few days before the end she sent for Lady Ritchie, that friend of so many years. She had indeed been the first to review her work in *Blackwood*, greatly to Thackeray's delight. Now she kissed her and sent her love to her children, and a little later borrowed from her a copy of Tennyson's *Poems* as she desired especially to read his *Ode on the Death of the Duke of Clarence.* " I think she is longing to go," Lady Ritchie wrote.

Then after her death Lady Ritchie wrote to Rhoda Broughton, telling her she had shown her note which " said truly what all our hearts are feeling " to the two nieces who were left to mourn her loss.

I am going to get ready now to go to the funeral—the letter continued, I have lost a life-long friend, and the world too, in that wise, tender and humorous woman whom all delighted to love and appreciate. She was to me one of those people who *make* life—so many unmake it.

John Oliver Hobbes

JOHN OLIVER HOBBES
(PEARL MARY TERESA CRAIGIE)

§

EVEN now, nearly thirty years after her sudden and premature death, it is not easy to estimate the ultimate position Pearl Craigie won for herself in literature. She herself was convinced that her books would live, and this assurance on the part of an author is a rare quality and is generally justified by the opinion of posterity.

But a new world has come into being since the days when those brilliant, wise trifles *Some Emotions and a Moral, A Study in Temptations* and *The Sinner's Comedy* broke upon an astonished London in the early years of the 'nineties. Concise, epigrammatic and dramatic, they had little in common with the three-volume novels of the day. Moreover, no one had ever heard of " John Oliver Hobbes " who had sprung thus suddenly to fame.

That epoch, so prolific in new writers, so daring in its disregard of tradition, is at once too near and too far for posterity to pass a conclusive judgment upon its group of brilliant, sad writers. But there is one thing for which her co-religionists must ever remember that new star, Pearl Craigie, with admiration and even reverence. She was definitely in England the pioneer of the Catholic novelist, and, as such, she can surely never be forgotten.

Her books are still read, perhaps by the few rather than by the many. Her reputation must ultimately rest, not upon the witty, epigrammatic trifles such as *Some Emotions and a Moral*, but upon those maturer works *The School for Saints* and its admirable sequel *Robert Orange*. Both these books were written many years after her conversion to Catholicism and they possess qualities of humanity, of deep, imaginative insight into the things of the spirit that were perhaps lacking in her earlier work.

Memory summons up a charming picture of her at a dinner where women writers were wont to assemble and at which on this occasion I think she presided. She was dressed in white ; her hair, dark and abundant, was plainly and even classically dressed, at a period when

233

most women wore theirs oddly puffed out over monstrous frameworks, so that the beautiful line of her little Greek head was unspoiled. She had dark, brilliant eyes, restlessly intelligent and remotely tragic ; there was something at once humorous and wistful in her smile. Without being strictly beautiful she possessed many of the attributes of beauty and she was extraordinarily attractive. Although she was below rather than above middle height, her small head set upon a slim neck made her seem taller than she actually was.

Another picture, and this time the scene is set in the Convent of the Holy Child, Cavendish Square, where at that time a little literary society, long since dispersed, held its meetings. Eminent Catholic writers, such as Monsignor Hugh Benson, Father Sebastian Bowden and Mrs. Katherine Tynan, were among those who read papers there. Mrs. Craigie's lecture was on " Dante and Plato," and she held the little assembly spellbound. But she looked tired and older. The slight exertion involved seemed something of an effort to her. The hint of tragedy had deepened in her eyes. She still, however, possessed that strangely alive, wise, if somewhat disillusioned, look that had struck me on the previous occasion of our meeting. . . .

The few years that had passed between those two encounters had been busy, active, crowded ones for her and had affected a physique that was never strong. Not only had she produced the second of her two masterpieces but she had written a number of other novels, had travelled extensively both in India and America, and had spent a great deal of time over those ambitious but ephemeral dramas, of which one, *The Ambassador*, was so admirably produced by the late Sir George Alexander.

Looking back one is inclined to regard those dramatic ventures as detrimental to her literary career. They absorbed a great deal of her time and strength ; she went hither and thither to be present at rehearsals, unduly taxing her delicate nervous system, suffering too from a kind of resentful depression when they failed to please. *The Ambassador* was the most successful, and ran for a considerable time ; it was produced with every advantage that a play in those days could hope to obtain. It was admirably staged ; the caste was a strong one. But I can remember hearing an indignant Frenchwoman say, as we left the theatre : " À Paris on ne le jouera pas douze fois ! " And her companion's " Comment ? Tu ne t'es pas amusée ? " lacked, to my thinking, adequate surprise.

§

The life of Pearl Mary Teresa Craigie was short, and in a sense, tragic. She was born at Chelsea, near Boston, Massachusetts, on November 3,

PEARL MARY TERESA CRAIGIE ("JOHN OLIVER HOBBES")
(From a photograph by Messrs. Elliot & Fry.)

1867, and she died in London in the early hours of August 13, 1906 in her thirty-ninth year. She was the eldest child of Mr. John Morgan Richards and of his wife, the daughter of Seth Arnold. On both sides she came of Presbyterian and Nonconformist stock.

She was a mere infant when her mother took her to London, where Mr. Richards was already engaged in business that had called him thither when his child was only two or three weeks old. London was to prove Pearl Richards's home for the greater part of her life. The little family lived first at Kennington Gate on the south side of the Thames, moving later as fortune smiled upon them to Upper Woburn Place, Bloomsbury, where three sons were born to the exiled American couple.

At that time Dr. Joseph Parker was minister of the City Temple, where the Richards family worshipped, and Pearl was only nine when she contributed two stories to the *Fountain*, a journal edited by Parker. Beginning thus early she continued to write stories and sketches and submitted them to various editors without consulting her parents in the matter, and remaining entirely unbaffled by the lack of success that attended these precocious ventures.

Her first school was at Newbury where she proved a clever, diligent pupil. When at home for the holidays she constantly went to the play and thus saw all the principal actors and actresses of the 'seventies while still quite a child, and this undoubtedly gave her her passion for the theatre. Her childhood was singularly full and interesting. Her education was conducted on broader lines than was customary at that period ; her recreations were less those of a child than of a grown-up person, and it is scarcely surprising that her first novel, written in her early twenties, should have proved such a mature piece of work. She seems indeed to have enjoyed all the advantages which accrue to the children of wealthy parents in our own day.

Nothing was spared to equip her for life. At seventeen she went to Paris to study music and became a brilliant pianiste. In the spring of 1886, when she was little more than eighteen, she returned to London and was presented at Court. That same year she returned to the States for the first time to act as bridesmaid to Miss Julia Randall Drake, the daughter of an old friend of her father's.

But her girlhood's days were nearing their end, and early in 1887, when she was nineteen, she married Mr. R. W. Craigie. The honeymoon was spent at Cannes where she had a most serious illness, and on her return to London she went straight to her father's house— that friendly asylum that never failed her—to be nursed back to health. Afterwards the young couple lived in a flat at Marble Arch

Mansions, moving a little later to a house at High Barnet. For two years after her marriage Mrs. Craigie contributed dramatic and art criticisms to a weekly paper called *Life*.

In 1890, when she had been married three years, Mrs. Craigie and her husband went to the Isle of Wight where Mr. Richards had recently purchased the beautiful property of Steephill Castle, near Ventnor, and there, at Rock Cottage, her only child, a son, was born. But in the following year she returned to her father's house in London, and informed her parents of her resolution never again to live with her husband. Although very little is known of her married life beyond the details that were subsequently revealed in the divorce proceedings which some years later ended it, one can judge that it was never a sympathetic union. But she obtained what was most necessary for her happiness, the sole custody of her child.

Mrs. Craigie was now in her twenty-fourth year. Broken, but by no means defeated, by the bitter experiences through which she had passed, and which must have been specially wounding to a woman of sensitive and imaginative temperament, she embarked upon a course of study at University College, London, under the kindly and sympathetic ægis of Professor Alfred Goodwin, who died in 1892, and to whose memory she dedicated *The Sinner's Comedy*. She rose early and worked for many hours daily.

§

Her first book, *Some Emotions and a Moral*, was published in 1891, the year of her separation from her husband. It was offered in the first instance to Macmillan, who suggested, perhaps justifiably, that she should revise the final chapter and also, with less foresight, that she should change that happy and intriguing title. She refused to do either and took it to Fisher Unwin. He accepted it for his new venture " The Pseudonym Library," of which it proved one of the outstanding successes. To people yet hardly weaned from the traditional " three-decker " these slight brilliant novels proved a welcome if challenging diversion. Indeed, it is on record that Joseph Conrad received his first impulse to write and to write in English after buying one of the series at Vevey station. One can only hope that his choice fell upon *Some Emotions and a Moral*.

The book appeared in July and before the end of the year six thousand copies had been sold. Witty, epigrammatic, unusual, with an undercurrent of profound if sad wisdom, it had only been out a week when Mr. Fisher Unwin was able to tell Mrs. Craigie : " Your book is a success for both author and publisher."

The author's name, John Oliver Hobbes, was completely unknown to the literary London of that day. But the little oblong book, with its yellow paper cover, unusual format, and challenging title, was to be seen in every house and was discussed and quoted at many a dinner-table. Her choice of a *nom-de-plume* requires some explanation. She took the name of John because it was that of both her father and her son, Oliver, out of admiration for the " warring Cromwell," and Hobbes principally on account of the philosopher, and also because of its homely sound.

This first venture was followed at no long interval by *The Sinner's Comedy*. After the success of *Some Emotions* she was naturally nervous as to its reception, and wrote as follows to her publisher :

I wish the book published as soon as possible, because I suffer so terribly from nervousness (a kind of stage fright) until a book has received a verdict, that it really amounts to an illness. The pleasure of writing is great, but the publishing is an agony long drawn out. . . .

It appeared in May, but after correcting the proofs, she sailed with her father in March for America, hoping to repeat her success on that side of the Atlantic. But curiously enough neither Scribner's nor Putnam's, to whom she submitted it, would risk its publication. Too long for a short story and not nearly long enough for a standard novel, her books failed to meet the usual trade requirements. She then discovered that Cassell's had a branch in New York and she immediately approached that firm, with the result that the contract was signed on April 26 and *The Sinner's Comedy* was published simultaneously in London and New York on May 16. Its success was immediate, and thenceforward Mrs. Craigie never had the slightest difficulty in placing any of her work ; it was indeed eagerly sought after by both publishers and editors.

In 1893 she published her third book, *A Study in Temptations*, and in her preface to the second edition she made a brief but poignant allusion to the circumstances in which it had been written :

A greater part of the book was composed under the strain of bad health and all of it in circumstances of peculiar anxiety. If the author had written as he felt and thought the result would have been very far from amusing. And his sole aim has been to amuse.

Work was necessary to her at that time as an escape from the haunting tragedy of her life. . . .

Later in the year she published a less attractive book *A Bundle of Life*. She preferred to make all the necessary arrangements herself without any assistance, and we find her writing to Mr. Clement Shorter in January, 1893, in a manner that suggests she did not always find the task too easy.

I find it so difficult to be at once a Christian, an author, and a woman of business.

In 1894 she published a much longer novel, *The Gods, Some Mortals and Lord Wickenham*, of which the charming early scenes were laid in a Roman palace.

§

Religion had always interested Mrs. Craigie since the far-off City Temple days when the genial Dr. Parker had encouraged her first essays in literature, and his wife had been amused and even a little shocked at the precocious child's quaint and sometimes impertinent speeches. In these later years, however, her steps were tending towards another path, and she was to be faced with a decision that must, she knew, definitely affect her whole future life, excluding her arbitrarily from any second marriage and the prospect—inevitable for such a young, beautiful and gifted woman—of any compensating love. It was characteristic of her that when the crucial moment arrived she displayed neither hesitation nor reluctance, and in July, 1892, the year after her separation from her husband, she was received into the Catholic Church by Father Charles Foster at St. James's, Spanish Place.

Father Gavin, S.J., the wise counsellor and director of her spiritual life, held the opinion that she read herself into the Church, and it was undoubtedly the philosophy of Catholicism that first attracted her keen intellect. He averred that she became a Catholic by study and conviction and in obedience to the dictates of her conscience, adding, too, that she was one of the cleverest converts who ever came to him for instruction.

" I was surprised at her decision," her father wrote in the Memoir he contributed to her *Life and Letters*, " but we never had one word of discussion on the subject ; she merely stated the fact." The abounding sympathy that existed between them was never more clearly shown than in this sentence. There was really no need for words between them. She was doing what she thought right and that was sufficient for him with his unshakable confidence in " Pearl."

One cannot pass by this episode without a word concerning the immense renunciation and sacrifice which Mrs. Craigie made of all future human happiness when she thus became a Catholic. She was not yet twenty-five, and she had just been freed from an unhappy and disastrous marriage. With her fame, her beauty, her wealth and arresting charm, it was hardly to be expected that she would not meet with a love that should compensate in some sort for that too-early matrimonial venture. Her vivid personality, her wit, her rapid rise to fame, had made her much sought after in the London society of her day. She knew everyone worth knowing, whether social, political or literary. But she deliberately and with her own hands raised an impenetrable barrier between herself and another marriage. Yet from our knowledge of her we can but be convinced that hers was no impulsive action ; she had counted the cost, and had the sacrifice been a thousand times more difficult, she would not have shrunk from it. It is impossible not to share her father's confidence in her wisdom and complete sincerity.

Often afterwards she would retire to a room she rented at the Convent of the Assumption, in Kensington Square, for a few days' rest and spiritual retreat.

" The Roman Catholic Faith," Lord Curzon said, when he un-veiled a memorial to her at University College, London, " supplied her with a philosophy of conduct and a rationale of existence. She found an inspiration in its ideals, and a solace in its authority."

§

All this time she pursued her work with unremitting diligence. In 1895 she made her first dramatic venture in a play called *Journeys End in Lovers' Meetings* founded upon a French one, but of which the dialogue was entirely original. It was produced at Daly's in June and the principal parts were played by Ellen Terry, Forbes Robert-son and William Terriss. Afterwards Ellen Terry, who became her intimate friend, bought the acting rights and played the piece with Irving both in England and America.

Mrs. Craigie still had eleven years to live, and they were very full and successful if anxious years. Her little son, her devoted parents, the love of her own family, supplied her with the sympathy that made her private life so serene and harmonious. She had hosts of friends and interests outside these things, but she permitted nothing to interfere with her writing. All authors seek an environment where they can best achieve their work, and with her it was the dining-room of her father's house in Lancaster Gate, whither he had moved when he gave up the one in Porchester Terrace. She liked the big table and often when alone would have her meals served at one end of it so that she was not under the necessity of moving her papers. At times she would seek a spot where there would be fewer interruptions, but always in the end she returned to her father's roof. She had a house of her own—Craigie Lodge—near Steephill Castle, rooms in the Albany, Piccadilly, and her little refuge in Kensington Square, but she rarely worked anywhere except in Lancaster Gate. Some authors require complete seclusion ; others need the inspiring stir of life about them.

In 1896 she published *The Herb Moon*, but it was not until some five years after her reception into the Catholic Church that she actually introduced a Catholic *motif* into her books. Her admiration for Disraeli—of whom she drew an admirable and convincing portrait in the *School for Saints*—may have prompted her to attempt the politico-religious novel such as he had written in *Lothair*, but with this difference. With her the Catholic Church played a very prominent and definite part in the lives of both her hero and heroine. She, however, achieved this with such consummate art that she never laid herself open to the accusation of " propaganda." Forsaking her early concise and epigrammatic style, she worked for the first time upon a crowded canvas, depicting a cosmopolitan group of people, politicians and minor royalties, who were engaged in foreign intrigues which especially affected the life of her heroine, Brigit Parflete.

She was thirty years old when the *School for Saints* appeared, and she already had some half-dozen novels to her credit. But this book was her first definite contribution to Catholic literature, and it gave evidence not only of imagination and increased power, but of deep study and of her profound love for the Church which was to her both solace and support.

Of course, it had its faults. The Carlist episodes and Spanish scenes, of which she had studied the topography with meticulous care, overweighted it with historical matter, detracting in some sense from the interest of the main theme and tending to confuse the issues. But who can read of the visit paid by Robert Orange in the company of Disraeli to the Bona Mors service at the Church of the Jesuit Fathers in Farm Street without sensing something of that profound love the writer possessed for the Faith ? Few, I think, could have read it without going thither afterwards to savour that little ceremony for themselves. Written at a time when the Catholic novel was looked askance at by publishers and libraries alike, ar ᵈ before the wave of conversion that swept over England in later yea , attaining to its peak during the Great War, had begun appreciably to be felt, that chapter must have guided many feet to the threshold of the Church, must have prompted many to seek for the first time the Divine Presence.

The light on the high Altar shone through the mist of incense as something wholly supernatural yet living and sacred. It seemed to breathe and vibrate, and was now a still blessing, and now a note of music too delicate to be told on instruments or uttered by human voice. It fell not upon the senses but upon the heart, and the faint sound that reached the ear was no more than the infinite soft murmur of many small candle flames.

Deliberately she proceeded to explain the rite of Benediction that followed, aware perhaps that her readers seeking to be present at it for the first time, whether from motives of curiosity or interest or from some higher and more inexplicable impulse, might find themselves bewildered and astray at the unaccustomed ceremony.

At its conclusion the priest mantled with the veil makes the Sign of the Cross over the worshippers. This Benediction is given in silence—to show that it is not the earthly but the Eternal Priest Who in the rite blesses and sanctifies His people. . . .

One of the most remarkable and dramatic scenes in the book is where Brigit Parflete, little more than a child, learns that her father was not, as she supposed, a Captain Duboc, but the Archduke Charles of Alberia who had privately married her beautiful mother, Henriette Duboc, a dancer, and whose legitimate though unacknowledged heir she is. Wishing to separate her from her husband, a worthless rake who has been discovered cheating at cards, the Archduke sends for his daughter, tells her the truth about her parentage and informs her that a divorce can be arranged and another husband found for her.

Brigit received this speech with profound resentment.

" As I am not a princess," she said, " and as I have no rights I may remain true to my marriage vows. The word divorce has no meaning for me. I am a Catholic. I implore you to let me go."

It was hardly to be expected that such a remarkable book should be followed by an even more brilliant sequel, but *Robert Orange* more than fulfilled the promise of its predecessor. Its technique was more assured, and it displayed an even deeper insight into humanity. It must always stand at the head of Mrs. Craigie's achievement. Perhaps, too, it might interest the present generation even more profoundly than it did her own.

Always slightly in advance of her time, Mrs. Craigie had been anxious to publish the *School for Saints* as a trilogy since it fell, she said, naturally into three parts. Twenty years later this would have been practicable, and the *School for Saints* and *Robert Orange* might most advantageously have been issued in this form so familiar in our own day.

We feel, when reading the book, that she was no longer writing merely to amuse, or to distract her mind from its own griefs ; she had a new aim, a more definite purpose. That purpose was undoubtedly to make the Catholic Church known in all its truth and beauty through the medium of fiction among readers to whom books of Catholic instruction were never likely to penetrate. She was the first to achieve this end, although Mrs. Wilfrid Ward, in *One Poor*

Scruple, and Monsignor Hugh Benson were soon to follow in the trail thus blazed.

In *Robert Orange* she wrote with a singular fearlessness :

The Catholic Faith which ignores no single possibility in human feeling and no possible flight in human idealism, produces in those who hold it truly a freshness of heart very hard to be understood by the dispassionate critic who weighs character by the newest laws of his favourite degenerate but never by the primeval tests of God. . . .

It may be said without exaggeration that *Robert Orange* is the finest Catholic novel written in the English language. It comes nearer than any other to real literature. It possesses passages of great beauty. The thirty-five years that have elapsed since its publication have in no sense detracted from its value and interest. It is not dated and possesses the elements of a sure immortality. Nor is its spiritual content the least enduring of its qualities.

§

Mrs. Craigie was still at work on this book when her most successful play *The Ambassador* was produced at St. James's Theatre. As we have seen, it enjoyed considerable popularity and had a longish run. On the first night the author was called for, and in response, she duly appeared. To many of the audience she was still John Oliver Hobbes, and failing to understand why a woman should thus appear, they continued to shout, " Where is John ? " The young slender woman dressed in white satin, with her dark hair and brilliant dark eyes, smiled at them, and then realizing that this was indeed the author, there were appreciative cries of " Pretty John ! "

Speaking once at the New York Lotus Club in regard to this name, she acknowledged wittily :

My jealousy of that creature is not to be expressed. However much I enjoy this party I know perfectly well it is not for me but for Hobbes. But for him I should never have been here. I will not say I dislike Hobbes —but even a woman is human.

The success of *Robert Orange* in 1900 did not, curiously enough, compensate her for the failure of her play *The Wisdom of the Wise*. This failure, combined with the dangerous illness of her little son, produced a complete collapse, and she went abroad that summer, spending some time in Switzerland and Italy. At Venice, " a wonderful place for tired nerves," she saw Duse act before a crowded house. D'Annunzio, who appeared at the end of each act, struck her as " an unpleasant person."

She was ever profoundly conscious that her life would be a short one.

Doctors told me some years ago that I should go out like a candle. My heart was broken with grief long ago, and although it is sound physically [an assurance which her sudden death was afterwards emphatically to disprove] and I ought to live by all the rules of the physical game, the laws of the spiritual game are more determined—if more elusive. No one was ever meant to see life as plainly as I see it and remain in it. . . .

While she would often work from eight to ten hours a day, suffering the while from the author's inevitable cerebral exhaustion which reacts so strongly upon the nervous system, there was little pause in her active life. Yet she often rose from her bed to attend functions where perhaps she was to be the " guest of the evening," and which she could thus hardly forgo. When, as did sometimes happen, she failed to appear, few imagined it was because the physical collapse was so complete that she had to lie for hours in a "hapless, brainless condition." There were days indeed when she dared not walk for fear of falling.

She was, like many authors, exceptionally sensitive to noise. She worked only while in the mood, but the mood must often have been often upon her, considering the amount of her output. Indeed, in the latter years of her life it was urgently necessary for her to earn money, as her father, unfortunate in speculation, had lost a good deal of his wealth.

And then she spent unstintingly in the cause of charity. She paid all the expenses of a little cottage home in the country where delicate children could be sent for change of air. She was ever ready to help the sick and ailing, and would often send nuns away for convalescent treatment after an illness. To the last she was a generous benefactress of St. Anne's, Vauxhall. But only those who were immediately concerned were ever aware of her innumerable charities.

§

Since her Paris days, music had always meant a great deal to Mrs. Craigie, and it did not fatigue her as it does so many brainworkers. It was at Bayreuth that she uttered the astonishing heresy (duly chronicled in Mr. E. F. Benson's *Mother*) that Wotan was a bore. Even before that she had written that " Wagner had desecrated every beautiful phrase in the great masters," and though she modified her opinion during a later visit, it is easy to see that the rather feverish atmosphere of adulation that prevailed at Bayreuth affected the clear sanity of her own vision very disagreeably. " I 'think the thing is on the whole mere sentimentalism of a rather vicious kind. In ten years Wagner will be ' off,' " she wrote to a friend.

" He was a great man," she wrote on another occasion, " but the greatest man is not so great as mankind. His art was too personal, nervous, overcharged. . . ."

The Serious Wooing was published in 1901 and *Love and the Soul Hunters* in 1902. During the latter year she went to India for the Durbar as the guest of the Viceroy and Lady Curzon—an old and dear friend. On arrival she went to the Viceregal camp at Delhi, but she disliked the life with its moderate comfort, its inadequate shelter during the bitterly cold nights that prevailed. Indeed many people were ill with pneumonia or sore throats. But she enjoyed the social side of the adventure, the State functions and balls and teas at which Royalty was present, and at which, as always, she came in for a good deal of attention and admiration. More than all perhaps she enjoyed the intimate talks with her beautiful friend. She had a profound admiration too for Lord Curzon, and her visit to India must certainly have proved one of the pleasantest interludes of her life.

Not that she was idle. She had been engaged to write a series of articles on the Durbar for the *Daily Graphic* (afterwards to be published in book form under the title of *Imperial India*) and she also planned a long historical novel dealing with the period of Warren Hastings and for which she had been promised access to documents of the first importance. This, alas, she never lived to achieve.

She returned to England in March, 1903, and wrote *The Vineyard*, which was serialized in the *Pall Mall Magazine*. She visited Spain that spring, and then spent the summer quietly at Ventnor with her boy, planning the *Dream and the Business*—the last book she ever published. At a bazaar, Princess Beatrice bought some books at her stall and was overheard to say as she turned away : " Who is that pretty woman ? "—a remark that could not fail to please her.

Her play the *Flute of Pan* was produced by Olga Nethersole at Manchester in the following year. It was, however, unfavourably received in London in the autumn, thus her ambition to be a successful dramatist remained unfulfilled. This was her last attempt to write a play.

In 1905 she went to the States to give a series of lectures. These included the *Art of Life*, the *Science of Life*, *Dante and Botticelli*, *Dante and Plato*, *St. Ignatius*, *Wesley* and *Tolstoy*.

It was in November, 1905, that she gave her first lecture on *The Art of Life* at Morristown, New Jersey. But the undue fatigue, the cold, the long hours of travelling, proved too much for her delicate physique, and after some weeks of strenuous effort she found herself unable to finish the tour. She sailed for England in February, 1906.

She was then very tired. Some premonition of the end seems to have been in her mind, since she wrote to a friend :

I don't believe I shall live much longer. There is nothing organically wrong with me, but I flag, the pulse stops.

Indeed, any undue exertion always made her collapse. Once, when as a much younger woman she had gone on a pilgrimage to Rome, she was so tired on arrival that she fainted on the floor of St. Peter's. The journeys to India and America with all the effort and work involved had undoubtedly debilitated her heart. The specialists, indeed, continued to warn her that her pulse might abruptly cease. Some of them even suggested that she was suffering from *le petit mal*—the earlier stages of epilepsy—but there was little to support this suggestion except the occasional loss of consciousness to which many delicate brain workers are liable. But the fact was she was worn out. She had made too heavy demands upon a nervous system that was never strong. The lecturing tour, although a great delight to her, should never have been undertaken, involving as it did such long nights in the train.

Please do not believe—she wrote once with a touch of pathos which was rare with her—that I have attained to any calmness in philosophy but by most bitter experiences. . . .

In March she wrote to a friend :

I thought I was dying last Saturday and I am sorry I did not. Please don't think I want a long illness and horrors. I want to die in harness and at work. . . .

She had her wish. The ink was hardly dry on the paper where she had written the last sentence of her unfinished book *A Time to Love*, when she died.

Soon after her return from America she finished *The Dream and the Business*, a mature piece of work that won favour from both critics and public. In it she used some of the Nonconformist experiences of her young girlhood. But in July she suffered a heavy blow from the death of her friend Lady Curzon, and from that time the sands of life began almost imperceptibly to run down.

August found her staying at Steephill Castle planning a motor-tour in Scotland for her boy's holiday. She drove and walked daily and began her book *A Time to Love*, adapted from a play, and for which she had visited Carlisle in order to obtain local colouring. The last entry in her Journal under date of August 12, 1906, ran as follows : *St. Wilfrid's*, 8.30.

It was a Sunday and the Feast of St. Clare, and she attended the half-past eight Mass and received Holy Communion at the Church of St. Wilfrid, Ventnor.　She spent the rest of the morning quietly, working a little at her book, and then took the afternoon train to London in order to fulfil a business appointment she had made for the following day.　The final arrangements for the motor tour had also to be made since it was her intention to start on August 15, her son's sixteenth birthday.

Just before leaving she went into her father's study to provide herself with a book for the journey.　Her choice fell upon Anne Brontë's *Tenant of Wildfell Hall* and one of the passengers noticed her reading it attentively on the boat between Ryde and Portsmouth.

Before retiring to rest she gave a telegram to the housekeeper at Lancaster Gate requesting that it might be despatched the first thing on Monday morning.　It ran as follows :

Excellent journey crowded train reached here by nine fondest love PEARL.

Acting on her instructions the servant sent the telegram early on the Monday morning before going to her room to call her.　When she did so there was no response.　Pearl Mary Teresa Craigie was lying as if asleep, her rosary in her hands.　Her face was quite peaceful ; there was no sign of her having stirred.　She had fallen asleep while praying and thus had died. . . .

The Requiem Mass was sung at the Church of the Jesuit Fathers at Farm Street, in accordance with her own wish.　Her body was laid to rest in St. Mary's Cemetery, Kensal Green, where every day Mass is said for the repose of the souls who lie there.　The granite pillar is surmounted by a cross, and the low kerb encloses a little plot of grass and flowers.

Katherine Mansfield

KATHERINE MANSFIELD

She is nothing but a little girl, sitting on the Tinakori hills,
dreaming. . . . (K.M.)

§

WHEN Guy de Pourtalès was finishing his admirable study
of Wagner he was staying at Montana, that high plateau
perched above the Rhône valley. The environment evoked
for him two figures, that of Rainer Maria Rilke, and—what is of more
profound interest to English readers—that of the "New Zealand
dove," Katherine Mansfield, who, as he said, trembled as she built
herself that mortuary-nest upon those rocks above Le Valais,
writing the while the stories which were to pay for her cure.

I have quoted this because it is significant of the deep impression
Katherine Mansfield made upon the men and women of her generation.

But it was a far cry from the little girl who once sat dreaming upon
the Tinakori hills, to the wounded dove who sought refuge in that
eyrie above Montana, watching the sequence of the seasons—the
deep snow of winter that tried her so cruelly, the delicate blossoming
of the spring orchards that reminded her of Karori, the riot of colour
offered by the alpine flowers in summer, the rich golden glow of
autumn with its odours of ripening fruit. It was there the cry
escaped her:

To write something that will be worthy of that rising moon, that pale
light. To be simple, as one would be simple before God. . . .

She had made a dark journey since she left the Tinakori hills, had
drunk deeply of the suffering of life. "The little boat enters the dark,
fearful gulf," she wrote, "and our only cry is to escape: Put me on
land again. . . ."

§

I have often wondered why Katherine Mansfield did not use the
story of her grandfather's early and somewhat romantic association
with New Zealand in one of her stories. Arthur Beauchamp inherited

249

his interest and holdings in that southern island from an aunt, Jane Beauchamp, who had been engaged early in the nineteenth century as companion to Lady Louisa Tollemache, daughter of the Countess of Dysart.

Lady Louisa had an unfortunate history for which she was in no sense to blame. She married in 1808 John Dalrymple, afterwards Earl of Stair, only to discover that he had formed a previous Scottish contract which invalidated the ceremony. Her so-called marriage was dissolved in 1809, and the lady retired to a dignified seclusion at Hamworth Park, together with Jane Beauchamp, her dogs and a parrot. Jane helped to tend these pets and also to look after the children—her employer's nephews and nieces—who from time to time came to enliven the place.

When Lady Louisa died, in 1834, it was found that she had bequeathed to Jane Beauchamp " now or late of Enfield," the sum of twenty thousand pounds, all her watches, such books, plate and furniture as she might choose, and those cherished canine creatures, Daphne and Zoe, as well as the parrot. Jane was further to receive an annuity of one hundred pounds during the lifetime of each dog and fifty pounds during that of the parrot. It will be seen that pets were not less adored by their owners a hundred years ago than they are to-day, and Jane Beauchamp profited by this passion to the extent of two hundred and fifty pounds a year. She thus found herself, on the death of her employer, a rich woman.

One of her co-legatees was Lady Laura Tollemache, afterwards Lady Ailesbury, a famous eccentric of Victorian times, who probably at the instigation of her cousin Algernon bought four sections of New Zealand land, he himself having acquired large tracts in that country. Jane, less prudent, purchased fourteen sections and a farm, her thousand acres costing her eleven thousand pounds. She quarrelled with her brothers and left all her personal estate to a distant cousin, but the New Zealand lands were bequeathed to her nephew, Arthur Beauchamp, who was the only member of her immediate family with whom she was on speaking terms at the time of her death.

Arthur was the second surviving son of Jane's brother, John. His elder brother Henry was in business and went to Mauritius and thence to Sydney, where he settled and where his famous daughter " Elizabeth," afterwards Countess Russell, was born. When Arthur was twenty-one, he too sailed for Sydney, reaching Wellington the following year. Algernon Tollemache appeared on the scene soon afterwards and found himself the owner of some of the most valuable land in the city. At that early stage New Zealand possessed far too many

KATHERINE MANSFIELD
By kind permission of Mr. John Middleton Murry.

lawyers, tailors, ribbon manufacturers and barbers, and was desperately in need, as all young countries must be, of farmers and builders.

Eventually the New Zealand Company surrendered its Charter to the Crown and Arthur Beauchamp was unable to make good his claim to Jane's lots. He returned to Sydney to take part in the gold rush, and during his absence Wellington was for the second time destroyed by an earthquake, the devastation being completed by an appalling tidal wave. But the early pioneers were not men to be easily daunted. They rebuilt the city with " square, wooden box-like buildings," low and earthquake-proof. We may observe the same precaution in the Avezzano of to-day—the ancient city having been almost completely destroyed by the earthquake of 1915.

In 1854 Arthur Beauchamp married Mary Elizabeth Stanley, a girl of eighteen, at Port Fairy, about a hundred miles from Melbourne, where a little later he established a shop and auctioneering business. Harold Beauchamp, the father of Katherine Mansfield, was the third and second surviving son of Arthur.

For some reason or other Arthur Beauchamp did not succeed in Australia. Gold-digging, shop-keeping, auctioneering, failed in turn to enrich him. In 1861 he took his family to Wellington and embarked for Picton, where he possessed a remnant of Jane's property and where Kathleen Beauchamp as a little girl was taken to see him. He was confined to bed then and she saw him lying there "like a very old, wide-awake bird."

§

Mr. Harold—afterwards Sir Harold—Beauchamp married Miss Annie Dyer in 1884. He was not then a rich man and at the time of the birth of his third daughter, Kathleen, in October, 1888, he was suffering in common with everyone else in New Zealand from a period of severe trade depression.

It was a Sunday, and a violent wind, known in those regions as a " south-westerly buster," was blowing over Wellington. When in after years Kathleen learned this, she seemed to see it as in a sense symbolic of her own life, so storm-tossed and tragic. And always she hated wind. . . .

Her mother who, as a young girl, was singularly lovely, was a delicate, imaginative woman who withdrew herself into a world apart. Like many people suffering from vague cardiac affection, she dreaded any kind of difficulty or emotion. Devoted to her husband, she relegated the care of her three little girls in large measure to her own mother, Mrs. Dyer, who lived with them. For those four years while

Kathleen, or " Kass " as she was called, remained, except for a brief interval, the youngest child, she received a devoted love and sympathy from her grandmother which she was never afterwards to forget.

She could remember with poignant vividness the arrival of her little sister Gwen two years after her own birth, and her consternation at discovering that Mrs. Dyer's arms were no longer at her disposal. But the child was very delicate and died shortly afterwards, and Kathleen remained the youngest for two more years, when her sister Jeanne and subsequently the only son, Leslie, were born. He was to meet the fate of countless only and beloved sons on the fields of Flanders in 1915, to his sister's eternal grief.

At the time of Kathleen's birth, the Beauchamps were living in Tinakori Road, Wellington, but when she was about five they moved to Chesney Wold, Karori, some three and a half miles from that city. The house stood eight hundred feet above the sea, and had a large garden with paddocks and an orchard of apple and damson-trees. We seem familiar with it from the charming account of it in *Prelude*.

There were beautiful views over the sea and mountains, indeed it was an ideal spot for the early years of a sensitive, imaginative child. Small wonder that when Kathleen Beauchamp looked back upon the past from her sick-bed in Italy, Switzerland or elsewhere, she was able to feel a deep gratitude for the fact that she had been born in a " new " country. It made a definite and very charming background for some of her best stories. She absorbed those scenes almost unconsciously, and later recovered them, sometimes with a stark and grim realism as in *The Woman at the Store*, sometimes with an almost unbearable pathos as in *The Doll's House*.

When far gone in consumption, fighting for life in the mountains above Sierre, she was able to look out at the damson orchards in their spring blossoming and remember Karori with a passion of nostalgia.

As a baby, Kathleen was yellow and sickly from an early attack of jaundice, but as she grew older she was a plump, healthy child in contrast to her second sister, Marie, who was eighteen months her senior and a thin, delicate girl. They were alike in feature as their photographs show, but not in colouring, for Kathleen was dark and pale, and Marie fair and rosy. Still less were they alike in temperament, for the two elder girls, Vera and Marie, were " good " children, sweet-tempered and amenable, while Kathleen was different and " difficult."

Il vaudrait mieux souvent avoir des vices qu'un caractère difficile.

But in most families there is an " outlaw," and the embryo author is by temperament ill-adapted to the herd discipline. Its need for solitude is regarded as abnormal, its inability to work much less to play in company is rarely considered. We know what Shelley suffered at Eton and how it affected his whole subsequent life since his natural impulse to rebellion was crystallized and consolidated there. The artistic temperament demands escape into the world of dreams. It cannot conform to type, and the effort to make it do so is bound to react unfavourably upon the psychology of the child.

§

The three little Beauchamp girls went to the primary school at Karori since there was none other available. Kathleen at five years old was placed in the first standard. All the children of the neighbourhood, irrespective of class, attended this school, which was fortunate, or we should never have had that masterpiece *The Doll's House.*

They took their simple luncheon with them, thick mutton-sandwiches and slices of " johnny " cake spread with butter. There Kathleen learned to read and there at eight years old she won the composition prize, the subject being *A Sea Voyage.* At this time she was devoted to her sister Marie who was a little backward on account of her delicate health. " I'm all tired in my elbows and feet," she used to say, and Kathleen suffered agonies when the other girls laughed at her in class.

About four years later the Beauchamps returned to Wellington, taking another and larger house in Tinakori Road. The sisters attended the Wellington College for girls which was at that time a private school. From her place in the second form, Kathleen could see the waves whitening beyond the harbour. She had all the islander's love of the sea. . . .

Mr. Beauchamp, whose affairs were now prospering, bought a country cottage on the shores of Day's Bay where his family could spend the summer holidays. We have a realistic description of it in *At the Bay*, written many years later but with a clear and accurate visualization of every detail. The story was, Kathleen said, full of sand and seaweed, bathing-dresses hanging over verandas and sand-shoes on window-sills. " And it smells (oh, I *do* hope it smells) a little bit fishy."

The tide was out ; the beach was deserted ; lazily flopped the warm sea. The sun beat down, beat down hot and fiery on the fine sand, baking the grey and blue and black and white-veined pebbles. It sucked up the little drop of water that lay in the hollow of the curved shells ; it bleached the pink convolvulus that threaded through and through the sand-hills.

. . . Over there on the weed-hung rocks that looked at low tide like shaggy beasts come down to the water to drink, the sunlight seemed to spin like a silver coin dropped into each of the small rock-pools. . . . Looking down, bending over, each pool was like a lake with pink and blue houses clustered on the shores. . . .

We can picture a grave, dark-eyed child with a wavy " smother " of hair, bending broodingly above those mysterious pools, watching, observing, memorizing.

When Kathleen was twelve she accompanied her sisters to yet another school situated in Fitzherbert Terrace and kept by a Miss Swainson. The head mistress was a Mrs. Smith, and the music master Mr. Robert Parker.

Mrs. Smith was one of those born school-mistresses who can be relied upon to mould the child to an accepted pattern. With the two elder Beauchamp girls she had no trouble at all, they were charming, amenable, affectionate. But she soon came to regard Kathleen as a " thunder-cloud " among them, " imaginative to the point of untruth, untidy, careless, lacking in concentration." Nor did she display any marked intellectual ability except that it was she who started and edited the first magazine of the school.

Emotionally, however, she developed early. She had a warm friendship for a beautiful young Maori girl, Maata, about whom she tried much later to write a novel. This was displaced when she came to know a boy prodigy, Arnold Trowell, who was already earning a reputation as a 'cellist. Plans were on foot to send him to Germany to complete his studies. A year younger than Kathleen he was the first to introduce her to the world of music. All the Beauchamps were musical without being musicians, but under the influence of this young genius, Kathleen studied the 'cello and became a competent performer. Indeed in those early years she was unable to decide which art should claim her—music or writing.

§

In 1903 Mr. Beauchamp took his family to England with the object of placing his three elder daughters at Queen's College, Harley Street, where some of their cousins were being educated. They made the voyage round the Horn, and were a party of eight, the parents, five children, and Mrs. Beauchamp's pretty sister, Belle Dyer, who obviously figures as " Aunt Beryl " in some of the stories.

Kathleen was in her fifteenth year, while her sister Vera was nearly eighteen and thus rather past school age. They lived in a boarding-house close to the college. There were about forty girls lodged in cubicles, one of the unfortunate governesses actually sleeping in a cubicle partitioned off from the bath-room which also contained the piano on which the girls practised. It seems incredible that only thirty years ago such a boarding-house should have been permitted to exist. The Beauchamps were more fortunate than their companions since they had a room to themselves. A passage on the top floor gave access to the college.

It was here that Kathleen Beauchamp met her life-long friend Miss Ida Baker whose selfless devotion to her throughout her long illness must have struck very forcibly all those who have read the *Letters* and *Journal of Katherine Mansfield*. She was the daughter of a retired army surgeon settled in Harley Street, and there is undoubtedly something of her in the Constantia of *The Daughters of the Late Colonel*.

Even then there would come upon Kathleen that urgent desire to be alone, to dissociate herself from the herd. " Don't bother me, girls, I'm going to have a mood," she would say. Then she would withdraw into herself, with set mouth and grave, dark, brooding eyes, while the land of dreams claimed her. Already she realized that such withdrawals were essential to her development ; the creative power was stirring within her.

If I could retain my solitude I should be profoundly happy. The great thing to do is to start as I mean to continue—never for one moment to be other than myself as I long to be.

Myself as I long to be. . . . To the end there was that desire for unity and truth, to realize what was best within her. But alas, this girl, immature, inexperienced, athirst for life, was to experience a harsh fate before she could attain to that ideal. She was like a lamb among wolves, not recognizing their ferocity. And as she grew in beauty and charm many must have thought of her future with misgiving and apprehension.

But never till the end did she abandon that endeavour to find her true self. The child " Kass " Beauchamp was lost in the famous writer Katherine Mansfield, and she fled into the wilderness to try to recover the forfeited identity of that little girl who once sat on the Tinakori hills, dreaming, dreaming . . .

She was happy enough at school if one may judge from her notes. When the year 1904 was born she wrote :

What a wonderful and what a lovely world this is. I thank God to-night that I am. . . .

But the routine of work appealed to her as little as it had done at Karori and Wellington. Afterwards she regretted that she had not

availed herself of the opportunity it offered for study. In a class of
forty girls she was generally fourth or fifth from the bottom, although
no one can doubt her ability to learn had she so chosen. In the English examination she was among the last. Music alone attracted her,
and as she was dissatisfied with the progress she made under the
Queen's College master she was permitted to study at the Royal
Academy of Music.

It is said she was nervous and excitable in those days, often
stammering a little when she spoke.

She wrote stories for the school magazine, revealing even then
something of talent. *One Day* was a picture of her own family, and
both this and *Your Birthday* were studies of children. For it was ever
the heart of a child she knew most surely to reveal, its agonies, its
futile protests against injustice, its inherent feebleness in a world of
giants and Olympians.

Thus she watched and observed, truthfully, if a trifle cynically.
I love watching and listening, she was to write many years later. And
despite her failure in class she would discuss Tolstoy, Ibsen and
Maeterlinck with the other girls, one of whom lent her a copy of
Dorian Gray. . . .

§

Certain of the more privileged girls were invited to the house of a
German professor. This domestic interior was of a kind that was
entirely novel to Kathleen Beauchamp as indeed to many others in
those days. It is difficult to divine the purpose which these people
had in view when they crammed the heads of adolescent girls with
the melancholy and so often decadent and corrupt fruits of the
'nineties.

Kathleen was at a singularly impressionable age ; her mind was
ripe for whatever of literature they chose to sow in it. She devoured
with eagerness, it is said, the works of Oscar Wilde, Verlaine, and
many more. Their perverted view of life did much to poison her
fresh beautiful mind. At sixteen and seventeen her notebooks
were full of quotations from Wilde. She had not yet learned to
eschew the evil, to retain the good. Afterwards there was to be a
reaction but not yet. This new world attracted her the more because
it differed so essentially from the conventional and sheltered life
she had known in New Zealand and which was far more common
everywhere in the early days of the century than it is now. Only,
at the present time, when girls go forth into the world at an early
age, they are adequately equipped for the adventure. But no one
could perhaps have been less prepared for it than the " little

Colonial " from New Zealand who now found herself abruptly
removed from that safe environment into a venue at once stimulating and exciting.

All this time she had corresponded regularly with Arnold Trowell,
and in 1906 she accompanied her aunt to Brussels to hear him give a
recital. During her last year at Queen's College he was in London,
frequently giving concerts at the Bechstein Hall. To Kathleen a
certain glamour hung over this youthful prodigy from the Antipodes.
Pale and with long red hair, dressed in deep black, he made a strange,
exotic yet attractive figure. His growing fame fascinated her.
They became secretly engaged and met under the ægis of one of the
older girls.

It was an uneasy period for Kathleen Beauchamp. She would
return from these encounters in an overwrought, almost hysterical,
state. She was seventeen and Trowell a year younger, so that there
was no question of marriage. Besides, she saw only too plainly that
she did not mean to him what he so profoundly meant to her. What
was this little immature schoolgirl to one who had earned the
plaudits of London and Brussels ?

Over that year a dark shadow hung. The girls had been in England
for three years, and Kathleen, the youngest, was nearly eighteen.
Their education was now finished ; it was decreed that they should
return to New Zealand.

Their father on seeing them so changed and developed, so unlike
the girls he had left at Queen's College three years earlier, declared
that he had lost them. But not one of them was so changed as
Kathleen. Not one displayed this fierce, vehement rebellious desire
to remain in England. It was the beginning of her tragedy. . . .

§

In the new and larger house in Fitzherbert Terrace, Kathleen
had a room to herself. There she kept aloof in an angry, mutinous
spirit among her pictures and bowls of flowers, playing the 'cello,
writing, reading, listening to the eternal plaint of the sea. Longing
for London, for the stimulating life, the friends she had left there. . . .

Her nostalgia was terrible. She was abruptly severed from all
those vivid and emotional interests that had centred round the
figure of Arnold Trowell and in a lesser degree those of her fellow-
schoolgirls.

And I listen and think and dream until my life seems not *one* life but a
thousand million lives, and my soul is weighed down with the burden of
past existence, with the vague uneasy consciousness of future strivings.

R

The voice one would say of Pater or Wilde. . . .

There were fewer people in the new home. The grandmother was living with friends, and Miss Dyer had made a rich marriage in England. The eldest daughter, Vera, was about to be married to a clever young Canadian geologist.

Mr. Beauchamp had prospered in those years. He had become a prominent figure in Wellington and was a director of the Bank of New Zealand besides holding various public posts. Despite the years of trade depression he had made good by his industry and single-ness of purpose and was now a rich man. Jane Beauchamp might have applauded *d'outre tombe* this great-nephew who had succeeded where his father had failed.

But he must have realized with bitter disappointment that his third daughter, Kathleen, was never likely to settle down to the life he was able to offer her. Over the house the shadow of that rebellious spirit hung. Hating New Zealand, she was fighting stubbornly to return to England.

She still continued to play the 'cello, receiving lessons from Mr. Trowell, the father of Arnold. Mr. Beauchamp's secretary, " Matty," was frequently requisitioned to play her accompaniments. She was one of the first to admire her, saying she had a " fine proud bearing, magnificent dark eyes, beautifully waved hair, and distinction."

But by the spring of 1907 Kathleen, who had then been only a few months at home, clearly saw that as a musician she would never rise to front rank.

Definitely I have decided not to be a musician. It's not my *forte*—I can plainly see. The fact remains at that. I must be an authoress. A. T. is losing hold of me.

She turned to writing, especially to poetry, and achieved a little book of child verse which was illustrated by her friend Miss Bendall, a girl slightly older than herself with a real talent for drawing children. It was always to musicians, artists and writers that Kathleen turned ; they were, as she said, " her people."

The book was sent to England, and though it was safely returned to her the illustrations were lost. She felt the rebuff very keenly. If she married " Cæsar " (as she called Arnold Trowell) she believed that she would prove many things. But Mr. Trowell, no doubt with some private knowledge of this too-early romance, told her somewhat enigmatically that Arnold's wife must share his glories and always " keep him on the heights."

Disquieting news of him reached her from England, and although he subsequently denied the truth of the report, it had an alarmingly depressing effect upon her, increasing her melancholy. Perhaps she had always had some subconscious fear of this, since she had written :

This loneliness is not terrible to me because in reality my outer life is but a phantom life . . . a world of intangible, meaningless grey shadow— my inner life pulsates with sunshine and music and happiness, unlimited, vast, unfathomable wells of happiness—and you.

But the fear emerged when she added at the end :

I am afraid even while I am rejoicing. . . .

Her family did all they could to make her more contented. Mrs. Beauchamp encouraged her to write, hoping that in work she might forget or at least ease her intolerable nostalgia for England. Her father spoke to a Mr. Mills, editor of the literary page in the *New Zealand Mail*, about her writing, saying that in his opinion she had been spoiling paper long enough. Mr. Mills consented to look at her sketches but it was some time before Kathleen could write anything to satisfy herself. Finally she sent him some verses and half a dozen stories which " a maturely and widely experienced woman of thirty might have written." He discerned their quality as well as the defects which might militate against their acceptance, but acting on his advice she sent three stories to the *Native Companion*, a monthly magazine published in Melbourne, and three to a London journal. Always before her eyes she had the wonderful success of her father's cousin who had achieved world-wide fame with her first book *Elizabeth and her German Garden. . . .* It must have seemed little likely to her then that she would ever win similar fame and yet the very fact of this example must have given her hope.

Mr. Brady, editor of the *Native Companion*, had the flair to perceive the original quality of these stories. He accepted them, and it was in his paper that *A Vignette, A Silhouette,* and *In a Café* were published. His interest in the young unknown writer was aroused ; he wrote and asked for personal particulars. In reply she told him that she was eighteen years of age, poor, obscure, " with principles as light as my prose."

Her father also wrote, thanking Mr. Brady for his encouragement and confirming the fact that his daughter was only eighteen. He added that she had been writing prose and verse since she was a child and had been educated for three years in London.

Even thus early in her career she told the editor she did not wish to publish under her own name but desired the stories should be signed Katherine Mansfield or simply K. M.

Sixteen years later in a letter to her father she wrote :

It is strange to remember buying a copy of the *Native Companion* on Lambton Quay and standing under a lamp-post with darling Leslie to see if my story had been printed.

Unfortunately at this time the elder Trowells left for England. They were the last links with that premature romance. " I used to think—as long as they are here I can bear it," she wrote.

She was so unhappy and restless that she was allowed to form part of a caravan tour through the Bush. It lasted for six weeks, and though she disliked her companions, and the famous geysers of Rotorua filled her with disgust, the expedition gave her that intimate knowledge of the wilder parts of New Zealand which she used later in her grim story *The Woman at the Store.*

During her absence her eldest sister left home to be married. When she returned the struggle for freedom was resumed. The conflict with her father massacred her, heart and soul. She wished herself dead. . . .

In July, 1908, she won her bitter victory at the sword's point and left for England by way of Montevideo and Teneriffe. Her father prompted, perhaps, by some fatidical instinct gave his consent with an extreme reluctance. She was not yet twenty, and in those pre-War days it was less usual for girls to live on their own than now. She was to receive an allowance of £100 a year, to be paid monthly, and she had every hope of adding to this sum by writing.

§

Katherine Mansfield, as she must now be called, lived at first in a hostel for unmarried women called Beauchamp Lodge. Then she went to stay with the Trowells in St. John's Wood.

I think it is the one darling part of London—she wrote many years later —but perhaps that is because I lived there in Carlton Hill for a long time when I was young and very, very happy. I used to walk there at night late—walking and talking on nights of spring with two brothers.

She stayed there long enough to know that Arnold Trowell's devotion was a thing of the past and that his brother Garnet had fallen in love with her.

She returned to the hostel. There ensued a time of very bitter anguish for her. It must have been on New Year's Day, 1909, that she sat weeping in the little garden at Leicester Square, hiding her face in her muff. A terrible little old woman in a jet bonnet who was sitting on the same seat presently said : " Well, that's 'ow it is, my dear ! "

Pretty, gifted, attractive, temperamental, little more than twenty years of age, always sheltered and cherished until that last disastrous journey to England when she found herself flung into a world alien to anything she had hitherto known, it might well be said of her that she " fell among thieves."

Probably she shrank from asking her father for more money and being desperately in need of it she sold her 'cello for two pounds. She tried various ways of earning her living, going on tour with an opera company—for she had a singularly sweet, soprano voice—acting as a super in motion-pictures, and trying always without success to sell her stories. But she was ill and frightened.

I am physically sick with no home . . . no place to say, " Here I belong," for there is no such place in the wide world for me. I can't rest—that is the agonizing part. . . .

It was in this hour of defeat that she turned to a man who had professed great devotion for her and married him at Paddington Registry Office in March 1909. Dressed from head to foot in deepest black, attired for a funeral rather than a wedding, she must have made a strange, sad little bride. She was accompanied by one attendant—Miss Baker. It was a pitiful gesture and all might yet have been well with her had she cared for her husband. But she could not return his devotion and in a few days she left him.

She was more homeless than ever. The hostel was closed to her since it received only unmarried women. Mrs. Beauchamp, hearing of the abrupt separation, hurried home. She found it useless to urge her daughter to return to her husband. Impossible too to take her back to New Zealand even if she had been willing to go. She went abroad to Bavaria, staying first in a convent and then at a pension, from which she derived the scenes for the sketches that composed her first book *In a German Pension*.

That the veil should have been lifted from that tragic period of her life is one of those lamentable instances of biographical indiscretion which all those to whom Katherine Mansfield was dear must deplore. But since it has thus been relentlessly revealed it is sufficient to add that during those months of exile she gave birth to a stillborn child, almost forfeiting her own life in so doing. And she who loved children so tenderly and with such deep understanding was destined never to have another. Yet throughout her journal we find poignant allusions to that dream-child that never ceased to haunt her.

Her sketches, for the most part written in Bavaria, met with a certain success. They attracted the attention of the late Mr. Orage, then editing the *New Age*, and he accepted *The Child who was Tired*—with its strong resemblance in plot to Tchehov's tragic *Sleepy*—for publication in his journal. It appeared in February, 1910, by which time Katherine Mansfield was back in England and had apparently returned to her husband since he accompanied her to the office of the *New Age* when she brought her story thither in person. A few months later she had a severe illness at Rottingdean—just at the time, as she said, of the death of King Edward VII—and this was followed by a terrible operation. Indeed from that time she never seems to have enjoyed normal health. Her heart was weak, she had constant attacks of rheumatism and at least one of " dry " pleurisy.

Mr. Orage had a keen flair for the discovery of young talent, and he especially admired the slightly cynical and disillusioned flavour of Katherine Mansfield's stories. But when he wished her to continue in that vein she refused to be thus restricted. It was ever her ambition to write other and different stories. And as the clouds passed she could not bind herself to be cynical any more than she could always be grim or tragic.

Those early stories were collected and published that same autumn under the title of *In a German Pension*. She received £15 as advance royalties but unfortunately her publisher failed soon afterwards, so that no subsequent payments were made.

She was lent a flat in Cheyne Walk that winter, and in the following year she rented one in Gray's Inn Road. Her parents came to England in 1911 bringing with them their son Leslie, then a youth of seventeen, handsome, full of promise and especially beloved by his sister. Later in the year she went to Switzerland to receive medical treatment after an attack of pleurisy.

§

It was at the house of the late Mr. W. L. George, the novelist, that Katherine Mansfield first met Mr. John Middleton Murry. They had previously corresponded when he invited her to contribute to a journal called *Rhythm*, a quarterly, published in Oxford where he was then an undergraduate. In response to this request she sent him that powerful little tragedy *The Woman at the Store*, and there is no doubt that its stark, grim landscape was the fruit of those unhappy caravanning days in New Zealand.

Thus when they first met, Mr. Murry was already deeply interested in her as a writer. A friendship sprang up rapidly between them, indeed it might be said of him that he fell in love with her at first sight. For a time he shared her flat in the Gray's Inn Road. He seems to have been without means except what he was able to earn by free-lance journalism. Nevertheless he abandoned his career at Oxford and threw in his lot with hers.

Katherine still had the allowance which was punctually paid by her father and which was often increased to meet the bills for her various illnesses. But she had little else at that time since her stories were regularly returned to her by all the editors to whom she submitted them. Their realistic simplicity, which did not at first betray their underlying profundity, left the editors of that day cold. And it must be said that only in one or two instances did her sketches conform to the accepted pattern of the magazine story. They were for the most part episodic. But she could capture a mood, a situation, a significant moment, and relate it with incomparable skill. And she could look into the past and transcribe it so faithfully that to use her own words, " the dead seemed to live once more. . . ."

The English public does not encourage the book of short stories ; it prefers the novel, and for choice, a very long one, whereas in France the "*conte*" has its definite and acknowledged place in literature, quite apart from the magazine story which in England, as in America, requires an almost stereotyped pattern. Thus few writers with us have risen to fame through the short story. Rudyard Kipling did so with his *Plain Tales from the Hills*, and W. W. Jacobs with his *Many Cargoes*. We must perhaps look back to that early success of Kipling's to find any short stories on a par with Katherine Mansfield's two masterpieces, *The Woman at the Store* and *The Doll's House*. For in these she combined a rare perfection of form with an almost stark economy of words. Both in their respective ways shock and bruise the reader, but as examples of child-psychology they are surely unsurpassed.

I do not think they were her own favourites. Where she most nearly satisfied herself was in *The Daughters of the Late Colonel* and *Je ne parle pas français*. Certain errors of taste are discernible in both these stories, but she could not be induced to alter anything in them. *Prelude* and *At the Bay* read like chapters of a novel that centres round the history of that delightful New Zealand family, the Burnells, among whom we can recognise Katherine as little Kezia.

Life was a hard struggle in those days ; she was ill and nervous and despondent. When a friend sent her a half-bottle of whisky and a box of cigarettes she burst into tears. She was hampered alike by lack of adequate means and by indifferent health. Indeed she once quoted from Jane Austen's *Sense and Sensibility* with bitter irony :

They were neither of them quite enough in love to imagine that £350 a year would supply them with all the comforts of life. " My God, say I . . ."

Sometimes she would go to parties with Miss Baker, but she was at odds with the world. Of one of them she wrote :

Pretty rooms and pretty people, pretty coffee, and cigarettes out of a silver tankard . . . I was wretched. I have nothing to say to " charming " women. I feel like a cat among tigers.

She liked solitude as most authors must, but never loneliness. " I have a real horror of people closing over me," she wrote once.

" She was young and yet old like a precocious child," Mrs. D. H. Lawrence wrote of her. But even she, who saw her frequently, never suspected the deep sadness underlying that charming child-like exterior.

During the summer of 1914 Katherine Mansfield stayed at Merryn, in Cornwall, but after the outbreak of war, which shocked her as it necessarily did all delicate and imaginative women, she rented a cottage at Missenden. She was much alone during that tragic winter of 1914–15, often ill, and always sad and depressed. She was twenty-six and recorded that she felt definitely old, no longer like a girl or even a young woman. Those past six years had been too full of bitter experience for her, and she had hardly known during all that time what it was to have a settled home.

The winter was cold and snowy and the cottage damp and uncomfortable. Her rheumatism was often so acute that she could not move in bed without crying out with pain.

This sad place is killing me. . . . My anxious heart is eating up my body, eating up my nerves, eating up my brain. I am never calm for an instant. . . .

§

In the early months of 1915 Katherine Mansfield spent a few weeks in Paris, believing that she would work better there. She returned thither in May, despite the air raids which then took place almost nightly. On the whole she seems to have been happier there although she found no market at that time for her stories.

In the summer she went back to London and was living in St. John's Wood when her brother arrived from New Zealand and spent a week with her before going to the Front. That was a time of pure happiness for Katherine Mansfield. They talked over old times, strolling about the little garden. Together they recovered something of the charm of their childhood spent in New Zealand. No detail was too trivial for them to recapture. Oh, they would go back there together when the War was over ! He was so confident that he would come through safely. " I couldn't not come back." He communicated something of this assurance to her.

Within a very short time of his departure Leslie Beauchamp was lying with the flower of England's youth in France. He was twenty-one years old. Details reached his sister later of those last moments, after he fell mortally stricken, and of how he had said : " God forgive me for all I've done. . . . Hold up my head, Katie, I'm dying. . . ."

The loss of this beloved brother for whom they all cherished such high hopes literally broke Katherine Mansfield's heart. She went to

Bandol in the South of France. Sometimes she would pray : " *Give me a hard heart, O Lord.*" One of the saddest entries in her Journal runs :

All this is a long uneasy ripple, nothing else, and below in the still pool there is my little brother. . . .

Even in the South it was bitterly cold with savage icy winds, Katherine Mansfield was ill-fed at the hotel as were all in war time. She used sometimes to have recourse to her old trick of looking at herself in the mirror and saying, " Courage, Katherine ! "

She was desperately lonely then, separated from all those for whom she cared. She dreamed of New Zealand as if possessed by some subconscious longing for the shelter of her father's roof. She wasn't of the stuff of which prodigal children are made. . . .

It was while she was still in the South that she resolved to embody the New Zealand experiences of her childhood in a story. She began to write the *Aloe*, afterwards given to the world as *Prelude*. It was that too brief meeting with her brother which had inspired her to reconstruct those days and she proceeded to do so with consummate art.

All that year—1916—was spent in wandering. Sometimes she was in Cornwall, sometimes in London. Early in 1917 she was living in a studio in Church Street, Chelsea. She was still at work on *Prelude*—that expression of the " perfect passion " she had for the island where she was born and to which her thoughts and dreams now turned. They were all scattered now, the children who lived again in those simple, yet brilliant pages ; three of the girls were married and the boy was dead. Return as she might she knew it must show a different and far sterner aspect to her. She could never again be the little girl who once sat dreaming on the Tinakori hills. . . .

When the story was finished she had it typed, feeling unequal to the task herself. " I threw my darling to the Wolves," she wrote, with a gleam of her old whimsical humour, for the Leonard Woolfs had then just started the Hogarth Press and had accepted *Prelude*, which was not, however, published till the following year when scant notice was taken of it. There were, it is said, only two reviews, thus it shared the fate of the Brontë poems. But the local printer who set up the story in type was struck by its quality of truth. " My ! But these kids are *real*," he exclaimed.

It was not a good moment for publishing books. Paper was becoming scarce. Gilt lettering on the covers of novels vanished. Few people, except the sick and the old, had time to read, and even to these books could give but momentary relief from the terrible newspapers with their guarded accounts of the fighting, their dreadful lists of wounded and dead. . . .

Katherine Mansfield's health had been failing all that summer. In November she went on a visit to a friend and caught a chill on the journey. Pleurisy developed, and the doctor warned her that she must never again spend the winter in England. He gave her a certificate—which was required at that time for anyone wishing to go abroad—saying it was absolutely essential for her to winter in the South. Unnecessary travelling was discouraged, the trains being required for the troops.

Miss Baker nursed her during that illness but as she was doing Government work she could not obtain permission to accompany her friend abroad. Katherine Mansfield therefore set out alone on what proved to be one of the most disastrous journeys of her life.

Her destination was Bandol. From Marseilles—where some soldiers made an ugly attempt to storm the train—she travelled with eight Serbian officers and their dogs. She caught a fresh chill and arrived to find that the hotel had changed hands. No one in the place seemed to remember her. Naturally everyone was pre-occupied with the War, and a sick, lonely woman could command little sympathy when thousands were enduring infinitely greater hardships.

Katherine Mansfield suffered both in body and spirit. Letters from England were delayed ; sometimes many days passed before the post brought her any. During those winter months of 1917–18 she must have plumbed the very depths of despair.

Definitely now she lived the life of a semi-invalid. She rose at noon, took a little walk after luncheon, and returned to bed directly after dinner. Yet her old mocking spirit did not even now desert her, for in writing to Mr. Middleton Murry on January 16, 1918, she told him : " *I did not compose a single farewell telegram last night in bed so that is* ONE UP."

But she coughed continually. The pain in her back increased. There were many days when she could not leave her room, and the privations she endured in that cold, uncomfortable hotel indubitably hastened the catastrophe.

At the end of January she felt nearer to her " writing self," despite the pain in her " wing " as she called her lung. *Je ne parle pas français* must be written and she did not spare herself. Every moment spent away from her work was misery to her. The effort, however, excited her so much that at the end of the day she felt " almost insane." When the mood was upon her she was capable of writing feverishly for hours at a stretch. Only, reading the letters she wrote at that time, we feel that she was subconsciously aware of the dark doom that was approaching her. On February 3 she wrote :

There is a great black bird flying over me, and I am so frightened it will settle—so terrified. I don't know exactly what kind he is. . . .

But, alas, she was very soon to learn. . . .

She finished the story, perhaps not one of her happiest ones, and with touches one would gladly have seen omitted, but it satisfied her and she was delighted when Mr. Murry, to whom she sent it, telegraphed his approval. Then she dreamed her short story *Sun and Moon* with title complete, and wrote it immediately, despatching it on the following day as if there were no time to be lost.

§

Miss Baker joined her—most fortunately as it proved—for on February 19, Katherine Mansfield had her first hæmorrhage. She had risen to open the shutters and had jumped back to bed when the abrupt movement made her cough. She was aware of a sinister, salty taste in her mouth. So did Keats learn the doom that had overtaken him.

And then she confided to her Journal that she had always feared it. She recalled the conversation of two women who had travelled with her to Marseilles, and who had expressed the opinion that the South of France was fatal to people suffering from lung trouble. Listening to them she forgot the thousands who had sought and found healing there ; these women had put fear in her heart, perhaps for the first time. . . .

She had had a bit of a fright and was still trembling, she wrote.

But it is certain that from that day forward the thought of death was never far from her, although she did not cease to hope—even to the end—for the " miracle " that should cure her.

Miss Baker was summoned back to England to her work in March, for that was a moment when not a single pair of hands could be allowed to remain idle. Frail and weak as she was, Katherine Mansfield resolved to travel with her rather than face the terrors of that journey home alone. They could not obtain places in the train until the 20th and thus arrived in Paris on March 21, the very day upon which the long-range bombardment began. No civilians were permitted to travel in that crucial moment so that further progress was impossible.

Katherine was desperately ill. " The fact that this *can* happen to me is so dreadful," she wrote. All these months she had been cut off from friends and from everyone dear to her, and this must have seemed the very climax of catastrophe.

She arrived in London ill and broken and incredibly changed on April 11. The next few weeks were spent in Redcliffe Road where Mr. Murry was then living.*

Prelude was not yet published but she now received the proofs of it. When she had read a few pages she said it all seemed so "once upon a time." But she had passed through very deep waters since she wrote that charming story of her child-life in New Zealand ; she was looking at the world with new eyes and as if from a great distance. . . .

London was considered impossible for her and to her grief she was sent to Looe where, however, she found her friend Miss Rice, who did all that was possible to enliven her solitude. She longed, as she said, "for our home, our life, and for a little baby." But she was never to know a really settled home for more than a few months at a time. Always, always, there was that desperate wandering in search of health.

That June she heard the news of her mother's death. "Such an exquisite little being," she wrote, "far too fragile and lovely to be dead for evermore. Ever since I heard of her death my memories of her come flying back to my heart."

And to a very old friend of her family she wrote :

In spite of her frailty and delicate hold on Life one really felt that she was an undying soul. She was such a part of life, especially these last few years. She seemed to live in everything and to be renewed with every Spring. And it was so extraordinary how close she kept to her children. Her last letters were quite uncanny. We seemed to be thinking the same thoughts at just the same time. . . . I wish we had not all lived so scattered —and it is dreadful to think of poor Father without his wife and his " Boy."

I shall be going abroad in the late Spring—the letter continues—for a more or less indefinite time. It will be such a relief to be strong again. I cannot bear an inactive life—and though of course I can do all my writing just as well with broken wings as with good 'uns, there are so many things besides that one longs to take part in

The letter of date December 30, 1918, was signed " Kass," as in New Zealand Days.

In 1919 Mr. Middleton Murry was appointed editor of the *Athenæum*, and Katherine Mansfield contributed both stories and reviews of books to it. When the spring came she said it made her " long for happiness." All that summer she was very ill and her cough became worse. It was evident to those about her that another winter in England would probably prove fatal to her. She suffered also from neuritis in her arm and shoulder and was sometimes physically unable to write. " I have felt so cut off from the world without a pen," she wrote.

* Katherine Mansfield had married Mr. Middleton Murry after the dissolution of her first marriage.

Finally it was decided that she should spend the winter in Italy, and a villa above Ospedaletti was taken for her. The Casetta Deerholm, as it was called, stood in its own olive orchard overlooking the sunny little Mediterranean town and the sea beyond. Miss Baker accompanied her.

It is on a wild hill-slope covered with olive and fig trees and long grasses and tall yellow flowers. Many lizards lie on the garden wall; in the evening the cicada shakes his tiny tambourine. . . .

At first she was happy enough in the warm sunshine. The healing balsamic air revived her, and the doctor who was called in pronounced a distinct amelioration. She was able to take short walks, and sometimes ventured as far as San Remo in the tram.

Then towards the end of October the usual cold spell, forerunner of winter, gripped Italy. The little exposed villa was very cold. A violent wind blew—she always hated wind—and this was succeeded by days of rain and fog and icy airs. The doctor's words rang in her ears: " Chill in your case would be a fatal disaster." She longed for her home and her husband who was now chained to his work in London. . . . Once she was immensely cheered by a visit from her cousin and a friend then living at Mentone. They motored over, bringing her father with them. To see him again, to be assured of his tender affection, was pure joy to her.

Father at last was wonderfully dear to me. I mean to be called my precious child was almost too much—to feel someone's arms round me and someone saying, ' Get better, you little wonder. You're your mother over again.' It's not being called a wonder, it's having *love* present, close, warm, to be felt and returned. . . .

And on the table as she wrote that letter, there was a little nosegay consisting of five daisies and an orchid which he had gathered for her and tied together with a bit of grass. That simple little gift touched her very heart.

§

It was a time of fierce unrest in Italy, tormented beyond belief by the long bloody struggle of the war. More than most countries did it feel that bitter upheaval as of a world wounded and battle-stained endeavouring to recover something of its ancient peace and poise.

Foodstuffs were still scarce and dear, and Italy was even then severely rationed lest the final catastrophe of famine should supervene. Strikes on the railway and at the post-office dislocated traffic and commerce. Three years were still to pass before Mussolini arose to straighten out the tangle and restore civic peace.

Katherine Mansfield suffered from the non-delivery of letters from England. She felt cut off, nevertheless she was unwilling to leave Italy although her cousin assured her that Mentone was warmer and more sheltered. She didn't want "a town and a band," as she expressed it.

She was haunted then by the thought of death :

It needs such a little push, hardly that, just a false step, just not looking, and you are over. Mother, of course, lived in this state for years. Ah, but she lived *surrounded*. She had her husband, her children, her friends, physical presences, darling treasures to be cherished—and I've not one of these things, I have only my work.

She longed anew for a home in England where she could live quietly, working side by side with her husband. Instead of which she was an exile in a strange land.

But she continued to review books—always with a certain cynical gaiety—for the *Athenæum*. And her criticism of contemporary writers was quite unbiased by the popularity they enjoyed. Indeed, few of us would quarrel now with her estimate of the *Saint's Progress*, one of Galsworthy's weakest novels.

It makes me feel queer sometimes when I read that *Saint's Progress* is one of the masterpieces of all time—she wrote in a letter—and yet I never feel for an instant I'm not right.

The centenary of George Eliot's birth occurred that year and Katherine Mansfield cavilled a little at some of her critics, one of whom she maintained had not "brought it off."

She was a great deal more than that. Her English warm ruddy quality is hardly mentioned. She *was* big, even though she was heavy too. But think of some of her pictures of country life—the breadth, the sense of sun lying on warm barns, great warm kitchens at twilight when the men came home from the fields, the peculiar passion she has for horses. . . . Oh, I think he ought to have been more generous ! . . .

This was the more significant as she had an almost savage dislike to "Amos Barton" in the *Scenes of Clerical Life*.

At the end of November she caught a chill and was seriously ill with pneumonia and fever. She was cheered, however, at the prospect of publishing a book of short stories. Grant Richards was willing to produce it, but Constable offered a higher price—£40 in advance royalties—and this was accepted. She was anxious that *Prelude* and *Je ne parle pas français* should be included in the collection which was ultimately published under the title of *Bliss* and at once brought name and fame to its author. Never again could she be ignored. Editors were alert for fresh work from her pen, and thenceforward she found a ready market for her short stories.

She had planned to go to Mentone for Christmas, but this attack of illness prevented her. Her husband, alarmed at the despondency of her letters, joined her at Ospedaletti, and spent a fortnight with her. After his departure she had a relapse. " My heart won't lie down," she wrote.

She acknowledged in her diary that those were the worst days of her whole life, which was saying a good deal considering how profoundly she had suffered in Bavaria. She could not sleep, and her past life came back to her with haunting vividness ; she re-lived those bygone scenes in anguish of spirit.

Entries such as these in her journal reveal the depths of gloom into which her malady had plunged her.

Black. A day spent in hell. Unable to do anything. Took brandy. Determined not to weep. Wept. Sense of isolation frightful. I shall die if I don't escape.

Nevertheless, she planned and partly wrote two stories, *Late Spring* and the *Man without a Temperament*. And despite the fact that she spent many weeks in bed she continued to review books.

§

The post-office strike in January, 1920, deprived her for many days of the letters from her husband upon which she so relied. It made her finally decide to leave Ospedaletti and go to Mentone, where she took a room at the " Hermitage." Her cousin made all the necessary arrangements and was there to welcome her on her arrival.

At first the large warm room, the better food, the pleasant surroundings, the constant visits from her cousin and her friend, brightened her outlook. " I've got away from that ghastly cloud. All is absolutely changed," she wrote.

But when she was sufficiently well to go downstairs for her meals the environment lost all charm for her. She found the place noisy and the food uneatable. She looked back upon the Casetta with regret. After all, the time there had not been wasted ; she had learned more about her craft and felt she was working with a finer, surer touch. She missed too the quiet, the solitude, the freedom of her own house.

It was at this point her cousin, Miss Beauchamp, came to the rescue. She and her friend, Miss Fullerton, were two Catholic ladies living then at the Villa Flora. Aware of the extremity of Katherine's need, her sick body and still more sick soul, they invited her to stay with them till May.

It was none too soon. Black depression had descended upon her.

The meals in company with the other invalids had become unendurable.

The waiters jerked her chair, offering food. It was no good. She left and went upstairs, but that was fatal. Had she a home? A little cat? Was she any man's *wife*? Was it all over? . . .

She needed human help, cut off as she was from the one person she loved. *" Oh, if they could only have known or seen her heart, that had been stabbed and stabbed. . . ."*

Her cousin's plan brought fresh hope to her. " I for the first time think I should like to join the Roman Catholic Church—I must have something "—she wrote in her journal.

After months of discomfort, the Villa Flora, exquisitely furnished and appointed, seemed like a dream. Her own room was decorated in grey and silver with touches of rose-colour. " You're going to get well here—please God we'll cure you," her cousin said.

The new environment cheered her after those months of misery at Ospedaletti. She could write with glee of the " Heron "—that dream-cottage which never materialized.

I feel we must keep bees and a cow, fowls, two turkeys, some India runner ducks, a goat, and perhaps one thoroughly striking beast like a unicorn or a dragon ! . . .

No one can live for very long as close to death as she did without giving profound thought to the immortality of the soul. Obviously, too, the spiritual atmosphere of the house affected her, since we find her writing :

I wish I could believe in a God. I can't. Science seems to make it impossible.

Had she no knowledge of the many great scientists who have set it on record that at every point in their researches they found themselves confronted by the Infinite and had thus been led to make their submission to the Catholic Church ? The cheap little science-mongers of the present day ignore those great minds. Katherine Mansfield had lived too long among free-thinkers, bereft of all spiritual assistance, but thenceforward she seemed to grope blindly towards the very Light she denied.

Her health improved in that fresh spring air. She enjoyed the long drives, especially the expedition to La Turbie.

It's up high, high, on the tops of mountains. It's a tiny ancient Roman town, incredibly ancient ! with old bits of pillars and capitals.

Had she read Dante she might have recalled his allusion to that unscalable rock, easy in comparison with the mountain that faced him in the *Purgatorio*.

*Tra Lerici e Turbia, la più deserta
la più romita via è una scala,
verso di quella, agevole ed aperta . . .*

On the way thither she saw many little houses that were surely
" theirs," with " terraces and a veranda—with bean-fields in bloom,
with a bright scatter of anemones in the gardens. . . ."

And all this time her old home in Fitzherbert Terrace, far away in
New Zealand, was " colouring beautifully with the years."

And I polish it and examine it, and only now is it ready to come out of
the storeroom into the uncommon light of day. . . .

While at Mentone she wrote *The Daughters of the Late Colonel.*
It was one of her favourite stories and she said afterwards that it was
written when she was " not so bad as usual. I was trying with all
my soul to be good." But she was terribly unhappy, and although
she had then ample leisure she wrote it as fast as possible for fear of
dying before it was finished.

Little creatures that we are—she wrote about this time—we have our
gesture to make which has its place in the scheme of things. We must
find what it is and make it—offer up ourselves as sacrifice. . . .

Perhaps those in England feared the influence of this pious Catholic
atmosphere for her and warned her against it, since a little later we
find her writing :

" Yes, it's true about Catholics—their world is not our world. My *duty*
is to *mankind*—theirs to a personal deity."

To combine the twin rôles of being at once a Catholic and a great
artist—as so many of the greatest artists of the world have done—
seemed impossible to her. Always, Catholics were not " her people."
She began to weary of the environment, and on April 27 she left
Mentone for England, greatly improved in health from the gentle,
assiduous care she had received.

Back to Portland Villas. . . . But the summer of that year was
chill and wet ; the weather affected her adversely. Her cousin had
taken a new villa in the Garavan quarter of Mentone and there was a
smaller house available in the grounds. She agreed to rent the Villa
Isola Bella and thither she went in September. There was a garden
with flowers and palm-trees. Mentone, she said, felt like home.

She was happy enough at first in a house of her own where she
was free to work and earn. And then as at Ospedaletti a profound
gloom overwhelmed her with its dark waves, as she realized more and
more the hopelessness of her own condition. No doctor would ever

s

tell her more than that she " still had a chance." Never could they honestly utter the word cure. She wrote in her journal :

I should like this to be accepted as my confession. There is no limit to human suffering. When one thinks : " Now I have touched the bottom of the sea—now I can go no deeper—" one goes deeper. . . . I thought last year in Italy, any shadow more would be death. But this year has been so much more terrible that I think with affection of the Casetta. Suffering is boundless ; it is eternity. . . . I do not want to die without leaving a record of my belief that suffering can be overcome. For I do believe it. What must one do ? There is no question of what is called passing beyond it. This is false.

One must *submit*. Do not resist. Take it. Be overwhelmed. Accept it fully. Make it *part of life*.

Reading her life side by side with *L'Histoire d'une Âme*—the autobiography of Saint Teresa of Lisieux, one of the most remarkable saints of modern times, and stricken at an even earlier age by the same malady—one can only regret that Katherine Mansfield was never to approach the same sources of spiritual consolation. Yet sometimes she seems to have come close to her sister-sufferer as when she writes :

If suffering is not a repairing process I will make it so. I will learn the lessons it teaches.

And then :

Everything has its shadow. Is it right to resist such suffering ? Do you know I feel it has been an immense privilege ?

Her mind was deeply preoccupied then with spiritual things.

I feel that only now do I desire to be saved. I realize what salvation means and I long for it. Of course I am not speaking as a Christian or about a personal God. But the feeling is . . . I believe (and VERY MUCH), help thou my unbelief.

Even more significant is the sentence :

I *long* for goodness—to live by what is permanent in the soul. . . .

§

In November she wrote *The Stranger*, a New Zealand story. How completely she identified herself with both scene and characters during the process of writing is evident from her own comments :

I've *been* this man, *been* this woman. I've stood for hours on the Auckland Wharf. I've been out in the stream waiting to be berthed. . . . It isn't as though one sits and watches the spectacle. That would be thrilling enough, God knows. But one IS the spectacle for the time. If one remained oneself all the time like some writers can it would be a bit less exhausting.

She was beginning to discover how strangely *craft* came into writing, " even down to details."

In Miss Brill I chose not only the length of every sentence but even the sound of every sentence. . . .

The Stranger, Miss Brill, The Young Girl, and *The Lady's Maid*— one of the most purely skilful sketches she ever wrote—all belong to this period of renewed mental activity. They appeared in the *Athenæum* and were collected and subsequently published in her volume of short stories *The Garden Party*, which contains also *At the Bay* and the *Daughters of the Late Colonel.*

The *Athenæum* ceased publication in January, 1921, when Katherine Mansfield had been for about four months at the Villa Isola Bella. Mr. Murry was free to join her, but she was very ill during almost the whole time of his visit. It was found that a gland was pressing upon an artery, and this had to be operated upon more than once. In April there was an alarming renewal of hæmorrhage. She began to dislike Mentone. There is evidence, too, that she was very unhappy there. Something happened, she told a friend later, that shook her world like an earthquake. " I lost faith and touch with every-body." There was also an enigmatic entry in her journal which indicates that some grief befell her in the spring of 1921 and that she was desperately unhappy in consequence. But she would leave no sign, of that she was determined. There had been a time when she would have written everything that happened to her after she left France, but now she would keep silence, " as Mother kept silence." But she confessed she had been almost out of her mind with misery. . . .

In May she left for Sierre accompanied by Miss Baker while Mr. Middleton Murry returned to England, having an engagement to lecture at Oxford.

She was ill at Sierre ; there were days when she could not bear heat or cold, noise or light. But ill as she was she reproached herself bitterly with idleness. She meant to write after tea (although her gland had been punctured that morning) but rested instead. A sense of guilt seemed to torture her because of those wasted hours.

Marks of earthly degradation still pursue me. . . . I am not crystal clear. . . .

Then the old spiritual longings broke out ever more painfully :

No, one can't believe in God. But I must believe in something more *nearly* than I do. As I was lying here to-day I suddenly remembered, O ye of little faith. . . . Not faith in a God. No, that's impossible. But do I live as though I believe in anything ?

To be stronger and better, to be *whole*, that was her one desire. " The soul's desperate choice," as she once called it.

It seems to me—she wrote to a friend—that there is a great change come over the world since people like US believed in God. God is now gone for all of us. Yet we must believe, and not only that, we must carry our weakness and our sin and our devilishness to somebody.

It was one of the tragedies of Katherine Mansfield's life that except for one brief interval she lived among people for whom God was " gone." Moreover she had come to believe that religion and any form of intellectualism were incompatible and could never be reconciled.

At the end of May her husband joined her and they moved up to a furnished châlet at Montana where they spent about ten months. Those days at the Châlet des Sapins were perhaps the happiest of her life. They were together, the husband and wife who had known so many separations, and both were hard at work in that mountain fastness. There were flowers—" all the flowers of the South "— and there were nightingales. Not very far away her cousin, Lady Russell, was living, and was a frequent visitor at the châlet. And the climate suited her. The strain was gone, she said. " One hasn't that feeling of dragging an endless rope out of a dark sea."

The Daughters of the Late Colonel, written while she was at Mentone during the previous year, appeared in the *London Mercury* for May. The *Saturday Review* pronounced it a " dismal transcript of inefficiency." One critic actually accused her of " poking fun at the poor old things." She could hardly have received a greater compliment as to their lifelike quality, but at the time these adverse notices depressed her. Perhaps living alone she had got out of touch, and " what seems to me lively is ghostly glee."

She was at work on a series of stories for the *Sphere*, then edited by the late Clement Shorter, whose encouragement of young writers will long be gratefully remembered. But her name was now fully established and her work eagerly sought. She was nevertheless too true an artist ever to be perfectly satisfied with her own productions.

It's always the next story which is going to contain everything, and that next story is always just out of reach.

While at Montana she wrote *At the Bay*, in which so many of her childish memories of Day's Bay were incorporated. One can little understand the New Zealand critic who pronounced it one of her feeblest stories. It is alive, authentic, sincere, and the characters come before us with a strange vividness.

It's about 60 pages—she wrote to a friend—I've been at it all last night. My precious children have sat in here playing cards. It's as good as I can do, and all my heart and soul is in it . . . every single bit. Oh God, I hope it gives pleasure to someone ! It is so strange to bring the dead back to life again. There's my Grandmother, back in her chair with her pink knitting, there stalks my uncle over the grass. I feel as I write, " You are not dead, my darlings. All is remembered. I bow down to you. I efface myself so that you may live again in your richness and beauty."

Between October 16 and November 21, 1921, Katherine Mansfield wrote her little masterpiece *The Doll's House*, perhaps one of the best short stories in the English language. No child-lover can read it without sensing a pity that comes near to tears. We leave the two forlorn little girls sitting on a big red drain-pipe by the side of the road. Kezia had shown them the famous Doll's House with its singular treasure, the little lamp, and her aunt had interrupted them and driven them away as undesirable companions.

Presently our Else nudged up close to her sister. But now she had forgotten the cross lady. She put out a finger and stroked her sister's quill ; she smiled her rare smile.
" I seen the little lamp," she said softly.
Then both were silent once more.

But, as has already been said, the reader emerges shocked and bruised because of that gratuitous act of unkindness to two small, poor girls.

§

But though she had come to regard that time at Montana as God-given, Katherine was aware that it could not last. She was troubled, as she confessed in her journal, by the daily thought of the proximity of death. Such cries as these escaped her : *Lord, make me crystal clear for Thy light to shine through.* . . . Such a beautiful spirit as hers needed faith to perfect it.

I am tired of the battle. No one knows how tired. . . .

She would sit there at the window, looking out at the " evening star, the cold, candid peaks," thinking of death. " Of life which is so lovely and of the fact that my body is a prison." And then :

This state of mind is *evil*. It is only by acknowledging that I, being what I am, had to suffer *this* in order to do the work I am here to perform. It is only by acknowledging it, by being thankful that work was not taken from me, that I shall recover. . . .

One of her most pathetic confessions was written to a friend in January, 1922 :

It's queer when I'm in this mood I always write as though I were laughing. I feel it running along the pages. If only the reader could see the snail in its shell with the black pen.

Stricken and emaciated as she was, she could yet smile at the folly and simplicity of some of her own creations. There was always that element of joy in her work that communicates itself to the reader.

She sold *The Doll's House* to the *Dial* in America, and to the *Nation* in England. She was very ill again in October, 1921, nevertheless she finished *The Garden Party*. She wanted, she said, to leave a solid body of work behind her, and despite her inherent hopefulness, she knew that in all probability the time for accomplishing this would be all too short.

This sudden attack of illness made her restless, dissatisfied with the climate. She wrote to her friend, Koteliansky, begging him to give her information about a Russian doctor, Manoukhin, who treated tuberculosis with X-rays in Paris. She was not then in the least deceived about her own condition. For more than a year she had not walked at all except to a carriage and back. Yet the thought of this new treatment gave her hope.

The bitter winter weather made her worse. A fierce wind blew about the châlet. The house was heated day and night, yet nothing could keep out those formidable, icy airs. Outside the snow lay to a depth of six feet ; even the tails of the birds were frozen.

She was working now at *The Dove's Nest,* of which only an amusing fragment remains. The scene was laid in the South of France.

Although the critics were often unfavourable, she received many appreciative letters from friends, known and unknown, about *At the Bay*—her " little family in the Mercury."

" I feel like Lottie's and Kezia's mother after the letters I have got this month. It is surprising and very lovely to know how people love little children—the most unexpected people."

During January, 1922, despite her illness, she wrote *Taking the Veil*, which appeared in the *Sketch*. And indeed it was necessary for her to earn money then, in view of the expensive nature of Manoukhin's treatment.

The time was drawing near for her to go to Paris on one of her last hopeless quests for health. She discussed the project with her husband, and a little to her surprise he understood. She said it was a proof that one must be calm and explain, and be *true*. . . .

Before leaving she wrote *A Cup of Tea* in a few hours. Ill as she was she reproached herself bitterly with idleness when a day passed and she had failed to accomplish anything. Most authors are afflicted with this sense of guilt, but she felt it to be almost a sin.

The last days in Switzerland were happy ones. " I feel there is much love between us," she wrote of her husband. " Tender love. Let it not change." She felt as if she had touched the zenith of

happiness on that last day of January, and she went away full of un-
conquerable hope and a firm conviction that this time the " miracle "
would happen, although there still lurked a little dark fear at the
back of her mind.

It was very beautiful on the way to Sierre. Then I kept wondering
if I was seeing it all for the last time—the snowy bushes, the leafless trees.

§

The journey shattered her and she and Miss Baker arrived late in
Paris. Fresh doubts assailed her. Was it any use ? She was staking
her all on this last hazardous throw.

Nevertheless she went to see Manoukhin that very evening. While
driving thither she suddenly realized her heart wasn't in it. She and
her friend went first to the wrong house, and had " one of their
famous quarrels."

Manoukhin was confident. He told her through his interpreter
that he could cure her completely. Cure ? The word she had so
long desired to hear. But it was too late—she refused to believe it.
Perhaps some secret knowledge convinced her that it couldn't be
true, " It all seemed suddenly unimportant and ugly."

Almost at once she began the treatment. It made her very much
worse at first, but of that she had been duly warned. She suffered
from agonizing neuritis. Then came a letter from her husband, still
at Montana, which plunged her into profound gloom. It kept her
awake nearly all night. He hadn't the smallest faith in the cure and
suggested coming to fetch her in May. " Well, if I am better there
will never be any more fetching, of that I am determined," she wrote
in her journal. One senses a woman utterly at the end of her
nervous tether.

Except for her visits to the clinic she spent her days in bed. She
wrote, read Shakespeare and Goethe, thought and prayed. She saw
clearly that it needed more than Manoukhin's X-rays to make her
whole. " I must heal myself mentally before I will be well." More
than ever was she conscious of that need of spiritual regeneration. . . .

Then her husband came to her. They resumed something of their
old life at the châlet. They read and played chess ; he accompanied
her to the clinic. But she was so ill that to lie down was agony.
" The worst of it is that I have again lost hope."

She was astonished to discover that the Russian colony in Paris
had become devoutly religious since the revolution, and this turned
her thoughts once more towards Christianity.

The more I study the religion of Christ, the more I marvel at it. . . .
If we want faith—and without faith we die—we must accept. . . .

It was the ultimate tragedy of her tragic life that she was bereft of all those spiritual influences which alone could have helped her in her hour of great need.

During the early months of 1922 *The Garden Party* was published and greatly enhanced her reputation. It brought her a fresh batch of letters of appreciation. Now she was able to resume her work for the *Sphere*, since Manoukhin's treatment was apparently having a beneficial effect. She had gained in weight, and was contemplating a return to Montana as she and her husband both had much work on hand.

They left Paris in June, but, alas, the air of Montana proved too rarefied for her and she was obliged to descend to an hotel at Sierre where Mr. Middleton Murry joined her for the week-ends. It was a time of blossom in Switzerland, and the damson-trees, she told her father in a letter, were the first she could remember seeing since Karori. Often a touch of nostalgia for New Zealand was apparent in those letters.

She was once more at work on *The Dove's Nest*, which was intended to be a longer and more important story than any she had hitherto written. Begun during the previous year with her memories of the South of France still fresh in her mind, she had often set it aside to fulfil her various contracts for short stories. She worked daily all the morning till half-past twelve, and then from four o'clock till supper-time. Her mental energy was still marvellous despite her frail, emaciated body.

Her friend, Miss Brett, joined her for a week, but after her departure, Katherine Mansfield was so ill that she resolved to go to London and consult her own doctor, Sorapure. No one was to know she was coming and she agreed to take part of Miss Brett's house at Hampstead.

Doctor Sorapure saw no cause for alarm, telling her there was nothing really wrong with her heart and advising her to walk a little and to move about as much as possible. He found her improved in health; she was fatter and had gained in weight as a result of Manoukhin's treatment.

Her father and two of her sisters were in London at the time. It made her very happy to see them again. She wished they could all foregather once more in New Zealand, but that, alas, was never to be.

September came, and with it colder weather. Katherine resolved to return to Paris for another course of Manoukhin's treatment. She took a room at the Select Hotel where she had spent those miserable weeks in 1918 during the long-range bombardment.

She was wretchedly unhappy. She longed, as she said, with all her

soul for a real life, for *truth*. . . . She was even dissatisfied with her
work, seeing that without a definite purpose nothing of lasting value
could be achieved. A journey without a goal—that was how she
expressed it. And as the shadows of death darkened about her she
looked round for some way of escape.

For she saw clearly now that Manoukhin who had cured others
could never effect her own " miracle." The life she had led that
spring in the Victoria Palace Hotel had resembled a living death.
She looked better but in many ways she was worse. New and disquieting symptoms betrayed this only too plainly. She suffered from
constant nausea and from ice-cold sweats when nothing could warm
her. And she wrote to a friend in a manner which displays only too
clearly her anxious, despondent state of mind.

In my heart I am far more desperate about my illness than I can ever
show you. . . .

§

There was at that time near Fontainebleau a Russian establishment called the Gurdjieff Institute for the Harmonic Development
of Man. It professed among other things to assist persons in
achieving a spiritual regeneration. But like so many enterprises of
the kind its processes and ultimate aims were slightly amorphous.
Yet as a reaction from her own bitter disappointment at the failure
of the X-ray treatment, Katherine Mansfield turned her dying
eyes thither in the pathetic belief that there she would " find "
herself. . . .

It was from every point of view a deplorable step. For if anyone
was in need of spiritual assistance it was Katherine Mansfield in that
forlorn hour. Actually, she had once expressed her sense of the *need*
of salvation. Over and over again the cry had been wrung from her
that she wished to praise God, to thank Him. She had lived long
enough to see with her own eyes the swift, appalling disintegration of
a world that has turned from God ; she had read with horror of the
happenings in Russia. Yet she still, unaided, pursued her " journey
without a goal."

There can be no sadder picture than this broken, emaciated, dying
woman, still so deeply in love with life, placing herself deliberately in
the Gurdjieff Institute with the intention of working with her
hands, " looking after animals and doing all kinds of manual labour."
Everyone who knew her must have been fully aware that in taking
this step she was signing her own death-warrant. She had hardly
walked more than a few paces for three years ; she had lived the life
of an invalid, spending many weeks in bed, suffering from fever,

s *

hæmorrhage and other ills.   Now she crept about that damp, chill, northern garden despite the re entless approach of winter.

She seems to have expected a moral rather than a physical change. Had she not always pretended to be one person when she was really another?   It had become more and more difficult for her to distinguish between the " ill me and the well me."   The life she had led of late in Switzerland and Paris seemed no longer possible for her—it was so far away, she said, it seemed to belong to another world.   Then came the pitiful confession :

I want to learn something that no books can teach me, and I want to try to escape from my terrible illness.

Perhaps, too, in the gesture there was something of that primitive instinct which constrains the wounded animal to seek some fastness where its death-agonies may be unobserved.   And like all persons aware of the proximity of death, a kind of detachment was discernible in Katherine Mansfield's letters as if already she had moved a little away from the persons and things that had hitherto meant so much to her, had taken, indeed, the first steps on her homeward journey. She had little wish to write, and even reading had become a weariness to her.   There were contracts with editors and publishers to be fulfilled ; she set their claims aside.

The novelty of the place and its enthusiastic inmates—for the most part Russians to whom its very privations must have represented luxury after their recent experiences—amused her at first. She could still listen and observe, and she showed a kind of radiant hopefulness, due no doubt to the change of atmosphere and mode of living.

Fortunately she had two friends in the Institute, Doctor Young and her former editor, Mr. Orage, with whom she had long conversations. She told him that she meant of course to write again but that when she did so her work must be " different."   She could not explain very precisely the form which this change must take, only that " goodness " must prevail.   A significant phrase escaped her in regard to her former stories : *There is not one I dare show to God.* . . .

She wished in fact to make the commonplace virtues as attractive as ordinarily the vices are made.   Hitherto she had been a mere camera—a selective camera—her observations coloured always by the trend of her own mind.   Her personal attitude determined, as she said, the selection with the result that " my slices of life have been partial, misleading and a little malicious."

This attitude must be radically changed before she could embark upon those new stories.   She must look at life with other eyes, aware of its heroic qualities, its spiritual claims.   " I wish the laugh to be with the heroes." And to write better she saw it was necessary to become *more*. " The greatest literature is still only mere literature if it has not a purpose commensurate with its art."

And she was tired, she wrote, of her little stories " like birds bred in cages." She needed that wider horizon she was so soon to know. Her last entry in the journal is singularly touching as well as prophetic.

I feel happy—deep down. *All is well. . . .*

§

As part of the disastrous " discipline " to which Katherine Mansfield was subjected at the Gurdjieff Institute we learn that she was given a small, chill, fireless room. She suffered so much from the cold that she wore her fur coat night and day. . . .

On the day following Christmas she wrote to a friend :

You see, if I were allowed one single cry to God that cry would be, I want to be *real*. At this present moment all I know really, really, is that though one thing after another has been taken from me I am not anni-hilated, and that I hope—more than hope—believe. It is hard to explain.

One single cry to God. . . . One can only pause on this significant phrase wrung from her in her agony, since it seems most surely to epitomize the aspirations of her last few weeks on earth. And then we can only wish that her steps had been guided to an environment more adapted to instruct her in that spiritual growth for which her soul yearned than the Gurdjieff Institute. It could not help her starved and suffering soul and it did most surely hasten the destruc-tion of her frail, delicate body. . . .

The year drew to its close. Early in 1923 Katherine Mansfield wrote to her husband inviting him to spend a few hours with her on January 9. It was well she did so. All who saw her on that day were struck by the peculiar radiance and beauty that informed her face. And that night when she went up to bed at ten o'clock she was seized with a violent fit of coughing, which culminated in a severe and fatal hæmorrhage. In half an hour she was dead. It was all over so quickly that perhaps she knew very little of that final agony of parting. The " miracle " was performed too swiftly and suddenly for her to be aware of it. . . .

She lies buried—this little girl who once sat dreaming on the Tinakori Hills—in the communal cemetery at Avon, near Fontaine-bleau. On her tombstone is inscribed her favourite quotation from the *First Part of King Henry IV*, Act II, Scene 3 :

But I tell you, my lord fool, out of this nettle, danger, we pluck this flower, safety. . . .

INDEX

285